PRAISE FOR

WIRED THAT WAY

Accepting how I was wired changed my life. It freed me from my
masks so that I could shine in the skin of my God-given personality.
This book goes beyond a quick look at our built-in styles. It spotlights the
bigger picture and teaches us the way to respond to others and revive our
relationships. Sound and sensible, filled with engaging personal stories,
Wired That Way is definitely a keeper. Prepare for dog-eared pages.

JAN COLEMAN
SPEAKER AND AUTHOR, *WOMAN BEHIND THE MASK: TRADING YOUR FACADE FOR AUTHENTIC LIFE*

What a relationship builder! *Wired That Way* equips readers to
understand that we are all wired differently, giving us a new understanding
for our mates, children and friends. Marita Littauer takes the guesswork
out of the thought process behind actions and encourages us to love
those around us just the way God made them.

LINDA GILDEN
AUTHOR OF THE *LOVE NOTES* SERIES:
LOVE NOTES IN LUNCHBOXES AND *LOVE NOTES ON HIS PILLOW*

Marita Littauer has done it again! She has tuned in to what we really
need to know and understand about ourselves and others and has then
translated that information into a practical, reader-friendly format that
will educate, enlighten and encourage us to fulfill God's purposes for our lives. *Wired
That Way* will free us to be all that God created us to be and to
graciously allow others to do the same. This book is a reminder that God has already
gifted us to fulfill what He has called us to do and that when we
operate accordingly, the Body of Christ will function in unity and power.

KATHI MACIAS
AUTHOR, *THE MATTHEWS AND MATTHEWS DETECTIVE NOVELS:*
OBSESSION, THE PRICE AND *THE RANSOM*

A great resource! *Wired That Way* will help you learn to connect with
people more effectively on personal, social and professional levels. You
might even learn something about yourself in the process!

CYNDY SALZMANN
NATIONAL SPEAKER
AUTHOR, *DYING TO DECORATE!* AND *BEYOND GROUNDHOGS AND GOBBLERS*

MARITA LITTAUER

WITH INSIGHTS FROM

FLORENCE LITTAUER

WIRED
THAT WAY

Revell

a division of Baker Publishing Group
Grand Rapids, Michigan

Published by Revell
a division of Baker Publishing Group
PO Box 6287, Grand Rapids, MI 49516-6287
www.revellbooks.com

Revell edition published 2014
ISBN 978-0-8007-2537-2

Previously published by Regal Books

Printed in the United States of America

The Library of Congress has cataloged the original edition as follows:
Littauer, Marita.
    Wired that way / Marita Littauer; with insights from Florence Littauer.
        p. cm.
    ISBN 0-8307-3840-1 (trade paper)
    1. Personality—Religious aspects—Christianity. I. Littauer, Florence, 1928- II. Title.
BV4597.57.L57 2006
    155.2'6—dc22   2006007436

20   21   22   23   24   25   13   12   11   10   9   8

This book could not have been written without my mother
pouring everything she knows about the Personalities into me.
Together, we have studied the Personalities for nearly 40 years.
My mother has given me the freedom to take this topic into
entirely new realms. We now have Certified Personality Trainers
in many countries—including, of course, the United States—
who are taking the message to the masses.

This book brings together both the basic teaching
on the Personalities that we have been sharing for years and
the newer developments that have come about through the
impact of our audiences' questions and the insights of
our Certified Personality Trainers—many of whom
you will hear from throughout these pages.

Thanks Mom. I hope I do you proud.

CONTENTS

ACKNOWLEDGMENTS

Thank you to my online reading group and my Certified Personality Trainers, who eagerly read each chapter in its roughest form, critiqued and commented, and added their stories, thus enriching the text and illustrating the points I was making. I appreciate each of you!

CHAPTER 1

FOUNDATION AND BACKGROUND

Have you ever noticed that there are people out there who are different from you? Perhaps you live with them. Maybe you work with them. But chances are that you have noticed differences and you have wished that you could change those people. You may have even gone so far as to try to "fix" them by suggesting that their way of thinking, attitude and approach to life should be more like your own. But these attempts usually end in futility and frustration. Those people's differences just seem to be hardwired into their Personality.

As you think about those people whom you may have tried to change (and as you reflect on your own personal growth), I want you to consider Romans 12:18: "If it is possible, so far as it depends on you, be at peace with everyone." I love how this verse is presented in three parts. The first part says, "if it is possible." It is as if God is giving us a disclaimer—as if He is saying that this is a goal we should try to reach. The second part says, "so far as it depends on you," making this our individual responsibility to—the last part—"be at peace with everyone."

If this verse simply said, "be at peace with everyone," it would be impossible for us to live out this teaching. We all have had situations with people in which we have tried everything we know how to do to get along with them, but nothing seems to work. No matter how hard we try, we cannot change those individuals. However, as this verse in Romans suggests, we can change ourselves—we can grow and improve. We can also change our approach to others so that we can, so far as it depends on us, be at peace with everyone.

Once we give up trying to change the people in our life—and accept that they are just wired that way—we can begin to understand others and improve our relationships with them. Likewise, when we are able to grasp the way we are wired, we can use that knowledge to grow beyond our natural tendencies and become better and more balanced individuals.

Personality: Learned or Inherited?

While each person is wired differently, there are many similarities that allow people to be grouped into general categories. The study of these differences and their interrelationship is known as "the Personalities."

A recent article in *Life* magazine stated that "Studies of twins and advances in molecular biology have uncovered a more significant genetic component to personality than was previously known."[1] Researchers have spent countless hours and dollars on studies in order to determine where our personalities come from. These researchers are now beginning to grasp what any parent or teacher will tell you: We all come with our own Personality, determined before birth within our individual genetic makeup. Environment plays a role in how that Personality is shaped, but the basics are predetermined.

I once met with a group of preschool directors and asked them if they had ever had several siblings go through their schools. Of course, the answer was yes. I then asked them to consider the fact that each of these children had the same parents, grew up in the same house, and went to the same church or preschool. Often, they wore the same clothes and slept in the same room as their siblings. But were they just like each other? The answer was a resounding no!

Despite having virtually the same environment, these siblings each had their own distinct Personality. Some were incessant talkers who liked to be the focal point and whom others wanted to emulate. Others were born leaders and liked to tell the other little children what to do and when to do it—these children would take over the class if the teacher let them. Others were more reserved and quiet, afraid to get messy, and avoided projects like finger painting in favor of tidy, methodical activities like building blocks or reading. Other quiet children were content with any activity and easily went along with the program, rarely initiating any ideas of their own.

These same patterns follow us throughout our lives. They are inborn Personality traits—the way we are wired.

It's All Greek to Me . . .

The study of inborn Personality traits is not a new science. During the golden age of Greece (around 400 B.C.), renowned Greek thinkers studied and philosophized about life and the universe. One of the areas that especially aroused their curiosity was the study of the differing natures of people. Just like the group of preschool directors that I met with—and probably just like you—they noticed that people are different.

GRANDMA KNOWS
RUTH CROW, CPT

Every grandmother knows what a joy their grandchildren are! I had the opportunity to take my granddaughter, Morgan, to her first day of kindergarten. From my experience, I know this can be a terrifying and traumatic experience for some children.

Morgan and I entered the room that morning and looked around. Some of the children were crying, some were clinging to their parents, and some were sucking their thumbs. Not Morgan—no, not Morgan! She took a few moments to size up the situation and then began telling the other children what to do, where to sit, who to talk to, what toy to play with, and what book to look at.

Morgan was five years old, a little girl, and the youngest in her family. No one had taught her how to be bossy, or how to be a leader. Watching Morgan's first day of school illustrated to me that Personalities transcend age, gender, birth order, environment, or learned behavior.

One particular Greek thinker, Hippocrates (known today as the father of modern medicine), theorized that what made people so different was their body chemistry. (Only recently have we come to learn that he may have been right on more counts than he has been given credit for!) He and other Greek thinkers believed that people could be categorized into four basic groupings and that their differing physical makeup (or "fluids" in their bodies) was what gave them the specific outward manifestations (what identified their Personality). Around A.D. 190, Galen, a Greek physician, built on Hippocrates's ideas and came up with what he called the four temperaments—four Personality types or moods that he said were caused by the imbalance of certain bodily fluids in people. He called these four temperaments Sanguine, Choleric, Melancholy and Phlegmatic.

Over the years, people have added to and expounded upon these concepts (often giving them different names so as to appear more clever or original), and today there are a variety of different teachings available on this general topic. For example, some of these "new" systems will refer to the Sanguine as Emotional, Influencing, Socializer or Expressive; the Choleric as Volitional, Dominant, Director or Driving; the Melancholy as Rational, Cautious, Thinker or Analytical; and the Phlegmatic as Personal, Steady, Relater or Amiable. However, regardless of the terms used, these basically all come back to these same four Personality types that were originally determined thousands of years ago. So, if you are familiar with one of these other systems, understand that we are all talking the same language, just using slightly different terms to mean the same thing (see chart below). You'll just need to translate as we go along.

Most people who are familiar with these other approaches find that this Personality program focuses more on the positives, rather than the pathology, and is more helpful in solving relationship problems.[2] While many Personality-typing programs give you a label, they do not tell you what to do with that information. The goal of this program, however, is to move you beyond the label and into application so that you can see real changes in your relationships. As you read, I trust that you will have fun discovering who you are and that you will be able to quickly apply the principles to grow beyond your natural Personality while improving all your relationships—both at home and at work!

Comparison Chart of
Different Personality Systems

The Personalities	Popular Sanguine	Powerful Choleric	Perfect Melancholy	Peaceful Phlegmatic
"Leading from Your Strengths" Behavioral Assessment	Otter	Lion	Beaver	Golden Retriever
DISC	Influencing/ Interacting	Dominance	Compliance/ Cautious	Steadiness
Color Code	Yellow	Red	Blue	White
True Colors	Orange	Gold	Green	Blue
Alessandra & Cathcart	Socializer	Director	Thinker	Relater
Larry Crabb	Emotional	Volitional	Rational	Personal
Merrill-Reid Social Styles	Expressive	Driving	Analytical	Amiable

Basic Personality Groupings

Let's start by looking at the basic Personality groupings, realizing that any time we take the entire population of the world and put all those people into one of four categories, we will be making generalizations—no one person will fit exactly into one box. But the thing about *generalizations* is that they are *generally* true! While we are all unique individuals, most of us do have our own set of colored glasses through which we view life and from which our decisions are made. This makes up our basic Personality.

In addition to our basic Personality, everyone has a secondary Personality and usually has a smattering of traits from some of the other categories (we will review the various combinations in chapter 4). The following chart will give you an at-a-glance review of The Personalities. Following the chart, I'll describe the characteristics of each Personality and provide a quick overview of each Personality. You will want to refer to these overviews from time to time as you familiarize yourself with The Personalities.

The Personalities

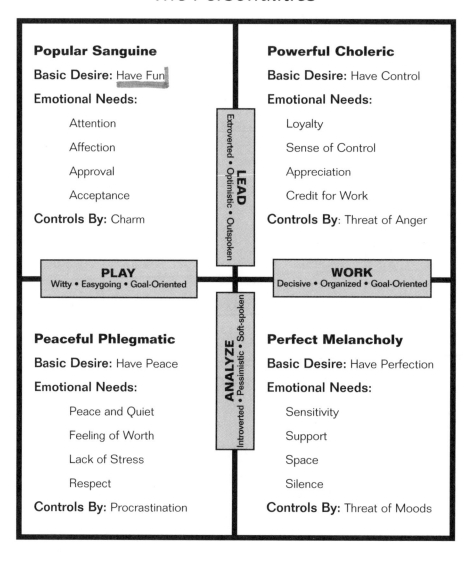

Popular Sanguine

Basic Desire: Have Fun

Emotional Needs:

    Attention

    Affection

    Approval

    Acceptance

Controls By: Charm

Powerful Choleric

Basic Desire: Have Control

Emotional Needs:

    Loyalty

    Sense of Control

    Appreciation

    Credit for Work

Controls By: Threat of Anger

LEAD
Extroverted • Optimistic • Outspoken

PLAY
Witty • Easygoing • Goal-Oriented

WORK
Decisive • Organized • Goal-Oriented

ANALYZE
Introverted • Pessimistic • Soft-spoken

Peaceful Phlegmatic

Basic Desire: Have Peace

Emotional Needs:

    Peace and Quiet

    Feeling of Worth

    Lack of Stress

    Respect

Controls By: Procrastination

Perfect Melancholy

Basic Desire: Have Perfection

Emotional Needs:

    Sensitivity

    Support

    Space

    Silence

Controls By: Threat of Moods

The Popular Sanguine

People with Sanguine personalities are typically high-energy people who are fun-loving and outgoing. These are the people who are always looking for the next gathering or get-together with their friends.

Originally, the ancient Greeks believed that people with this Personality type behaved this way because they had red-hot blood coursing through their veins; hence the name "sanguine," which relates to the blood. Today, the word "sanguine" is also used to describe someone who is optimistic or confident.

Because the word "sanguine" isn't commonly used in speech today, throughout this book it will be coupled with the word "Popular" when it is being used to represent a Personality type. Of course, if you are familiar with this teaching from another source and are accustomed to just the word "Sanguine," feel free to use it. Or simply use the term "Popular" if you find Sanguine cumbersome.

Remember, it's not about labels or how we refer to the Personality types—it's about understanding ourselves and also improving our relationships.

The Powerful Choleric

People with Choleric personalities are naturally goal-oriented and live to achieve those goals. They are highly task-oriented and well-organized, but they are also outgoing, just like the Popular Sanguines. However, in addition to having these positive traits, Cholerics also tend to have a short fuse and to be bossy.

Hippocrates and the Greek thinkers believed that people who displayed this type of Personality had yellow bile in their bodies that gave them these specific traits, like a baby with cholic or a person with cholera; hence the name "choleric." (Choleric is pronounced like "collar" on a shirt, not like "calorie.")

For the same reasons as "Sanguine" above, throughout this book the term "Choleric" will be coupled with the word "Powerful" to better define this strong Personality type: the Powerful Choleric.

Popular Sanguines
"Let's do it the fun way."

Representative Color: yellow (like a "happy face")

Desire: to have fun

Key Strengths: ability to talk about anything at any time at any place, bubbling personality, optimism, sense of humor, storytelling ability, enjoyment of people

Key Weaknesses: disorganized, can't remember details or names, exaggerates, not serious about anything, trusts others to do the work, too gullible and naïve

Emotional Needs: attention, affection, approval, acceptance

Get Depressed When: life is no fun and no one seems to love them

Are Afraid Of: being unpopular or bored, having to live by the clock, having to keep a record of money spent

Like People Who: listen and laugh, praise and approve

Dislike People Who: criticize, don't respond to their humor, don't think they are cute

Are Valuable at Work For: their colorful creativity, optimism, light touch, cheering up others, entertaining

Could Improve If: they got organized, didn't talk so much, learned to tell time

As Leaders: excite, persuade and inspire others; exude charm and entertain; are forgetful and poor on follow-through

Tend to Marry: Perfect Melancholies who are sensitive and serious, but whom they quickly tire of having to cheer up and by whom they soon tire of being made to feel inadequate or stupid

React to Stress By: leaving the scene, going shopping, finding a fun group, creating excuses, blaming others

Recognized By: their constant talking, loud volume, bright eyes

Powerful Cholerics
"Let's do it my way."

Representative Color: red (like a fire engine)

Desire: to have control

Key Strengths: ability to take charge of anything instantly and to make quick, correct judgments

Key Weaknesses: too bossy, domineering, autocratic, insensitive, impatient, unwilling to delegate or give credit to others

Emotional Needs: sense of obedience, appreciation for accomplishments, credit for ability

Get Depressed When: life is out of control and people won't do things their way

Are Afraid Of: losing control of anything (e.g., losing a job, not being promoted, becoming seriously ill, having a rebellious child or unsupportive mate)

Like People Who: are supportive and submissive, see things their way, cooperate quickly, let them take credit

Dislike People Who: are lazy and not interested in working constantly, buck their authority, become independent, aren't loyal

Are Valuable at Work Because: they can accomplish more than anyone else in a shorter time, are usually right

Could Improve If: they allowed others to make decisions, delegated authority, became more patient, didn't expect everyone to produce as they do

As Leaders: they have a natural feel for being in charge, a quick sense of what will work, a sincere belief in their ability to achieve, a potential to overwhelm less aggressive people

Tend to Marry: Peaceful Phlegmatics who will quietly obey and not buck their authority but who never accomplish enough or get excited over their projects

React to Stress By: tightening control, working harder, exercising more, getting rid of the offender

Recognized By: their fast-moving approach, quick grab for control, self-confidence, restless and overpowering attitude

The Perfect Melancholy

People with Melancholy personalities tend to be quiet, deep and thoughtful. They strive for perfection in everything they do that matters to them and believe that if a job is worth doing, it's worth doing right. Because people with this Personality type focus so much on perfection, they often find themselves more disappointed—and even more depressed—than the other Personalities.

The Greek thinkers believed that people who displayed this type of Personality behaved this way because of the black bile in their body—thus the name "melancholy." Today, this word is often used to describe people who are depressed or have negative mood swings. To focus on the positive aspects of this Personality, throughout this book the term "Perfect" will be coupled with "Melancholy" to describe this Personality type.

The Peaceful Phlegmatic

People with the final Personality type—the Phlegmatics—are a bit harder to identify than the other Personalities. While the Popular Sanguines, Powerful Cholerics and Perfect Melancholies tend to live life to the extreme, individuals with Phlegmatic personalities tend to be more balanced and contented with life. As such, they often do not feel the need to change the world or alter the existing status quo.

People who display this type of Personality are often viewed by the more driven Personality types as being slower and more thoughtful, which may be why Hippocrates and the other early Greek philosophers believed that people who displayed this type of Personality had phlegm in their bodies—thus the name "Phlegmatic." Because this word is often foreign to most us, throughout this book the term "Peaceful" will be coupled with "Phlegmatic" to better describe these balanced, steady and easygoing individuals.

Remember, these terms are listed here in order to provide us with some form of shared vocabulary so that we can better discuss each of our Personalities. The goal here is not to label anyone or put them in a box, but just to give some general characteristics that are common among people who share these different Personality types.

Perfect Melancholies
"Let's do it the right way."

Representative Color: blue (like deep water)

Desire: to have it done right

Key Strengths: ability to organize and set long-range goals, to set high standards and ideals, and to analyze deeply

Key Weaknesses: easily depressed, spends too much time on preparation, is too focused on details, remembers negatives, suspicious of others

Emotional Needs: sense of stability, space, silence, sensitivity, support

Get Depressed When: life is out of order, standards aren't met, no one seems to care

Are Afraid Of: no one understanding how they really feel, making a mistake, having to compromise standards

Like People Who: are serious, intellectual, deep and can carry on a sensible conversation

Dislike People Who: are lightweights, forgetful, late, disorganized, superficial, prevaricating and unpredictable

Are Valuable at Work For: their sense of detail, love of analysis, follow-through, high standards of performance, compassion for the hurting

Could Improve If: they didn't take life quite so seriously, didn't insist that others be perfectionists

As Leaders: they organize well, are sensitive to people's feelings, have deep creativity, want quality performance

Tend to Marry: Popular Sanguines because of their outgoing personality and social skills, but whom they soon attempt to quiet and get on a schedule

React to Stress By: withdrawing, getting lost in a book, becoming depressed, giving up, recounting problems

Recognized By: their serious and sensitive nature, well-mannered approach, self-deprecating comments, meticulous and well-groomed looks

Peaceful Phlegmatics
"Let's do it the easy way."

Representative Color: green (like the grass)

Desire: to avoid conflict, to keep peace

Key Strengths: balance, even disposition, dry sense of humor, pleasing personality

Key Weaknesses: lack of decisiveness, enthusiasm or energy; a hidden will of iron

Emotional Needs: sense of respect, feeling of worth, understanding, emotional support

Get Depressed When: life is filled with conflict, they have to face a personal confrontation, no one wants to help, or when the buck stops with them

Are Afraid Of: having to deal with major personal problems, being left holding the bag, making major changes

Like People Who: make decisions for them, recognize their strengths, do not ignore them, and give them respect

Dislike People Who: are too pushy, too loud, or expect too much of them

Are Valuable at Work Because: they mediate between contentious people and objectively solve problems

Could Improve If: they set goals and became self-motivated, were willing to do more and move faster than expected, faced their own problems as well as they handle those of others

As Leaders: they keep calm, cool and collected; don't make impulsive decisions; are well-liked and inoffensive; don't cause trouble; don't often come up with brilliant new ideas

Tend to Marry: Powerful Cholerics who are strong and decisive, but whom they soon tire of because they realize that they don't like being pushed around and looked down upon

React to Stress By: hiding from it, watching TV, eating, tuning out life

Recognized By: their calm approach, relaxed posture (sitting or leaning when possible)

In the next few chapters, we will go into more detail regarding each of the Personalities. However, before proceeding, I recommend that you pick up a copy of *Wired That Way Personality Profile* and complete it so that you can determine which Personality type best fits you. By completing the Personality Profile, you will be able to apply the discussions in the following chapters to your own life, and also to those with whom you interact every day.

YOU ARE HERE
KATHRYN ROBBINS

Completing the Personality Profile may seem like taking a test, but it's a tool that will help you find a starting point. Think of it as going to the shopping mall. First, you need to decide to go to the mall (you need something). You park your car and walk in (do the profile). Now, if you don't know exactly where you are, you might wander around in circles. So a helpful thing to do is to look for the directory board and find the "You Are Here" sticker (add up your totals).

Once you figure out where "You Are Here" is, you then can make a Personality Plan for getting from where you are to where you want to be. You may find you're on the wrong end of the mall (living in weaknesses), which means it will take a little more time to get where you want to go (living in strengths). The journey may be long or short, but at least you're not aimlessly walking around in circles anymore. While most people live with a mix of their Personality strengths and weaknesses, what you want to become is a well-balanced individual who is living in his or her strengths, not wallowing in weaknesses.

This book is your Personality Plan. While you are wired a certain way, you can use the tools and techniques in this book to overcome natural tendencies that hinder you from making the connections in your wiring that turn the lights on. Yes, "You Are Here." But, here is not where you will want to stay. Apply the Personality Plan and enjoy living in your strengths!

Notes

1. George Howe Colt, "Were You Born That Way," *Life* magazine, April 1998, pp. 39-50.
2. To determine the nuances of your own Personality in this program, you will want to use the *Wired That Way Assessment Tool*, the complete and comprehensive Personality Plan that will help you understand yourself and improve your relationship. This tool is available at www.classervices.com.

VISIBLE
CLUES

Now that you know your Personality, you are probably wondering about which basic personalities fit your friends, family members and coworkers. If you all get along, you can pass out individual Personality Profiles and have them all take one—like a game! In fact, in my office, we have a big increase in the sale of Personality Profiles around Christmas time. As families gather together, one member of the family orchestrates the "Personality Party" aspect of the holiday.

But what if that person whom you want to learn to understand—the one you need to get along with better—is resistant to taking a "test"? If you are in a difficult relationship with someone, it is awkward to go to that person and say, "I am having a tough time with you. Would you please take this profile so I can figure you out?" Or what about the people with whom you come in contact on a casual basis: the server at your favorite restaurant, the checker at the grocery store, your child's teacher, or the receptionist at your doctor's office? Can you figure them out without the benefit of the Personality Profile? Can you use the knowledge of the Personalities to adjust your approach to those individuals and become their favorite person because of how you treat them? The answer is yes! You can learn to identify a person's basic—and often secondary—Personality by learning to watch for the visible clues.

Research shows that people will be more likely to respond favorably to you if they like you. So even those with whom you come in contact only occasionally are worth the little extra investment of time that it takes to understand their Personality and to consequently adjust your approach to them. John Maxwell says, "Those who add to us, draw us to them. Those who subtract, cause us to withdraw."[1] When you can identify the Personality of others and then adjust your approach to them accordingly, you become a positive in their lives.

The Patient from Hell

I have used this knowledge over and over in my life, and as a result I have gained favor with people. Recently, I even found that my approach worked when I went to the dentist! I had moved from one side of town to the other, and I was looking for a new dentist who was nearer to my new location. When I asked around for a referral, a couple of my employees referred me to a man who had been their dentist for years. "You'll love it there," they told me. "It is an office full of Sanguines." That piqued my interest, as my experience in the past with dentists was that they were usually Perfect Melancholies/Peaceful Phlegmatics. As a Popular Sanguine/Powerful Choleric, I always feel stupid around dentists because I do not floss enough (who does?) and I hate the out-of-control feeling I have while reclined in that chair, my mouth filled with hands and tools.

But I liked the prospect of a Sanguine dental office, so I called and made an appointment with Dr. Hearn. As I sat in the waiting area, my cell phone rang. I glanced around, because most dental offices frown on people using cell phones while in the office. I was the only one in the waiting room, so I took the call. It was a return call from a friend who was trying to assist me with some computer problems. As we discussed the computer problem, Joanne, the receptionist at Dr. Hearn's office, chimed in, "I hate it when that happens," making it clear that she had been listening to my conversation. The tone of her voice did not indicate to me that she was irritated that I was on the phone in the office, but rather interested and involved in my conversation. I made some jovial comment back to her and continued my conversation until I was called for my appointment. On my way out, Joanne and I chatted about our mutual computer problems. We bonded.

From just that brief interchange, I knew that Joanne was a Popular Sanguine. If a Perfect Melancholy had listened to my phone call, he or she never would have participated in a conversation on which he or she had been eavesdropping. If a Perfect Melancholy had been in charge of the front office, I would not have been on the phone in the first place, as there would have been signs posted about the prohibition of cell phone use. If I had not noticed the signs and answered my call anyway, I would have been scolded and told to turn off my phone. But in this particular office, the receptionist's cheerful involvement in my conversation told me that she was a Popular Sanguine, as my staff had predicted. Because I now knew she was a Popular Sanguine, we had an interchange that made us new "best friends."

When I had to go back for some additional treatment, I was late for my appointment. I miscalculated how long it would take to get there from my new house. On top of that, I could not remember which street the office was on or what the doctor's name was, so calling information wasn't an option. I called my office to see if anyone there could find this out for me, but the two staff members who went to this particular dentist were not in yet. Eventually I got the information and made it to the dental office—albeit late. I told the receptionist my saga. She laughed appropriately and took me in without any reprimand.

A month later, I was scheduled to return to have my permanent crown fitted. I never looked at my calendar, but the day before, I had overheard one of my staff members, Pam, take the call from the dentist office confirming my appointment. Pam had even put a Post-it Note on my purse with the reminder—which I never looked at. I was sure the appointment was at 4:00 P.M.

The next morning, I was driving into town—heading into my office and yakking with my friend on the phone—when the "call waiting" sound beeped. I took the call. The receptionist, Joanne, was on the other end. She said, "We've run out of time to wait for you. We no longer have time to get your crown on." I gasped, "What do you mean? My appointment is at 4:00!" After a brief chat, we figured out that my appointment had been scheduled for 8:40 A.M. When the call had been received in my office the previous day, I had heard Pam say, "4-0." I planted that information in my brain as 4:00 P.M, when in fact she was actually confirming that the appointment was at 8:40 A.M.

Fortunately, Joanne let bygones be bygones and offered me an appointment at 1:30 P.M that afternoon—an appointment that I accept-ed and was subsequently late for! I had to call to verify the street and cross street, as I was sure I had passed it—and I had. I sound like the patient from hell, don't I? No sane dental office would want me as a patient. But Joanne and I had bonded. She welcomed me with no repercussions and no missed appointment charge. I got favor, because she liked me. I had identified her Personality and taken time to chat with her, during which time we connected.

Wouldn't it be great if everyone with whom you interacted actually liked you? While you can't change those other people, you can figure out their Personality and then change the way you approach them based on that information. But first, you must take the time to figure out what that Personality is—just as I did with Joanne at the dentist's office. You do this by watching for the visual clues: people's clothing, mannerisms and personal pace.

Once you know what to watch for, you will be able to identify their Personality almost as accurately as if you had them take a Personality Profile. Most adults have a lot of baggage when it comes to who they think they are, and these misconceptions can color the words they select on their profiles. They can be influenced by what their parents, their teachers, their bosses and their spouses have wanted them to be—and they all probably verbalized different expectations. But when you're watching others—whether friends, coworkers, a spouse—from the out-side, you begin to know them better than they know themselves.

Often, everyone else sees our traits, but we have difficulty owning who we are—especially our weaknesses. This is where knowing what to watch for is so helpful. In the remainder of this chapter, we will exam-ine some of these visual clues as they relate to each of the Personality types.

Popular Sanguine

Popular Sanguines are first in the list, not because they are the most important, but because they are the most obvious to identify. In a crowd, these are the individuals who you see and hear. They are the ones about whom Chuck and I often look at each other and say, "NTN," meaning "No Test Needed." Their Personality is so obvious that it just pops out of them!

Rufus is one of those NTN people. He is a gate agent for an airline. Most gate agents simply take your ticket and look to see if your carry-ons meet the regulations. If they are having a good day, they may say, "Have a nice flight." But not Rufus. Even at a distance, you could tell that he was different. He was a splash of individuality in a uniform world. His black-and-white-checkered glasses really made him stand out.

I met Rufus while boarding a flight for a trip. As I approached the doorway, I noticed that he was cheerfully chatting with each customer as they passed by him. When it was my turn to board the plane, he reached out, gave me a hug, and said, "God bless you." Now, I had never seen Rufus before—or since—yet he hugged me and blessed me. Yes, Rufus was an NTN Popular Sanguine, and he was in a job that was perfectly suited to his Personality. While his bosses might have been frustrated with his chatty nature and wished that he'd get serious, I am sure his frequent-fliers appreciate the cheer that he brings to the arduous task of flying.

Not every Popular Sanguine will be as easy to identify as Rufus, but when you know what to look for, you can identify this Personality type just as successfully. There are two key words that will help you spot the Popular Sanguines in a crowd: "loud" and "open."

Loud

Popular Sanguines naturally have a loud voice that can be heard above the crowd. My Personality is about 50 percent Popular Sanguine. When Chuck and I were dating, he was constantly shushing me when we were out in public (I find that nearly all Popular Sanguines have been shushed most of their lives). If we were in a restaurant and I was telling some entertaining story of what happened during my day, Chuck would encourage me to tone it down, as others around us were listening. If I observed people at other tables straining to hear my story, I'd speak up so they did not have to strain. I liked a bigger audience—the more the merrier. That might be part of the reason why we Popular Sanguines naturally have a loud voice!

One of the greatest fears of the Popular Sanguine is that they might blend in—that they might not be noticed. They are naturally attracted to loud clothes, bright colors and big prints—which may be why Rufus wore those checkered glasses. A Popular Sanguine woman may have big hair and wear dangly earrings or "sparklies" on her clothing. One day, I was in a store looking longingly at a plaid and striped mixed-print outfit when two ladies came down the aisle and looked at the same outfit. One said to the other, "I just hate it when they do this. It looks so confused." She was definitely *not* a Popular Sanguine!

A Popular Sanguine woman also likes theme dressing—selecting a different theme each day so as not to get into a rut and to keep others guessing. She may be equestrian one day (complete with riding boots) and a Mexican Señorita the next (with an off-the-shoulder peasant blouse, a full skirt and hoop earrings).

Due to regional differences and professional requirements, not every Popular Sanguine will be dressed loudly, but when you see someone dressed this way, you can be pretty sure you have found a Popular Sanguine. My friend Gayle lives in Pennsylvania, near Amish country. When she came to New Mexico with her husband for a business conference, she succumbed to the environment after about a week and bought a southwestern outfit with a broomstick skirt. She loved the outfit and wore it often while she was visiting, but when she wore it for the first time after she returned home, she told me that she felt foolish in it due to the conservative nature of the particular region in which she lived.

Women have more fashion freedoms than men, so their clothing is more likely to identify them as having a Popular Sanguine Personality. However, even a Popular Sanguine man will usually find a way to express some individuality when it comes to fashion—even when his profession, like Rufus's, requires a uniform. Let me give you an example.

At a grocery store where I used to shop, there were two managers with whom I interacted. They were required to wear blue oxford shirts, dark slacks and ties. One manager looked very traditional in his pressed, long-sleeve shirt and regimental stripe tie. His hair was perfectly combed and sprayed. The other manager had the same basic uniform but he wore a short-sleeved oxford shirt, frequently sported a novelty tie with a hula girl (complete with a grass skirt that wiggled when he moved), and combed his hair casually over his balding spot. He met the dress code, but still managed to express his personal individuality. Freedom to express oneself is important to a Popular Sanguine.

Open

The other key thing to watch for in identifying the Popular Sanguine is that they are open. For one thing, the Popular Sanguine has an open mouth. They are uncomfortable with dead air and often feel compelled to fill the silence—a trait that has earned Popular Sanguines the moniker "the Talker."

Due to my heavy travel schedule and rural residence, I do a lot of mail-order shopping. I flip through catalogs while I am on the plane and tear out the pages that interest me. When I get home, if I still think I need a particular item, I call and order it. I find that while I am placing the order with the person on the other end of the phone, there is often dead air while he or she keys in the information or looks something up. So I fill that gap. I tell this complete stranger why I am buying this, whom it is for, whether it is late or on time, and so on.

When Chuck hears me carrying on like this with people at the other end of the line, he says, "Marita, they don't care." So now I tell the sales-people, "You probably don't care, but I'm the type that is going to tell you anyway." Typically, they humor me and tell me that people like me make their job much more interesting. Whew! I am not the only one who does this. We Popular Sanguines save the customer service representatives from boredom.

Not only do Popular Sanguines have an open mouth, but we also have an open life. Popular Sanguines have no secrets—and if you have one, it is best not to tell a Popular Sanguine. This is not to say that we are malicious in sharing a confidence: Popular Sanguines just have a very short distance from their brain to their mouth. What comes into their brain comes out their mouth with no processing in between.

If you are talking to someone and he or she is telling you intimate personal details of his or her life—details that you have no business knowing—that person is probably a Popular Sanguine. It is for such folks that the term "TMI" (too much information) was created.

One of Chuck's favorite nicknames for me is "Miss Free Information." I have received this title due to my willingness to tell anyone anything, at any time. For example, due to all the travel that I do for speaking engagements, I spend a lot of time on the phone with airline agents. Because I am usually dealing with the special frequent-flier service desk, they are especially nice. I often tell them, "My husband's favorite nickname for me is Miss Free Information, but actually I am a motivational speaker and I get paid quite well for my information. So tonight, you are getting a free seminar!" They laugh appropriately, and we banter throughout the remainder of the call.

So, the Popular Sanguine has an open mouth and an open life. They also have open body language. They are the huggy, kissy, touchy, feely ones. Popular Sanguines will run toward you with open arms as if they have not seen you in a year, even though you might have had lunch together last week. They are the ones who physically hold on to you while they are talking—usually because they are afraid you will leave before they finish the story!

Cluttered

Another way that you can spot Popular Sanguines is by their cluttered personal space. Their home, office or car will usually be littered with personal paraphernalia—pictures of the dog, the kids, the last vacation; name tags from various functions; a dead plant or two; and maybe a toy. The car of most Popular Sanguines is like a rolling diary of every fast-food restaurant they have been to in the last week or two, with drink cups and crumpled-up bags carelessly tossed into the back seat.

Chuck, my Perfect Melancholy husband, often looks at my desk and asks, "How do you work here? I get a headache just looking at this desk."

But for those of us who are at least 50 percent Popular Sanguine, if it is out of sight, it is out of mind. We must keep everything that we are working on that has to get done out where we can see it every day.

Popular Sanguines are the ones who attend organization seminars. When I am speaking on this topic, I like to ask those in the audience who are Popular Sanguines why they go to these conferences, to which they shout back, "Because everyone tells us to!" They know that they need to get their act together, but when they go home and do what the organization expert tells them to do, they end up not being able to find anything. When it was under the dead plant, they knew exactly where it was, but when they get it into a system, they are lost. Popular Sanguines function best in their own litter—even though others with their best interests at heart are always trying to help them get their act together.

So, let's review: The keys to identifying the Popular Sanguine are a loud voice and loud clothing; an open mouth, life and body language; and personal space that is littered with personal paraphernalia. If you find someone with most of those characteristics, you've found yourself a Popular Sanguine—NTN!

Perfect Melancholy

Perfect Melancholies have the second most obvious Personality trait, so let's look at the visible clues to identify this Personality type. Take a look at "The Personalities" chart in chapter 1 (see page 16). If you look at this chart, you will find that the Popular Sanguine is located diagonally across from the Perfect Melancholy. This is intentional, as the Perfect Melancholy and the Popular Sanguine are like polar opposites. In particular, where the Popular Sanguine is loud, open and cluttered, the Perfect Melancholy is quiet, closed and neat and tidy.

Quiet

The Perfect Melancholy is quiet . . . and that quiet manifests itself most noticeably in a quiet voice. One of my best friends is a Perfect Melancholy. When I am on the phone with her, I can hear her clearly at the beginning of the conversation. But as we go on and she gets comfortable in the conversation, her voice drops. I find myself saying, "Huh? What did you say? I can't hear you." For those of us who are Popular Sanguines, our voices are naturally loud, and we have to work to tone it down. The Perfect Melancholy is just the opposite—he or she has to work to project his or her voice.

The Perfect Melancholy also likes quiet clothes. Chuck has five pairs of khaki pants and thinks he needs more because they are not all perfect anymore. He has also proclaimed that all the best colors are found on a schnauzer. Hmm . . . that would be gray, black and white.

Perfect Melancholies like classic styles, traditional colors, and enduring value. One day while shopping with my Perfect Melancholy friend, I was admiring some cute, fun, hip, trendy outfit. As I was trying to determine if I could afford it—or even needed it—she asked, "Why would you buy that? It's going to be out of style next year," to which I flippantly replied, "Darn! I hate it when that happens. I'll have to go shopping again next year." Perfect Melancholies and Popular Sanguines see things from a totally different perspective—they are wired completely different. I plan to go shopping next year and *want* to go shopping next year, while my friend prefers to make selections that will last.

One time, my friend heard me recount this story when I was speaking at a seminar near her home. Afterward, she came up to me to defend her methods.

"You know that green suit I have?" she asked.

"Yes," I affirmed. She went on to explain that it was an expensive suit and that she had probably paid too much for it, but it was a really good fabric and even after six years, it was still like new. "And I am so sick of looking at it," I quipped.

My friend hasn't worn it around me since. She is pleased that a suit she has been wearing for six years is still like new. I don't know why you'd want to wear the same thing for six years. Neither view is right or wrong—they are just different.

Closed

As much as Popular Sanguines are open, Perfect Melancholies are just as much closed. They fully embrace the adage that "silence is golden" and keep their mouths closed. Recently, when Chuck and I watched the movie *Ever After*—a redo of the classic Cinderella story—a few lines in the film about the tone in which a lady of breeding should speak caught our attention. One of these was that lady should not speak "any louder than the gentle hum of a whispering wind." The other was that a lady should "not speak unless [they] can improve the silence." Knowing the Personalities, Chuck looked at me with a smile. "I like it," he said. To a Perfect Melancholy, not much could improve the silence.

Chuck is a Licensed Professional Clinical Counselor. In the 23 years that we have been married, I have learned to differentiate between when the time he comes home and reports on his day and the times that he is really hoping I will learn the lesson he had to teach his clients. Of course, as a Perfect Melancholy, he is very concerned about boundaries, and so I never know who these people are.

One day, Chuck was telling me about a couple who was in his office. He was explaining that the combination of their Personalities was very similar to our own. He said, "I was telling the wife that she needs to learn to play the silence."

"Play the silence?" I asked.

"Yes," he replied, "You Sanguines . . . [that was my clue that this was something I was supposed to learn, not just a report on his day] need to learn to make a conscious choice to play the silence, like you play the radio. When you get into your car, you reach over and play the radio. You need to learn to make a choice to play the silence."

My mental reaction to this teaching was to think to myself, *I am a big girl; I can do this.* So now when we are in the car together and I have been quiet for a while, I say, "Have you noticed? I have been playing the silence." We laugh about it, because we understand each other.

In addition to having a closed mouth, the Perfect Melancholy also has a closed life. When Chuck and I met, he was in the military, which suited him very well because the armed forces operate on a "need to know" basis. Perfect Melancholies will not tell you intimate details about their life, even if they are intimate with you. I have found that being married to a Perfect Melancholy—and wanting to be included in his life—is like being a junior talk show host: "What did you do today? Then what happened? How did that make you feel?"

When you meet folks who are Perfect Melancholies, you will notice at once that they also have closed body language. They do not use flailing gestures. In fact, if they use gestures at all, they will be small, precise and close to the body. I like to think of the Perfect Melancholy folks as the greatest respecters of space. They will stay out of your space—and they will expect you to stay out of theirs. Let me give you an example of how this works.

Once when I was speaking in Freeport, Maine, I went to Friendly's, a favorite dining experience from my childhood. At the table next to me was a family that looked as if they could have come out of an L.L. Bean catalogue. The mother and father were conservatively dressed in colors befitting to northern New Englanders. They had a baby in a high chair who was fairly well-behaved. And then there was Owen. Owen was about three, and he was all over the place. Now, let's be clear: He wasn't behaving badly—he was just being a toddler. I was clear on his name, because I heard, "Owen, stop that!" several times during dinner.

After Owen had eaten all that he wanted to eat—and his mother had eaten all that she was going to get to eat—Owen moved to her side of the table. He climbed up into her lap, and then got down. Then up. This obviously Perfect Melancholy mother had clearly had enough of Owen. She stood him in front of her, looked into his perky little eyes and said, "The lesson for today is personal space. I have my personal space and you have your personal space. This is my personal space." She swept her hands in front of her to indicate the territory that Owen was to stay out of. She then waved around Owen and said, "This is your personal space. You are to stay out of my space, and I will stay out of yours."

I watched in fascination as this mother attempted to keep her energetic toddler from crawling all over her. It worked for a few minutes, and then we were back to "Owen, stop that!" Yes, the Perfect Melancholy is the greatest respecter of space—though I doubt the concept means much to a toddler.

When we Popular Sanguines come at Perfect Melancholies with our arms outstretched and lips pursed for a kiss, they will reach forward and offer a handshake. It is as if they are holding out their hand and saying, "This far and no farther." If we should be so aggressive as to penetrate their boundaries and actually hug them, it is as if we have just hugged a pole, and we instinctively back off. We know we have done something wrong.

I used to wonder why Perfect Melancholies are like that—until I watched Chuck iron his khakis. It is like art. He mixes his own starch—using an empty spray bottle, water and a gallon of starch—so that he can get the right formulation. He double-starches his khakis. When you go through that much effort to iron, you do not want people hugging you—you might wrinkle!

Neat and Tidy

The personal space of the Perfect Melancholy is, well, perfect, neat and tidy. Whether it is their car, home or office, Perfect Melancholies like everything to be in order. Perfect Melancholies do not multitask well, for they find it hard to do anything right when too many things are going on at the same time. They cannot work in a messy, cluttered environment.

When Chuck and I were dating, he bought a brand-new car. One day, we went to a drive-through restaurant, and to my surprise, he parked the car.

"What are we doing?" I asked.

"Going inside," he said.

"Why?" I asked, since, in my opinion, the fast food was not worthy of the investment of time to go inside.

"You cannot eat in the car," he told me.

"Why not?" I said. "Why would they make drive-through restaurants if you cannot eat in the car?"

"Because," he said, "once a car smells like French fries, it always smells like French fries." Up to that point in my life, I had been unaware that *Eau de French Fry* was a bad smell.

Now, 23 years later, Chuck again has a brand-new vehicle. If I get into his truck with a beverage, he is constantly reminding me not to spill it. If we go somewhere together, I really prefer taking my car so that I do not have to worry about possibly messing up his.

Although I have been teaching this information for years, recently I got an entirely new appreciation for neatness when it comes to personal space. I was in Knoxville, Tennessee, and our entire team had been invited to the home of one of the committee members for dinner the night before a seminar. The home was lovely and was, of course, neat and tidy. However, when I went into the guest bathroom, I noted some extremes in the neat and tidy realm. Across from the toilet was an electrical outlet. It was directly in my line of vision while I was using the facilities, so I noticed it immediately. Down in the bottom right corner was a small label with a number on it.

As I stood at the sink to wash my hands, I noticed the switch plate cover for the light also had a small number on the lower right-hand corner. There was also an electrical outlet near the sink and it, too, had a number. Puzzled, I determined to inquire about it when I got to the main room. Before I stepped out of the guest bathroom, I happened to catch a glance into the wastebasket—which I had not used. In the bottom of the wastebasket was a piece of fabric that was hand-crocheted, like a doily.

I was so amazed at this new level of "neat and tidy" that I challenged two of my colleagues, Kathryn and Georgia, to go into the bathroom to find the two items that took the Perfect Melancholy's neat and tidy to a new high. I later asked the host what the numbers were for and discovered that they were used to tell the position of that particular outlet on the electrical schematics. If there were ever an electrical problem, he'd know exactly which breakers to flip.

Kathryn and I—both Popular Sanguines/Powerful Cholerics—thought that this was an amazing waste of effort. She declared, "I have a similar system. If I have a problem with the wiring, I have one of my kids stand in the room while I go to the basement, flip switches and holler, 'Is it on yet?!'" Georgia, on the other hand, is a Perfect Melancholy, and her house has been hit by lightning. While Kathryn and I were trying to hide our giggles, Georgia was getting information from our host on how the system works.

Ah, but you've got to love these Perfect Melancholies!

Powerful Choleric

Powerful Cholerics are not as easy to identify as the Popular Sanguine or the Perfect Melancholy because their defining characteristics are not as obvious. While there are some clothing and body-language clues for people of this Personality type, the best way to identify the Powerful Cholerics in your life is by the atmosphere they create.

Energy

Powerful Cholerics do not enter a room unnoticed. If the Powerful Cholerics in your life are a positive influence in your life, they will bring a sense of energy and excitement with them. If they are a negative influence in your life, they will bring a sense of energy with them, but not the good kind—they will bring stress and tension. Regardless of the effects Powerful Cholerics have on you personally, they will never leave any doubt that they are currently occupying the same room as you are.

My friend Wendy reported that she could feel the Powerful Choleric energy from her son Andrew even before he was born. When he was awake, there was no way she could sleep, as his movements were like a jolt to her system—"stronger than caffeine!" she said. When he was asleep, it was if a part of her became quiet and still. She and her husband, Mike, refer to Andrew as "the Force." Even from across the house, she can tell when he wakes up from a nap—the energy level just seems to rise. In the car, she knows when he has dozed off, even without looking. "There is a drain in the force," Wendy will say, and when Mike looks back, yes, Andrew will be sleeping.

Body Language

Powerful Cholerics can also be identified by their body language. They are heavy-footed. The floor shakes when they walk. I spend a lot of my life on airplanes, and some Powerful Choleric flight attendants walk so strongly and purposefully that they wake me up as they go past.

Powerful Cholerics may also often have a scowl on their face. This is not necessarily because they are angry (although they may be, as Powerful Cholerics do have a shorter fuse than the other Personalities) but because they are focused, intense, and not easily distracted. Powerful Cholerics never go from point *A* to point *B* and ask themselves, "Why am I here?" Unlike Popular Sanguines, who frequently forget where they are going and why, Powerful Cholerics do everything with a purpose.

In addition to the walk and the scowl, Powerful Cholerics have three gestures that are unique to them: pointing with their fingers, putting their hands on their hips, and pounding with their fist. If someone in your life regularly does any one of the preceeding three gestures, no test needed—you have found yourself a Powerful Choleric.

The expression "in your face" was developed to describe the person with Powerful Choleric traits. Powerful Cholerics like to wag their fingers in your face. When they are in your face, your natural reaction will be to back up. Then they will move forward. Then you will back up. This curious dance will go on until you are backed up against a wall. If the Perfect Melancholy is the greatest respecter of space, the Powerful Choleric is the greatest invader of space.

Function over Fashion

While these body language clues are the best way to identify a Powerful Choleric, there are some clothing and personal-space clues. If you understand that the Powerful Choleric is basically more interested in function than fashion, it is easy to grasp how he or she feels about clothing and décor. The Powerful Choleric values production and makes fashion decisions based on whether the selection will help with productivity or hinder it.

When it comes to clothing, a Powerful Choleric woman would never wear pointy toed, spike-heeled shoes. You cannot walk like a Powerful Choleric in shoes like that—you'd snap the heel off! In fact, most Powerful Choleric women have only a few basic pairs of shoes that they wear with everything: a beige pair, a brown pair and a black pair. Likewise, they will have one gold chain or a string of pearls that is their all-purpose jewelry. They see no need for five pairs of hot-pink shoes.

The same is true for décor. Many years ago, my parents were moving from an older office to a brand-new one. My mother, a Popular Sanguine, wanted my father, a Powerful Choleric, to have new matching office furniture in the new office. But my father was resistant to shop for new furniture because he was quite happy with the odd collection he had amassed for himself over the years. He had an old dark-wood desk with thick, green glass on top. He had a big black executive-style chair with a spring that had worn out long ago. The chair had two positions: upright and—with one false move—all the way back!

My father kept his phone and related supplies on a reproduction antique oak icebox. Behind his desk, he had created a credenza from two old two-drawer file cabinets (complete with contrasting fake wood finishes), bought from the building-supply store next door. Across from the file cabinets, he had a hollow-core door in a deep burgundy type stain—probably something he had also picked up at the building supply on clearance. You can see why my mother did not want to move that mishmash; but for my father, it worked, and he did not want to part with it. (We all prevailed upon him, and eventually he did relent—he got all new matching pieces.)

When identifying people with the Powerful Choleric Personality, remember to look for people with energy and who dress in a "function over fashion" manner. Also, watch for the body-language clues: heavy-footed walk, pointing, "in your face," hands on hips, and fist pounding.

Peaceful Phlegmatic

Peaceful Phlegmatics are often the most difficult Personality types to identify, for their traits are not as obvious as the other personalities. Each of the other three Personality types lives life in the extreme: the Popular Sanguine is extremely loud, outgoing and fun-loving; the Powerful Choleric is extremely strong, goal-oriented and driven; and the Perfect Melancholy is extremely neat, organized and detail-conscious. But the Peaceful Phlegmatic is not *extremely* anything. He or she is steady, even, balanced and consistent—and, as a result, harder to identify. Truly, the best way to identify a Peaceful Phlegmatic is by process of elimination. If a person does not fit any of the other categories, he or she is probably the Peaceful Phlegmatic.

Chameleon-like

When trying to identify Peaceful Phlegmatics, the process is often complicated by the fact that they are also the chameleon of the Personalities. Because their traits are not as extreme, it is easier for the Peaceful Phlegmatic to be flexible to whatever the task at hand demands. Yet this in itself is a clue that you're dealing with this Personality type.

Before I developed the "chameleon concept," I had a hard time identifying the Personality of my friend Melanie, who worked in the building next door. She was vice-president of operations for a nationwide ministry. She did the hiring and firing—a task you might think of as belonging more to the Powerful Choleric. She cajoled the donors and increased donations—a task you might think more suited to the Popular Sanguine. She took care of the finances and issued the paychecks—a task you might think would be done most efficiently by a Perfect Melancholy.

Although Melanie did all these things well, she did not love any of these tasks. She liked her overall job, but at the end of the day, she was often too exhausted to cook dinner or clean the house. All day long, she had to pull from the depths of her resources to be someone whom she was not. As an intelligent human being, she could perform these tasks. As a Peaceful Phlegmatic, she was worn out from having to be someone all day that was not in her nature. Like a chameleon, she could turn the color she needed to be at the appropriate time. When she finally quit that job, it took her months before she was ready to tackle a new position. Her diverse roles made it hard to pinpoint her Personality. That in itself was the best indicator that my friend Melanie had a Peaceful Phlegmatic nature.

Another friend, Susan, found that "chameleon" was an accurate description of her Peaceful Phlegmatic Personality. She wrote me the following note:

I'm always having to adapt to the personalities around me so that the atmosphere will be "balanced." If someone is quiet and withdrawn, I will be more Sanguine around them to draw them out. If someone is over-the-top and loud, I back off. If someone is Melancholy, I try to be sunny. We have joked for years that my life verse is "Blessed are the peacemakers," and it really is true! I think Peacefuls like to keep things at an even keel all the time, so we're constantly changing with each situation.

Cool, Calm, Collected

Another way to help recognize the Peaceful Phlegmatics is that these individuals are opposite of the Powerful Choleric. Whereas the Powerful Choleric brings a sense of energy and excitement—or stress and tension—to a room, the Peaceful Phlegmatic brings a sense of peace. Most of us who have a good portion of Powerful Choleric in our personalities need Peaceful Phlegmatic friends whom we can call when we are all—as my grandmother used to say—"gee-hawed up." (My grandmother was a Peaceful Phlegmatic who was always telling us kids not to get "all gee-hawed up"—she wanted us to stay calm, cool and collected.)

Linda, the Executive Director at CLASS, is like that. Like my friend Melody, Linda can do anything—she doesn't like it all, but she can do it. No matter what stress or problem I come up with, just Linda's tone of voice will assure me that it will all be okay. On the flip side, Linda has used voice exercise/coaching tapes to help her learn to project her voice when she speaks. When the coach worked with her individually, he pointed out that she drops her voice at the end of her thoughts. When preparing for a speaking engagement, Linda draws an arrow, point up, in her notes to help her remember to lift her voice. Her natural voice is gentle and calming. When she needs to be firm or when she needs to project, she has to consciously work at it.

Comfort Trumps All

Another area in which the Peaceful Phlegmatics differ from the Powerful Cholerics is in their motivation for selecting clothes. While the Powerful Choleric prefers function over fashion, the Peaceful Phlegmatic prefers to dress for comfort. Whatever the occasion, the Peaceful Phlegmatic will usually be dressed on the more casual end of the acceptable spectrum of attire. Peaceful Phlegmatic women like those crinkly broomstick skirts because the skirts are supposed to wrinkle!

Several years ago, I was speaking at a function in downtown Charlotte, North Carolina, and had lunch in a local restaurant. At a table next to me were four businessmen. One was Perfect Melancholy and another was Peaceful Phlegmatic, no test needed. The Perfect Melancholy man had on neatly pressed khaki slacks and polished loafers. He was wearing a properly creased, blue oxford shirt with his initials monogrammed on the cuff. He had a red-striped tie, and his hair was arranged perfectly in place. He sat with perfect posture throughout the meal.

Across the table from him was the Peaceful Phlegmatic. He, too, had on the blue shirt and khaki slacks uniform. But he wore a short-sleeve shirt with no tie, and athletic shoes. I am sure that his shirt must have said "permanent press" on the label—but he took it literally! His hair was wind-blown casual and, true to his Personality, he was as close to being reclined as possible throughout the group's post-lunch discussion.

Relaxed

Body language is another point of radical difference between the Powerful Choleric and the Peaceful Phlegmatic. Power Cholerics are heavy-footed, while Peaceful Phlegmatics "flow" when they walk. Like the businessman mentioned above, Peaceful Phlegmatics have an unwritten rule: Why stand when you can sit; why sit when you can lie down.

A group of us were at a conference at the Opryland Hotel and decided to stop in at the hotel restaurant for a late dinner. It was near closing, and the restaurant was almost empty. Our waiter, Andre, took good care of us. He kept trying to get our order in, but we were too tired to actually make a decision. Andre patiently waited for us to place our orders. While we were discussing the menu options—he suggested that I not get the lasagna—we noticed that he leaned against a large square column next to our table. His eyes were closed. My mother asked him, "Are we wearing you out?" to which he replied, "No, I'm just catchin' myself a lean. You gotta do it when you can." Andre couldn't lie down on the job, but he could catch a lean.

Andre was very much like my friend's teenaged son, Aaron, who is most definitely a Peaceful Phlegmatic. He worked for me for a year before he found his true niche in life: working an office job that allowed him to sit in his chair. On the wall next to his desk, there were always black footprints from where he pulled out the bottom drawer of his desk and rested his feet.

One day, my mother and I were in my office and Aaron needed to ask one of us a question. When he entered my office, my mother exclaimed, "Look what just rowed in!" I looked up, and there was Aaron in his desk chair. His chair had wheels on it, and he was using an empty wrapping paper tube as an oar to "row" in to see us. My other staff informed me that he frequently rowed down the hall to the offices in the back.

One day, I asked Aaron to make copies for me. I needed 12 copies of 10 different originals. As I walked by, I noticed that Aaron was sitting in a chair in front of the copier, which was on a counter just above head-level where he was seated. When one set of copies was finished, he reached up, pulled the original out, placed the new master on the glass, closed the lid, and then pressed the green button to start the next set. When I asked him why he was seated, he said, "It is more comfortable this way."

Like Aaron, Peaceful Phlegmatics like to have things in their personal space all within reach. If it's not within reach, they scoot across the room so they can get what they need without having to get up.

While Aaron rowed around the office to avoid having to get up, Chuck, a pastor who also serves with us on the CLASSeminar teaching team (not my husband), brought the Peaceful Phlegmatic personal space thing to a new level. At the time, he was changing churches and in the process of moving from a parsonage to a home that he had purchased. His former church did not yet have a new pastor, so they were not pushing him out of the parsonage. When we all got together in September, we asked him how he liked his new house—which we knew he had bought in June.

"I don't really know," he said. "I haven't really lived there yet. I am still moving."

"Still moving?!" all the Powerful Choleric women gasped.

"Yes," he said, "I don't have to be out of the parsonage until October."

He took *four months* to move one town over. Betty and I had each moved within the last year, and we each began recounting the laboriousness of moving. (Both of our husbands pack everything in boxes, securely tape them shut, and then label them for an across town move. Betty and I stick full drawers in our car and drive to the new house.)

We were all shocked at Chuck's attitude toward moving but became even more so when he began to describe his process. Rather than packing all his stuff into his desk (or on top of it), Chuck and his sons lifted the whole desk—full of stuff, with his papers and phone still on the top— carried it to the U-Haul, and drove it to the new house. Then all he had to do was set it in the right room, and he was ready to work. He could see no reason to pack all that stuff just to unpack it again.

If you're like me, you probably find the Peaceful Phlegmatic difficult to relate to. Yet the world would be an unhappy place without their calm presence and peacemaking tendencies.

Ready, Set, Identify That Personality

I trust that from these descriptions, you have been able to identify the primary Personality—and maybe the secondary as well—for most of the people with whom you live and work. Perhaps reading over these traits has helped you get to know your own Personality more objectively.

Another way that might be helpful in determining the Personality of the people in your life is to think of a blind date. If you were going to set up your friend on a blind date, how would you describe that person? For example, when I think of my friend Georgia—who is single—I describe her as lovely, gracious and elegant. She is sensitive, deep and thoughtful. She is a classic dresser with a quiet voice. She will not bowl you over, but she is strong and determined. Based on the descriptions in this chapter, can you guess Georgia's primary Personality? Secondary Personality? If you guessed Perfect Melancholy as her primary Personality and Powerful Choleric as her secondary Personality, you are correct!

So think about this: How would you describe your friends if you were setting them up on a blind date? How would they describe *you*?

Note
1. John Maxwell, *Twenty-five Ways to Win with People* (Nashville, TN: Nelson Business, 2005), n.p.

CHAPTER 3

STRENGTHS AND
WEAKNESSES

If we all lived in a perfect world, we'd only have strengths. But as we interact with others, it becomes painfully clear that we all have weaknesses. These strengths and weaknesses are a big part of what makes us who we are—they are part of the way we are wired.

As you are gaining insights into your own basic Personality—you know what your Personality is right now and you can quickly identify the Personality of your friends, family, coworkers, and even those with whom you interact on a personal and professional basis—it is time to begin to understand what's in it for you.

Remember, the process of identifying Personalities is about more than just labels. It is really all about relationships. Once you know your own Personality, you can use that knowledge as a tool for growth—moving from where you are to where you want to be. Once you can identify the Personalities of others, you can begin to understand them and adjust your expectations of them.

In this chapter, we will look at the strengths and weaknesses inherent in each Personality type. We will not fully address each and every trait, but the "Personality Strengths and Weaknesses" chart on pages 48-49 will give you a good overview of how each Personality functions.

Personality Strengths

	POPULAR SANGUINE The Talker	POWERFUL CHOLERIC The Worker	PERFECT MELANCHOLY The Thinker	PEACEFUL PHLEGMATIC The Watcher
EMOTIONS	Appealing personality Talkative, storyteller Good sense of humor Memory for color Physically hold on to listener Emotional and demonstrative Enthusiastic and expressive Cheerful and bubbling over Curious Good on stage Wide-eyed and innocent Lives in the present Changeable disposition Sincere at heart Always a child	Born leader Dynamic and active Compulsive need for change Must correct wrongs Strong-willed and decisive Unemotional Not easily discouraged Independent and self-sufficient Exudes confidence Can run anything	Deep and thoughtful Analytical Serious and purposeful Talented and creative Artistic or musical Philosophical and poetic Appreciative of beauty Sensitive to others Self-sacrificing Conscientious Idealistic	Low-key personality Easygoing and relaxed Calm, cool and collected Patient, well-balanced Consistent life Quiet, but witty Sympathetic and kind Keeps emotions hidden Happily reconciled to life All-purpose person
WORK	Volunteers for jobs Thinks up new activities Looks great on the surface Creative and colorful Has energy and enthusiasm Starts in a flashy way Inspires others to join Charms others to work	Goal-oriented Sees the whole picture Organizes well Seeks practical solutions Moves quickly to action Delegates work Insists on production Makes the goal Stimulates activity Thrives on opposition	Schedule-oriented Perfectionist, high standards Detail-conscious Persistent and thorough Orderly and organized Neat and tidy, Economical Sees the problems Finds creative solutions Needs to finish what he starts Likes charts, graphs, figures, lists	Competent and steady Peaceful and agreeable Has administrative ability Mediates problems Avoids conflicts Good under pressure Finds the easy way
FRIENDS	Makes friends easily Loves people Thrives on compliments Seems exciting Envied by others Doesn't hold grudges Apologizes quickly Presents dull moments Likes spontaneous activities	Has little need for friends Will work for group activity Will lead and organize Is usually right Excels in emergencies	Makes friends cautiously Content to stay in the background Avoids causing attention Faithful and devoted Will listen to complaints Can solve others' problems Deep concern for other people Moved to tears with compassion Seeks ideal mate	Easy to get along with Pleasant and enjoyable Inoffensive Good listener Dry sense of humor Enjoys watching people Has many friends Has compassion and concern

Personality Weaknesses

	POPULAR SANGUINE The Talker	POWERFUL CHOLERIC The Worker	PERFECT MELANCHOLY The Thinker	PEACEFUL PHLEGMATIC The Watcher
EMOTIONS	Compulsive talker Exaggerates and elaborates Dwells on trivia Can't remember names Scares others off Too happy for some Has restless energy Egotistical Blusters and complains Naïve, gets taken in Has loud voice and laugh Controlled by circumstances Gets angry easily Seems phony to some Never grows up	Bossy Impatient Quick-tempered Can't relax Too impetuous Enjoys controversy Likes to argue Won't give up when losing Comes on too strong Inflexible Is not complimentary Dislikes tears and emotions Is unsympathetic	Remembers the negatives Moody and depressed Enjoys being hurt Has false humility Off in another world Low self-image Has selective hearing Self-centered Too introspective Guilt feelings Persecution complex Tends to hypochondria	Unenthusiastic Fearful and worried Indecisive Avoids responsibility Quiet will of iron Selfish Too shy and reticent Too compromising Self-righteous
WORK	Would rather talk Forgets obligations Doesn't follow through Confidence fades fast Undisciplined Priorities out of order Decides by feelings Easily distracted Wastes time talking	Little tolerance for mistakes Doesn't analyze details Bored by trivia May make rash decisions May be rude or tactless Manipulates people Demanding of others End justifies the means Work may become his or her god Demands loyalty in the ranks	Not people-oriented Depressed over imperfections Chooses difficult work Hesitant to start projects Spends too much time planning Prefers analysis to work Self-depreciating Hard to please Standards often too high Deep need for approval	Not goal-oriented Lacks self-motivation Hard to get moving Resents being pushed Lazy and careless Discourages others Would rather watch
FRIENDS	Hates to be alone Needs to be center stage Wants to be popular Looks for credit Dominates conversations Interrupts and doesn't listen Answers for others Fickle and forgetful Makes excuses Repeats stories	Tends to use people Dominates others Decides for others Knows everything Can do everything better Is too independent Possessive of friends and mate Can't say, "I'm sorry" May be right, but unpopular	Lives through others Insecure socially Withdrawn and remote Critical of others Holds back affection Dislikes those in opposition Suspicious of people Antagonistic and vengeful Unforgiving Full of contradictions Skeptical of compliments	Dampens enthusiasm Stays uninvolved Is not exciting Indifferent to plans Judges others Sarcastic and teasing Resists change

Accentuate the Strengths

As you read this chapter, look specifically for the strengths and weak-nesses of your own Personality type. Most of us have an easier time embracing our strengths ("Oh, yes, that is me!") than we do our weak-nesses ("I don't do that!"). Unfortunately, unless you have spent a good portion of your life in a self-improvement mode, if you have strengths, you probably have weaknesses too.

One of the goals as you look at your own Personality is to accentu-ate the strengths and minimize the weaknesses—not just use the weak-nesses as an excuse for bad behavior: "Oh well, that is just how I am. You better get over it." This is called "refining your Personality," or living in your strengths. Just like sugar is sugar, whether it is raw or refined, your Personality is still your Personality, but it can be raw or it can be refined. As you mature, the goal will be for you to acquire the strengths of all four Personalities but not have any of the weaknesses.

Years ago, I dated a guy who was into self-improvement and person-al growth. He was in sales. Salespeople tend to go to lots of seminars to learn how to be better at their craft, and this guy went to every acclaimed sales training program, consulted every personal-growth expert, and read every book on the subject—and he really applied the information. We dated for two years, but I never could really figure out his Personality. It was as if he did everything right. He had pulled himself out of his impoverished background and had learned how to behave in every situation, yet there was something phony about him. I never really felt as though I knew him. Every now and then, I meet someone like this guy—a person who has been so molded, massaged and made over that it is difficult for anyone to know who he or she really is.

When I talk about refining your Personality, I am not saying that you should become a phony person. Rather, I am encouraging you to build on who you are naturally. Trying to be someone you are not is emotionally expensive. It is like trying to make your hair curly when it is not. You can do it—you can get perms or use a curling iron or hot rollers—but there is a cost: Perms are expensive, and they damage your hair. Plus, if you get tired of fighting it and let up, the straight hair comes back, but the damage remains. Trying to be someone else is exhausting, and the damage often comes in the form of stress-related illnesses.

That is what happened to Debi. She had a concept in her mind of what a perfect woman was supposed to be, but it was not who she was. She told me:

> As a young adolescent, I was often told that I was too bossy, loud and unforgiving. I was told that I needed to be gentler in my approach with people and that a real lady didn't always need to be in control. I took all this "advice" and devised in my mind what I needed to do to change those negative things about me to become a better person. I began to observe other women whom I felt were the example of this ideal woman—what I was supposed to be.
>
> I truly felt there was something wrong with me. I struggled so hard to be the pleasant, compliant, peaceful wife and mother I admired in those other women. I would try. And fail. And try again. And fail harder. I would sit and sweetly give calm, quiet and loving answers to my other women friends. I would keep quiet even when I knew something my husband did was totally wrong! I would smile and say, "Everything is fine." This behavior went on for years, to the point that my husband asked if I might have a mental disorder.
>
> Then one day I learned about the Personalities and took the Personality Profile to find out what my Personality was. What a relief it was to finally be able to embrace who I was! I began to realize that the way I was wired had many strengths that I hadn't even been aware of. Somehow, I had thought I was all bad and had to be someone else.
>
> Even more important than understanding myself was the understanding I began to have for the people around me: my husband, children, coworkers and friends. I learned that not only am I okay, but that they are all okay, too. It has been many years now since I began learning about me—how I can operate and be the best me that I can be, by living in my strengths while working to eliminate my weaknesses.

Take some time to get to know the basics of your Personality. Look at your strengths and build them up, and then work to whittle away your weaknesses. Don't wallow in them. Use the knowledge of other people's strengths and weaknesses to better understand them and adjust your expectations of them. This is not to excuse their behaviors, but to eliminate some of your frustration in dealing with them. When you understand what to expect, you will take the actions of others less personally.

I've mentioned Linda, our Executive Director at CLASS. She is a Peaceful Phlegmatic, and she is in charge of setting up all of our conferences. Whenever we hold a conference, the facility administrator usually wants a diagram of how we want the room set up. For one particular conference, the Glorieta Christian Writers Conference, my sister Lauren, a Powerful Choleric, was running the Resource Center. Linda wanted to make Lauren happy by trying to guess how Lauren would want the room set up. I advised Linda not to bother. "Just put the tables in the middle of the room," I told her. "Lauren won't know how she wants the tables set up until she sees the room and gets a feel for it, so when she gets here she will just rearrange them anyway." Because Linda understands the Personalities—and therefore understands Lauren—she no longer frets over trying to please Lauren. Instead, she makes her life easier by just letting Lauren do it her way.

So as you review the following sections, think about which of these specific traits not only fit you but also the people with whom you interact on a daily basis. How can you use this knowledge to grow? How can you use it to adjust your expectations of others?

Popular Sanguine
Strengths

Emotions: **Natural Curiosity**

Those of us who are Popular Sanguines have a naturally curious, inquisitive nature. While we mean no harm, our curiosity often gets us in trouble.

One day, Chuck and I visited one of his friends. After we left, I made a comment—as though it were a known fact—that this friend colored his hair. Chuck looked surprised and asked, "How do you know?" I explained that besides the obvious fact that the hair coloring dripped down his face when he sweat, I had seen the Just for Men box under his sink in the bathroom. My Perfect Melancholy husband was aghast at the mental picture of his wife foraging through the cabinets of his friend's bathroom. "What were you doing looking under his sink?" he gasped. It seemed perfectly logical to me. While I was using the bathroom, I saw that there were no magazines or catalogs on the floor for me to peruse. So, without giving it a thought, I opened the cabinet door and just had a look.

When Chuck heard me tell this story at a conference, he realized by the reactions of others that I am not the only one who does this! And this reality hit home the year we received a card that played Jingle Bells when you opened it. Chuck decided to take that little music maker and put it in the drawer next to the toilet in the guest bathroom. We joked that you could tell who the Popular Sanguines were when you heard Jingle Bells ringing through the door!

Work: **Energy and Enthusiasm**

When you look at the Popular Sanguine portion of the chart under the Strengths/Work section, you will see that coming up with positives in this area required a bit of a stretch! Each of these strengths is rather shallow, implying that even though Popular Sanguines look good on the surface, they seldom live up to expectations. Work is not really the strong suit of the Popular Sanguine!

In fact, I had great difficulty coming up with a story to illustrate the Popular Sanguine's strengths at work! I had to send a pleading e-mail to my readers. Fortunately, Cheri, one of our Certified Personality Trainers, sent the following story to me:

> Since I work with preteens and teenagers every day, I consider energy and enthusiasm two of my greatest assets at work. It doesn't matter how much I know about dangling participles or comma splices; if I can't get these kids revved up about their own writing, I won't be an effective teacher.

Recently, my principal showed up in my classroom, unannounced, to observe me for the class period. Although I was a bit unnerved, I proceeded with my lesson plan, which called for me to read a story in a hysterically absurd picture book, *The Secret Knowledge of Grownups*. Yes, I read a children's book to my junior high students! I threw myself totally into the reading, using my best dramatic voices, pauses and inflections. The story concluded with the dire warning, "Eat your vegetables, or be eaten *by* your vegetables."

We'd all been laughing throughout the story, but this line brought down the house (and, to my relief, my principal joined in the merriment!). My students then began a creative writing assignment of their own. Pens scribbled rapidly and occasional giggles scattered across the room. After 10 minutes had elapsed, most of the students had written a full page, and many begged me for more time because their stories were "getting so good." When I asked for a show of hands from those who felt they'd written something better than they thought they could write, virtually every hand shot up.

When my principal met with me to share the results of his observation, his focus was not on my subject-area knowledge or on my ability to keep the students quiet and obedient. He lavished praise on my ability to infect my students with my own unbridled enthusiasm for reading and writing.

I felt greatly rewarded when a few months later, one of my students took Best in Class in four of the seven Creative Writing contests she entered at our county fair. The Popular Sanguine enthusiasm my students caught translated into tangible results!

As Cheri's story illustrates, one of the best strengths that the Popular Sanguine has at work is the ability to turn "work" into "play."

Friends: **Makes Friends Easily**

When I first moved to New Mexico, I was invited to speak to a group of teachers in Santa Fe. I was new to the area, so I planned, uncharacteristically, to arrive early. But when I arrived in the college parking lot, I saw only one other vehicle—and a woman unloading boxes from it. I asked her if she was there for the teacher's conference. She replied that she was and indicated that she knew where we were supposed to be.

I unpacked my books and followed her into the building. We set up our tables next to each other (she was selling insurance and I was selling books) and visited while the other sessions were taking place. I found out that her name was Debbie, and as we chatted, we discovered that we had a lot in common—including having recently moved to Albuquerque from California. We bonded.

During my speech, when I was talking about Popular Sanguines, I told everyone about my new best friend, Debbie. After my session was over, people went over to Debbie's table and asked if she was the "new best friend" to whom I had been referring. At first, she had no idea what these people were talking about, but she quickly caught on and agreed that she was. At the end of the day, Debbie and I exchanged cards and promised to stay in touch.

When I pulled into the garage that evening, Chuck was working on a project. As I got out of the car, he asked, "How was your day?" I gushed on about how great it was, especially because I had made a new best friend. Knowing that Chuck is a Perfect Melancholy and a therapist, one would have expected him to reply with something like, "Oh, Sweetheart, I am so glad you made a new friend. You are new here in Albuquerque and do not know anyone." But instead, he firmly told me that I could not make a new best friend every day—that new best friends take years to develop and I could only have one or two in a lifetime. Crestfallen (but not deterred), I told him about Debbie anyway.

I sent Debbie a Christmas card, but she did not send one to me. It was kind of like dating—I like you; do you like me? Months went by, and I never heard from her. One day, I had about 15 minutes before I had to be somewhere and I found myself right in front of where I understood her office to be. I stopped in, and she was there. The moment she saw me, she jumped up from her desk and exclaimed, "Oh, Marita!" as she gave me a hug. We were like new best friends all over again, catching up on what had happened since the last time we had seen each other.

That was years ago. I haven't seen or heard from Debbie since. But for that day, we were, again, new best friends. The thing about Popular Sanguine instant best friends is that there is no guilt and no, "Why didn't you call me?" You just pick up where you left off—and if you never see each other again, it was fun while it lasted!

Weaknesses

Emotions: **Egotistical**

While Popular Sanguines can be energetic or enthusiastic, sometimes these beneficial traits can evolve into weaker traits like egotism or pride.

Tammy was going to drive from Midland, Texas, to the Dallas area to attend a Women's Professional Bowling Regional Tournament for which she had recently qualified. Her husband, an ICU nurse at the local hospital, was unable to get off work on such short notice, which meant that Tammy would have to drive to the tournament alone. Concerned for her safety on the trip, Tammy's husband begged and pleaded with her to get a cell phone before she left. Tammy was insulted. After all, she was a big girl and perfectly capable of driving four-and-a-half hours by herself without a phone—and she made sure that her husband knew that!

Reflecting back on that day, Tammy told me:

The more I thought about it, the more the idea of being able to chat with my buddies while making the trek and show off my advanced technology became appealing! I finally gave in. I headed for Dallas with the big suitcase-type model in the front seat.

I had a wonderful trip and bowled well—I finished in fifth place. I was so excited. It had been a great time. As soon as I got in the car, I started calling my friends to report on my success and show off my new phone. It was nearly dusk, and when I got on the freeway from Dallas to Fort Worth it was raining. The rain poured down so hard that I could only drive about 25 miles per hour. All of a sudden, the car started sputtering, and I realized I had not gotten any gas! I knew that my gas gauge was broken (it was stuck on "full"), but in all the excitement, I had forgotten that little fact. I managed to get to the side of the road, but I was terrified that someone might hit me in the blinding rain.

I got on the cell phone (that I didn't think I needed!) and called my husband at work to relay my tale, ending with, "What do I do? HELP!" After a few minutes, he managed to calm me down and, in his Peaceful Phlegmatic way, explained how to call the tow truck. I did as he instructed, and after what seemed like hours, the driver arrived, hooked up my car, and took me to the gas station. The driver refused to unhook the car until he was sure it only needed gas, so after we filled up the tank, he took my keys to start it up. He left the car running and shut the door, locking the keys in the car in the process. After about 20 minutes, we finally got the door open, and I started home.

Now it was dark. I was scared and nervous. I talked to my husband most of the way home on that "unneeded" cell phone. About 10 miles from home, I told him that I was fine and would be home soon. About 5 minutes later, I rounded a turn and the car began sputtering again! I had been so distracted on the phone and with the rain that I had once more failed to stop and get gas. I had to call my husband, again, and ask him to bring me gas. Boy, was I glad I had that "unnecessary" phone.

Work: Wastes Time Talking

I used to have an employee named Kathy. I frequently told her, "Kathy, you give Popular Sanguine a whole new meaning!" She was strong Popular Sanguine, with little of any other Personality type mixed in. Amazing things happened to Kathy on her way to work each day. She drove the same route that many others drove, but for her, stuff just happened. When she got to the office, she could hardly wait to tell us about the morning's adventures. If anyone came in after she arrived, she would tell her story all over again—sometimes several times each day.

Knowing that Kathy was a Popular Sanguine, I knew that I could not keep these stories from bubbling out of her. So I told her to wait until everyone got into the office, so that we could all be there and pay attention while she told us her tale. This plan pleased her because she now had a bigger audience, and it pleased me because she was now working instead of telling 10 different renditions of her daily story.

I recently chatted with Kathy to get permission to use this story in print, and I asked her if she had any additional stories that I could share. She told me that my timing was good, for she had just been laid off from a pharmaceutical company. When the layoffs came down, she was the only employee who went and hugged her boss to thank him for laying her off. She had not yet found her passion, so she welcomed the opportunity to seek a new career path. Now, her old company keeps calling to ask her to come back. When I asked her why, Kathy said that it was not because they miss her or her productivity, but because they miss her stories!

Friends: **Fickle and Forgetful**

Popular Sanguines live in the moment, and this carries into their friendships. As easy as it is for Popular Sanguines to make friends, it's almost as hard for them to maintain those friendships. With Popular Sanguines, it's out of sight, out of mind—it could be one day, one year, or one decade between contacts. Popular Sanguines seem to feel that if people are their friends, time makes no difference. They expect to just pick up the friendship where they left off.

For other Personalities, this extended absence may be taken as a personal affront. As I previously mentioned, Perfect Melancholies invest a lifetime into the few friends they have, and because of this, they are more likely to be wounded when they find their investment forgotten in the flurry of Popular Sanguine activity. When faced with the fickle friendship of a Popular Sanguine, Powerful Cholerics cut their losses and go elsewhere—they don't have time for what they perceive to be the "pettiness" involved in maintaining the friendship. The Peaceful Phlegmatics generally put up with the Popular Sanguine's flighty tendencies, as they tend to be natural grace givers. After all, for them it is too much work to hold a grudge—and Popular Sanguines are such fun!

The whole concept of time (not to mention being on time) is a problem for Popular Sanguines. Cassandra, one of our Certified Personality

Trainers, is a Powerful Choleric who had a Popular Sanguine friend. Because she understands the Personalities, she learned to expect her friend to be tardy all the time—but it still bothered her. But rather than dump the relationship, Cassandra decided to make a plan:

> My husband and I enjoy going out for dinner and a movie. My friend Nancy and her husband often join us. The first time her tardiness caused us to miss the opening of the movie, I wrote it off. But after the second time, I realized that Nancy did not have any built-in sense of time. In true Powerful Choleric fashion, I decided to take matters into my own hands and relieve some of the pressure that I knew her husband was under trying to get her out the door (not to mention the safety of all who rode in her car as she tried to make up for being late by driving very fast).
>
> The next time we planned to go to a movie, I decided to implement a master plan. If a movie started at 9:15 P.M., I would tell Nancy that the movie started at 8:45 P.M. This would allow extra time for her running late, and we would still walk into the theater in time to get a good seat and see the previews. This plan worked well, and from then on we have always made it to the movies on time. And to my knowledge, I do not think that Nancy has ever caught on to my plan!

Powerful Choleric
Strengths

Emotions: Exudes Confidence

I have said before that you always notice when a Powerful Choleric enters a room. This is often due to the fact that they have great confidence.

Even as a child, the Powerful Choleric's confidence shines through. Nothing illustrates this better than the story of Kayleigh, a young girl who has difficulty behaving in youth church. She prefers to do her own thing.

However, knowing that Kayleigh is motivated by rewards, one day her mom told her that if the teachers didn't have to get after her that Sunday, the whole family would go on a picnic at the lake near their house after church. Kayleigh, being the confident Powerful Choleric that she is, accepted the challenge and met the goal. When her mom picked her up, Kayleigh immediately began to tell her that they needed to go to Wal-Mart right away to get all the items necessary for the picnic.

As they went through the store, Kayleigh told anyone who would listen that she and her family were going on a picnic. She then began to invite everyone she met, ending her story with, "You can come, too!" One of the stockers laughed at her excitement and played along with her.

"I would love to come, but I have to work," he told her.

"But they give you breaks so you can go," she explained. "Where's your boss? I'll tell him that you have a picnic to go to and can't work right now!" He laughed and humored her by saying that he'd come.

A few aisles later, Kayleigh stopped and told her mom, "We have to go back! We didn't tell him where we would be at the park." To ease her expectations, her mom told her that it was okay. If the young man did decide to join them, he would probably want to picnic with his own family—just like their picnic was just for their family.

From that point on, Kayleigh continued to tell people about the picnic and kept inviting them to come, but she added that the picnic was just for their family. "But," she said, "you can picnic near us, and we could share food if you wanted us to." She even told one mom who was shopping that "someone else is already going to be picnicking beside us on the right, but you could sit on the other side if you want to." When the mom explained that she wanted to join them but probably couldn't, Kayleigh replied, "Well, if you want to, you should do it. Your kids aren't getting any younger."

Work: **Goal-Oriented**

There is an old saying that states if you want something done, ask a busy woman to do it. I'd like to improve on that: If you want anything done—and done well—ask a Powerful Choleric to do it! Once you read about my friend Sheryl, I think you'll see why this is true.

For six months, Sheryl served as the interim children's director at a large church where her husband was an associate pastor. The church had more than 350 slots that needed to be filled with volunteers for the weekly children's programs. This one task had worn out the previous director and driven her to the brink of a nervous breakdown. Sheryl, thinking the past director must have been weak, was determined to get all the spots filled and prove herself worthy.

Being very task-oriented, Sheryl completed hours of phone blitzes to fill the incessant openings. As a result, she was able to keep the departments fully staffed for many weeks. However, after the first few weeks, Sheryl realized just how overworked the past director had been. Minutes before the volunteers were to be on duty, Sheryl would receive phone calls saying that there had been a family emergency and that they could not make their shift. The volunteers had been told to find their own substitutes, but this policy had not been enforced. They constantly called Sheryl with apologies for the short notice, and they rarely had a substitute lined up.

Because of her desire to excel in her role, Sheryl would stand at the back of the services and pray over the congregation, asking God to show her who He would have her recruit. And God always proved His power in bringing fabulous volunteers with humble servant's hearts to Sheryl—often just in time for class to start!

Friends: **Excels in Leadership and Organization**

Inside every Powerful Choleric is a hero just waiting for a chance to show what he or she is made of. In an emergency, the Powerful Choleric's quick thinking, fast action, sheer guts and fortitude often save the day. This is good, because the Powerful Choleric's need for adventure and rescuing others requires all these attributes. Most of the time, they are willing to go around, leap over, dig under, plow through, endure pain or move an obstacle for the sake of fixing a problem. I'm sure that many of New York's "finest" are Powerful Cholerics.

Powerful Cholerics are not only effective in rescue-type occupations but also are good at problem solving. A paper jam in the printer at work can put everyone behind. Tah-dah! Powerful Choleric to the rescue! The offending piece of paper is out, the tray is reset, and everyone can go back to work. Powerful Cholerics make it look so simple. Even as small children, this quick ability to size up a situation, figure out a plan and act on it is already evident in their Personality.

Katie recalls a fun-filled childhood vacation at Lake Leach, Minnesota, that she spent with countless aunts, uncles and cousins. As usual, when you have that many people and activities in one place, some of the younger kids are bound to get into places that they should not be. One day, when all the kids went out on the dock to see the fish that were swimming around, Donovan (a two-year-old who shouldn't have been there) wiggled off the dock and fell into the water. It was instant winter—everyone froze. Diane, Donovan's older sister, started screaming, "Someone get him! Hey! Someone! Donovan is drowning!" Without giving it a second thought, a nine-year-old named Katie jumped into the deep water, grabbed Donovan, got his head up above the water, swam to shore, and deposited the frightened baby back into his mother's care. "How did you know how to do that?" the adults all asked her. She replied, "I didn't. I just knew that he had to get out of the water." To this day, Katie reminds her cousin that he owes her one.

The Powerful Choleric's ability to do everything themselves—and usually do it better than anyone else—often translates into a lack of friends. When Sheryl found herself in this place, she used her Powerful Choleric strength of leading and organizing to solve her problem.

Sheryl, a pastor's wife and a mother, was frustrated with her lack of friends, intimacy and meaningful relationships at church. Although Sheryl served in her husband's ministries, opened their home for small groups, made meals for the church potlucks, and met with women who needed lay counseling, she knew that something was missing in her life. She was lonely for women friends.

As a pastor's wife, Sheryl knew that she had to be selective about who she could trust with her prayer requests and burdens. Sheryl wondered if the wives of the other pastors on staff felt the same way. After praying about her next step, Sheryl called the wife of one of the other pastors and asked if she might be interested in meeting regularly for fellowship and prayer—maybe even for a Bible study. Sheryl explained her feelings of isolation and frustration. The other pastor's wife said, "I feel exactly the same way!"

The pastors' wives began meeting once each week in Sheryl's kitchen. They met right before Sheryl's kids needed help getting ready for school, from 6:00 A.M. to 7:30 A.M. on Friday mornings. They talked and prayed for their husbands, their children, and themselves. They enjoyed the fellowship and the blessing of bonding in their unique roles as wives of pastors.

Sheryl has seen her Powerful Choleric strengths of leadership and organization taker her to the place in which God has called her to minister. She continues to speak to women's groups, is working on a devotional book for pastors' wives, and serves on the Ministers' Wives International Network. By confronting her frustration at the lack of meaningful friendships with women in her life, Sheryl was able to come up with a solution that has helped many others.

Weaknesses

Emotions: Unsympathetic

Powerful Cholerics have a difficult time expressing empathy, especially for those who are sick with an illness such as the cold or the flu. I tell my employees that they should come to work if they just have the sniffles. I tell them, "You will be miserable alone at home. You might as well come to work and be with people who love you." In contrast, Chuck, my Perfect Melancholy husband, thinks it is inconsiderate for people to come to work with colds because they spread germs around the office.

Chuck likes to tease me that Powerful Cholerics are the only ones who fake being well. We do not want anyone to know that we are sick, and we will deny it if asked. Because of this, we assume that others will feel the same way, and so we have little sympathy for their ailments. We view sickness as a weakness—something that we hate to admit.

When I was a child, my friends' mothers would bring their children soup and ice cream if they did not feel good. My mother, on the other hand, would send me to my room if I had a tummy ache and tell me to come out when I felt better. My siblings and I used to say that she had a lack of "nurseness," but it did cut down on our skipping school unless we felt truly terrible. For me, whatever I was trying to avoid at school was usually better than staying home in my room alone.

In my early childhood, my family attended a church that taught that all sickness was in people's heads. If people wanted to be well, they would be. While I do not subscribe to that church's overall teaching, that part did kind of stick with me, and to this day I have little patience for sick people.

I have two get-well cards that I like to use when teaching on this topic. The first is a Mary Englebright card that features a Powerful Choleric-looking girl on the front. Her hands are on her hips, and she appears to be scowling from underneath her wide-brimmed hat. On the front of the card it says, "Snap out of it." On the inside, it says, "And get well soon." The other card also captures the overall Powerful Choleric attitude toward being sick. It is a Hallmark Shoebox greeting card that features "Maxine," that mostly-Powerful Choleric curmudgeon. The front of the card says, "Heard you're sick." Inside, it simply says, "Wimp."

Work: **May Be Rude or Tactless**

Chuck used to work for an insurance company that provided behavioral health services. He had a coworker who was great at her job, and she got more work done than anyone else. Part of her job involved denying claims, while another part involved her inspecting the premises of the providers of the services to make sure that the services being paid for were actually being performed. After she had been at one facility, they called the management at the insurance company and requested that she never be sent there again—she had left too many of their staff members in tears. When this was brought to her attention, she could not comprehend why she had been reprimanded. After all, she had just done what she was supposed to do.

Friends: **Can't Apologize**

When you realize that Powerful Cholerics are usually right, it becomes easier to understand why it is often so difficult for them to apologize.

For those of us who are Popular Sanguines, we are always in trouble, and we have grown up apologizing. Plus, we want everyone to love us. We will sometimes apologize even if we were not in town the day the infraction occurred. We figure, *If you will be quiet and quit whining, I'll apologize.* But Powerful Cholerics rarely get into trouble—and if they do, they do not realize it. As a result, they seldom see the need to apologize.

If you are in a "discussion" with a Powerful Choleric and you come to the place in which an apology would be their next appropriate comment, the Powerful Choleric is more likely to say something like, "I am sorry you got so upset over what I said." Somehow you feel worse after you hear that kind of "apology" than you did before.

I have learned that with Chuck (whose secondary Personality is Powerful Choleric), he seldom actually says, "I'm sorry." But when we are at the point in the discussion where others might apologize, he will become very solicitous of me. He'll offer to do the dishes or take out the trash, or he'll suggest that I go take a bath and read a book. I have learned to accept this change of attitude as a full-on apology, just as if he were asking for forgiveness.

I found a Powerful Choleric apology card. On the front it says, "I'm sorry." On the inside, it says, "But you know, it really was your fault."

Perfect Melancholy
Strengths

Emotions: Sensitivity to Others

Of all the Personalities, Perfect Melancholies feel the full spectrum of emotions. This ability to feel emotion makes them perfect sympathizers to other people's pain or problems. Unlike Powerful Cholerics, who feel the need to fix the situation, Perfect Melancholies will sit and listen quietly to you, and then sympathize with your struggle. This acute sensitivity can be both a benefit and a disadvantage, as Perfect Melancholies can often misunderstand that many of the things they are feeling are "borrowed" and not their own. It may take time for them to figure how to live with this gifting.

This gift of sensitivity gives Perfect Melancholies the ability to decipher the smallest differences in taste, textures, misspelled words, improper grammar, mathematical stress loads, and the details of legal fine print. When Perfect Melancholies apply these emotions to the arts, masterpieces are born. Take to a deeper level this ability to be sensitive, and Perfect Melancholies can communicate in metaphor, which may be lost on the shallowness of the Popular Sanguines or the bottom line of the Powerful Cholerics. No other Personality type has produced more brilliant artisans and poets.

Work: **Likes Charts, Graphs and Lists**

The Perfect Melancholy is often predisposed toward a love of charts, lists and graphs. One day, I was talking to Chuck while he was sitting at his desk in his study at home. I noticed a yellow Post-it Note hanging off one of the little cubbyholes; on the note were written the names of two electronic items he had recently purchased.

"What is that?" I asked him, pointing to the note.

"That's my list of things waiting to get on the list," he explained.

I was puzzled. "Your list of things waiting to get on the list?"

"Yes," he said, pulling open a file drawer and removing a slim file with a neatly typed label. He opened the file to the one piece of paper it contained. "This is my inventory," he continued. "Sometimes when I buy a new item, I do not have time on the day I make the purchase to update the inventory list. So I make a list of things waiting to get on the list."

It seemed so logical the way he explained it to me, but I would never have thought of doing anything like that.

Friends: **Deep Concern for Other People**

Even though Vicki, a Perfect Melancholy nurse, had only seen my colleague Georgia two other times, she had a profound impact on Georgia's life. Georgia was in the doctor's office to receive the results from another biopsy. She was exhausted from her battle with cancer six months earlier, and the thought of a reoccurrence was especially scary. Her Powerful Choleric doctor came into her examining room, pronounced that the biopsy revealed a reoccurrence of the cancer, and then added, "This is serious. You have a 2 percent chance to be alive in 10 years."

At that time, Georgia's only child was just 8 years old. Georgia quickly realized what this dire prognosis meant. She broke down, sobbing, "I won't get to see my son graduate. I want to see Kyle graduate." The doctor, uncomfortable with Georgia's display of emotion, quickly slipped out. But Vicki, the nurse, had the Perfect Melancholy trait of deep concern for people. She held Georgia and let her sob. She didn't tell Georgia that she would see Kyle graduate, and she didn't tell Georgia that she wouldn't. She simply allowed Georgia to cry, provided her with tissues, and comforted her until she calmed down.

Georgia did beat the odds. Today, she often speaks to oncology caregivers groups and tells the story of how Vicki's deep care for her and her tenderness made all the difference during a very traumatic time in her life. It's been more than 15 years since that day in the doctor's office, and Georgia still remembers Vicki's comfort and compassion.

Weaknesses

Work: **Spends Too Much Time Planning and Is Hard to Please**

Perfect Melancholies are perfectionists that can make a simple project into a big task. Let me illustrate.

Fourteen-year-old Keegan came home from high school and announced that he needed a photo of himself for his English class. His Popular Sanguine mom quickly produced one in which she thought he looked "darling." But to Keegan, that photo would not do. He spent all weekend poring over shelves filled with photo albums.

Finally, on Sunday night, he told his parents, "I can't believe I can't find a good picture for English class!" Frustrated with the time his son had invested in such a simple task, his Powerful Choleric father pointed to the 35 albums on the shelves and barked, "If you can't find a good picture in there, you won't find one anywhere. Stop trying to find the perfect picture. Just go in and pick one out!"

Keegan finally found one photo that he could accept. It was the "darling" one his mother had shown him on Friday night.

Emotions: **Can Be Moody or Depressed**

My Perfect Melancholy friend Georgia and I were spending a few days in paradise before heading to a seminar in the Seattle area. We were staying with Georgia's brother on San Juan Island, and he had plans to give us the grand tour and take us sailing. Before we crossed over to the island on the ferry, we stopped in the tulip fields between Seattle and Anacortes and took pictures of ourselves with the sun on our faces and the snow-capped mountains in the background. The weekend promised to be perfect.

On our second day there, I awakened to sounds of whimpering. Georgia and I were sharing the guestroom, and it was obvious that she was crying. "Georgia," I said quietly, "what's wrong?" Through sobs and several tissues, she told me what had made her so depressed—even when everything around her was so wonderful.

As I mentioned, Georgia nearly died from cancer and the subsequent treatments. She was 40 years old at that time, and all of her friends had thrown big parties for their fortieth birthdays. Since, because of her illness, Georgia could not have one, she had promised herself that if she lived to be 50, she would have a big party to celebrate the fact that she made it to the big "5-0." This morning, she had awakened to the realization that she would be turning 50 in a few months, but that she didn't have the strength to put the party together herself or the money to have it catered.

Once I heard her tale of woe, I offered to organize the party for her. I made all the plans. I flew across the country and cooked the food, and 50 people celebrated her life in her beautiful garden. Georgia's story had a happy ending. But left to herself, Georgia's propensity for sadness might have kept her paralyzed and unable to even think about having that party!

As a Perfect Melancholy, my husband likes to defend the Perfect Melancholy viewpoint. One morning, we were both in the bathroom getting ready for the day. I was at the sink and Chuck was in the shower. Through the shower spray, I heard him declare, "Anyone who isn't at least a little bit depressed doesn't understand the gravity of life." While he was seriously contemplative, I nearly died trying to keep from laughing out loud. Finally, I asked, "That's a great line. Can I use it?"

Friends: **Suspicious of People**

When Chuck and I moved to New Mexico, we spent a long year in Carlsbad, which is located in the southeastern portion of the state. While we were there, I made five friends—each of whom were under the age of 10. When they learned that I worked at home, they would come visit me after school and before Chuck got home. If I overbaked some cookies—Chuck likes them soft—my little friends were happy to eat his rejects. They taught me how to rollerblade and kept me from feeling lonely and isolated.

One day when they came over, I met them on the front porch and explained to them that they shouldn't come to our house during the Fourth of July weekend. I told them that Chuck and I had left many of our possessions in California, and so we needed to rent a truck to go back and bring more of our stuff to New Mexico. I told them that we would be gone all weekend.

When I got in the house, Chuck looked at me with one of those "if looks could kill" kind of looks. I knew that I had done something wrong, but I had no idea what it was.

"What did I do now?" I asked.

Chuck simply shook his head and said, "You are hopeless—you are never going to learn."

"What? What did I do now?" I again asked.

"I cannot believe you!" he said. "Standing on the front porch broadcasting to the entire neighborhood that we are going to be gone for five days."

"Chuck," I said, "those are children!"

"Yes," he replied, "but we do not know what kind of families they come from!"

Peaceful Phlegmatic
Strengths

Emotions: **Good Listener**

Ruth, one of our Certified Personality Trainers, served as a medical social worker for a home health agency. Her responsibility was to visit patients in their homes to provide them with information about resources available to meet their needs and to look for ways to improve the patients' quality of life.

One of Ruth's patients, Mrs. Jones, was obviously a Powerful Choleric with a lifetime of experience meeting her own needs. She was loud, abrupt and very capable of expressing herself. A series of social workers and nurses had visited her and tried to assist her, and Mrs. Jones had sent many of them away with instructions to never return. However, despite her history, Mrs. Jones liked Ruth and had requested more visits from her.

This puzzled Mrs. Jones's doctor, who was well aware of the difficulty that the social workers and nurses had while trying to assist her. After several visits, he asked Mrs. Jones why she wanted Ruth to return when she had told so many others to leave and never return. Mrs. Jones said the reason was that Ruth listened to her when she visited. "I talk and she listens," she said. And that is how it was. Mrs. Jones had a wealth of experience and knowledge and did not need a social worker coming to tell her how to run her life. But she was lonely and cherished the time when someone—anyone—sat and listened to her. As a Peaceful Phlegmatic, Ruth was the perfect social worker for Mrs. Jones.

Work: **Competent and Steady**

Dan has been involved in law enforcement for more than 30 years, and the majority of those years have been spent working with tough gang members and at-risk youth. Dan has been blessed to see the fruits of his efforts in the form of many rehabilitated young people who now are living productive lives and making positive contributions to their communities.

Dan's wife, Sherri, told me, "Before I understood the Personalities, I used to think this was just Dan's 'calling' or that he just had a 'heart' for troubled kids. I realize now that it is largely his Peaceful Phlegmatic Personality that has led to his great success on the job." This is very true: Dan's cool head and calming influence allow him to mediate any situation—whether it be a family argument, a heated staff meeting, or a potential gang war. He has the ability to keep his head in any situation.

He is a great listener, never betrays a confidence, and always respects others. He is competent and consistent and can be trusted to take charge whenever necessary. Yet Dan has no need for control or recognition. And when things get tense, his dry sense of humor can lighten the mood by pointing out the absurdity in the situation.

Dan has worked on many of the negative aspects of his Peaceful Phlegmatic Personality. He used to be so drained by the time he got home that all he wanted to do was have his dinner in front of the tube and immerse his brain in hours of mindless television. He could easily sleep away the weekend, and it was difficult to motivate him to do household chores, much less go out on the town. In fact, he would let Sherri know in no uncertain terms what a sacrifice he was making when she wanted him to do something "fun" with her. He could get stubborn and would occasionally be sarcastic. He also liked to rebel against dressing professionally, opting instead to dress in cords, a sports shirt, and tennis shoes.

One day, he sauntered into the courtroom while still wearing his sunglasses, looking as if he had gotten lost on his way to the beach. The judge commented on his casual attire and gave him a subtle hint that he needed to show the court a little more respect. Sherri finally solved his clothing dilemma by hanging two sports coats and an assortment of ties in his office. Whenever he had a court appearance, his secretary would then graciously select a matching coat and tie that he could throw on as he headed for the door.

As Dan has sought to be the man God has called him to be, many of his "rough edges" have been smoothed. Dan knows that he battles fatigue, often lacks motivation, and has a tendency to be reclusive. When he lived in the weaknesses of his Personality, he could be stubborn and selfish. Now, he knows that to stay motivated and have optimal energy, he needs to do certain things: exercise regularly, take vitamin supplements, and be consistent about praying and reading God's Word. He sets goals and stays on task, knowing that at the completion he can treat himself to a nap or a *Law and Order* marathon, if that is what he wants. Dan still needs his quiet time and probably would still prefer life as a recluse, but he recognizes that compromise is necessary to function in a world (and a household) made up of all types of Personalities.

Sherri says, "As a sometimes shallow Popular Sanguine and often overbearing Powerful Choleric, I have learned many valuable lessons from my precious Peaceful Phlegmatic husband. While everyone loves me at the family gatherings for my great stories and my ability to keep everyone laughing, Dan has always been the favorite. While I'm a great 'fair-weather friend,' he is the trusted, constant shoulder that countless family members and friends have leaned on throughout the years. What a blessing it is to live and work with a Peaceful Phlegmatic who has learned to operate in his strengths!"

Friends: **Easygoing and Relaxed**

One day, one of our Personality Trainers, Christy Largent, was speaking to a group of plumbers. When she got to the part in the program in which she described how laidback the Peaceful Phlegmatics are—that their motto is "Why stand when you can sit, and why sit when you can lie down"—the plumbers all started laughing and pointing their fingers at Timmy. "Timmy, Timmy, that is so you! That is so you!" they exclaimed. Timmy was leaning back relaxed in his chair. He looked around, slowly smiled and quietly drawled out, "Heck, yeah . . . I've been looking for a way to have a wheelchair get me around."

Weaknesses

Emotions: **Indecisive and Have a Quiet Will of Iron**

Peaceful Phlegmatics do not feel the need to make decisions and are usually content to allow others to tell them what to do. However, once they do make a decision, you can be sure that it is well thought out and that they are not likely to change their mind. Sometimes, this stubborn will of iron can lead others to believe that they are Powerful Cholerics, but in fact the Peaceful Phlegmatics are really the ones with a will of iron.

Cassandra is a Powerful Choleric who is married to a Peaceful Phlegmatic. When they were first married, Cassandra tried hard to be a good wife. She would offer her husband options on his beverage choices with dinner, saying, "Coffee, tea or milk?" Her husband would look up with a smile and say, "Yes." After several nights, this started to make Cassandra crazy. So the next night when she asked the usual question and he simply said yes to coffee, tea or milk, she gave him all three—in one cup. She can still remember the look on his face when he took a big gulp, expecting coffee. After 30 years of marriage, she has learned not to give him too many choices. Sometimes, even two choices are too many.

While the Peaceful Phlegmatic is uncomfortable making a decision, when they do, it is for keeps. Lynette was a woman who put up with a great deal in her life. For years, she watched passively as her husband humiliated her and made a fool of himself. Everyone in town knew that her husband was a womanizer (he did nothing to hide his extramarital relationships) and he was also a heavy drinker, frequently passing out before he made it to bed. Sometimes, his drinking made him do foolish things, like racing the train to see if he could cross the railroad tracks without getting hit, or walking long distances in freezing weather, wearing nothing but a sports coat.

Her husband's behavior only seemed to get worse with the passage of time. The birth of their son did little to curb his activities. But now that she had a child, Lynnette realized that there was a high likelihood that she would end up as a single parent—that her husband's pattern would eventually get him killed. Even worse, she realized that her husband might begin to hurt her son, just as he had hurt her.

Motivated by a desire to protect her son, Lynette began to take courses at the local college. There, on the college campus, she felt a deep sense of peace that she had not experienced in years. It made her realize just how long it had been since she last had that sense of calm and just how crazy her life at home had become.

One night after class, she went home and found her husband in bed with his boss's wife. That was the last straw. Lynette packed her things, took her son, and left. She had no plans for divorce and no idea of what she was going to do. However, once she was out of that environment, she knew that she was never going back. Although her husband begged and pleaded and promised to change, Lynnette was firm. She had finally made up her mind, and she wasn't about to go back. And she still hasn't.

Lynette's son is now an adult. Looking back on her life, Lynette now realizes that before she left her husband, she had never stood up for what was right. No wonder everyone who knew her thought she'd be back! But like the old country western song, she took a long time leaving, and she's been a long time gone. A Peaceful Phlegmatic, Lynette had been pushed around for a long time. When she was finally backed against a wall, her will of iron made itself known to the world.

Work: Not Goal-Oriented

Kim worked at home in a home-based business. Her husband was in sales, and while he traveled quite a bit, he also had an office in the home. They were both driven and goal-oriented, and they were quite disciplined about getting to their desks and staying focused. Brandon, their nine-year-old son, always knew not to bother them when they were working. He grew up this way and didn't know any other way of going about life.

When Kim's father retired, her parents decided to build a home in the same area where she and her husband lived. While the house was being built, her parents moved into Kim's guestroom. Each day, her parents got up when they wanted and did not seem to have any set agenda. Brandon watched this with fascination and finally asked, "Grandpa, what do you do?" His grandfather replied, "I'm retired. I don't have to do anything." This clicked with Brandon. As a Peaceful Phlegmatic, his parents had always struggled with getting him motivated. But now, Brandon had a goal: to retire!

FROM A NOTE CARD FOUND
IN A MASSACHUSETTS GIFT SHOP:

"His favorite chair was always a bit wobbly, but he decided that accepting things with their quirks was much more enjoyable than trying to fix things."

Friends: **Stays Uninvolved and Is Indifferent to Plans**

Michael, a Peaceful Phelgmatic, shared several insights with me that helped me to understand the apparent disconnectedness this Personality type has in group situations. He explained:

> It is easy for me to avoid situations in which I don't feel comfortable. While I can get lost in the details and options available, I am comfortable with the idea of having lots of options. I am amazed that Powerful Cholerics seem to only see one way to get things done. It never seems to cross their minds that there might be more options. When I am in a group and the Powerful Choleric discards a new idea because it is not the way he wants it done—ignoring that there may be some other way—I grow cynical and quit investing in the process. I don't share my ideas or insights, but keep them to myself. I just endure the process and get out as quickly as possible.

Those of us who are not this Personality type may view Peaceful Phlegmatics as uninvolved and indifferent to plans. However, the truth is that if they do not feel their ideas are being heard, they won't see the point in sharing them.

Strengths Carried to Extremes Become Weaknesses

Hopefully, this quick overview of the various strengths and weaknesses that go with each Personality has helped you to confirm your assessment of your own Personality and that of those people with whom you interact on a regular basis. I could fill all the pages of this book with additional entertaining and enlightening stories, but these few examples should help deepen your basic understanding.

As you look at your own Personality and seek to grow, realize that any strength can be carried to an extreme. Carefully consider whether this might be true in your life. What you may see as a strength, others around you may view as a weakness.

I know a man who is in the network marketing business. He can be very charming and does well in this kind of business. He is very good on stage and can get people to sign up for his program. Just from the brief snippet I have shared about this man, you can probably guess that he is a Popular Sanguine. He has a magnetic personality, is an entertaining storyteller, and is the life of the party.

It would be easy for someone like that man to look at the Personality traits chart and pat himself on the back, thinking, *Look what a great person I am—I have all these amazing traits*. However, these very same strengths often get this man into trouble. He relies on his charm and wit, and therefore he is a poor planner. In fact, he has had so much financial trouble in his life that one of his adult children has had to take over his bookkeeping and provide his father with an allowance. And while he is an entertaining storyteller, if you are in a one-on-one or small-group conversation with him, it is hardly a conversation, as he is constantly talking.

The "Living in Strengths" chart on the following page will help you develop a mental image of what each Personality type looks like when people are living in their weakness (raw) versus when they are living in their strengths (refined). Use this chart to help you examine your life. If you have the indicated strengths, ask those around you whom you can trust whether the accompanying extremes are something you need to watch out for. Rather than feeling criticized over the weakness, work to dial it back to the strength.

The Popular Sanguine man in the network marketing business that I introduced to you has done just this. He has now become aware of his offensive behaviors. As he has learned these deeper insights, he has worked to dial back the extremes and bring his traits into balance.

I have had to do the same thing. As a Popular Sanguine I naturally have a loud voice, which is very good to have as a professional speaker, but not so good in social settings because I can easily come across as brassy and obnoxious. Chuck has helped me to become aware of this by pointing out people in social settings who were "behaving badly" and then showing me how much like them I can be. Once I saw the flaw and how offensive it could be, I wanted to correct it. Now, when I am heading into the extreme mode, Chuck taps me on the shoulder and then uses his hand to make a subtle ges-

Living in Strengths

POPULAR SANGUINE		POWERFUL CHOLERIC	
LIVING IN WEAKNESS	**LIVING IN STRENGTH**	**LIVING IN WEAKNESS**	**LIVING IN STRENGTH**
Loud	Energetic	In your face	Productive
Shallow	Warm	Know it all	Visionary
Impulsive	Enthusiastic	Angry	Multitasker
Monopolizes	Approachable	Bossy	Open-minded
conversation	Inviting	Belligerent	Leader
Erotic	Cheerleader	Untouchable	Organizes people
Undependable		Argumentative	and resources
Overly dramatic		Usurps authority	Purposeful/focused
Self-centered		Offensive	Motivates others
Superficial		Controlling	Constructive
Irresponsible		Narrow-minded	
Easily distracted		Manipulative	
"It's all about me"			

PEACEFUL PHLEGMATIC		PERFECT MELANCHOLY	
LIVING IN WEAKNESS	**LIVING IN STRENGTH**	**LIVING IN WEAKNESS**	**LIVING IN STRENGTH**
Dull	Loyal	Hesitant	Empathetic
Boring	Faithful	Fearful	Succinct
Indecisive	Witty	Uptight	Analytical
Spineless	Dependable	Fragile	Organized
Lazy	Steady	Hermit	Compassionate
Wishy-washy	Consistent	Moody	Good listener
Sarcastic	Willing	Hypochondriac	Reliable/
Obstinate	Patient	Emotionally	trustworthy
Passive-aggressive	Calm	vulnerable	
No initiative		Self-righteous/aloof	
		Critical	
		Obsessive	

ture, like turning a dial, to indicate that I need to "tone it down." Because I am aware of this potential weakness in my Personality, I do not resent his behavior—instead, I appreciate him helping me. I now use my loudness as a professional asset, but I dial it back in settings in which it isn't appropriate.

By being aware of my tendency to be loud, I have learned to judge whether my loud voice will be well received or whether it will turn others off and cause a negative response. In the same way, when you learn to dial back the extremes and control the various degrees of your positives, you move beyond just a Personality label and head toward the goal of living in your strengths.

Living in Your Strengths

As I teach this material, I have often found that people get confused that one person of a specific Personality may seem very different from another person who seems to have the same basic Personality. Of course, everyone is unique and, as we will address in chapter 4, the secondary Personality and the percentage it has in the mix will play a big part in the way a person's Personality presents. But another major factor in the different manifestations of the same Personality is whether the person is living in their strengths or wallowing in their weaknesses.

If a person grew up in a home in which she was disciplined and taught right from wrong, her offensive behaviors were probably curbed. However, if a person grew up in a home in which she was allowed to do whatever she wanted, her rough edges were never smoothed. As a child, she was out of control—and as an adult, she is living in her weaknesses.

If you know people of a certain Personality who are living in their weaknesses, they may give you a bad impression of everyone who is that same Personality. That is what Diana discovered. She recently attended one of our CLASSeminars. I stopped by her small group and made a comment about her group leader, Craig. Everyone loves Craig, and the group was telling me what a great guy he was.

Because of her negative past experiences, Diana commented that she was surprised Craig was a Peaceful Phlegmatic. I explained to her that the difference was that Craig was a Peaceful Phlegmatic who was living in his strengths, not wallowing in his weaknesses. After the seminar, Diana sent me this note regarding my casual comment: "My negative experiences with people who are Peaceful Phlegmatics had given me a negative view of all Phlegmatics. God used your offhand comment to transform my thinking, and I can sure use all the help I can get!"

Now that you have a good idea of your Personality—including your strengths and weaknesses—you can use this knowledge as a part of your Personality Plan to help get you from where you are to where you want to be. As you begin to understand your Personality and the Personalities of others, you can use this knowledge to dial back the extremes, live in your strengths, and give grace to others.

CHAPTER 4

PERSONALITY
BLENDS

While some people fear that tools such as the Personalities put them in a box, the truth is really just the opposite. We all start with four basic Personalities, but within each of us is a unique mix of these traits, allowing for a full spectrum of individualities. Just as all colors are made from a few basics—red, yellow, blue—the variety of men, women and children with whom we interact day in and day out have Personalities that are made up of a few basics: Popular Sanguine, Powerful Choleric, Perfect Melancholy and Peaceful Phlegmatic. Within these basics comes a color wheel filled with different individuals and Personality types.

If we look at these different components as drops of color, we can find ourselves on the Personality color wheel by finding our basic primary color and then determining the other colors that are mixed into our Personalities—our secondary Personality traits. Think about it this way: We know that mixing red with blue makes purple, while mixing red with yellow makes orange. Purple and orange share the same base color—red—but they are nothing alike. Our personalities are the same way: I have a Powerful Choleric/Popular Sanguine mix, while a friend of mine has a Powerful Choleric/Perfect Melancholy mix. My friend and I share the same basic "color," but we have very different personalities.

If we add into the mix a little nature and nurture, we will change the hue of our color. Think of "nurture" as adding a bit of white into the mix and "nature" as adding a bit of black. We can soon see how the intensity changes. Nature and nurture play a huge part in forming our Personalities.

Understanding Secondary Personalities

As we discussed in chapter 1, most of us have a primary Personality and a smattering of traits from each of the other Personality types. For me, I am close to 50 percent Popular Sanguine and 50 percent Powerful Choleric. The role I am playing determines which of my faces you might see. When I am running an event, you will see my Powerful Choleric side. When I am not in charge, or when I am with my friends, you will see my Popular Sanguine face. Because my Personality blend is fairly even, I can switch from one to the other easily. When I have a choice, I prefer not to be in charge (as long as the leadership is competent) and to just play. However, because of my lot in life, I frequently am in charge of activities and events.

My husband's primary Personality is so strongly Perfect Melancholy that it took a few years of marriage before I could figure out what his secondary Personality was. Many of my friends thought that he might be a Perfect Melancholy/ Peaceful Phlegmatic mix because he is always in the background when they see him at the events I am running.

But I finally figured out one day while I was visiting my friend Bonnie that this was not the case. Chuck and I share a lot of similarities with Bonnie and her husband, Jack. Bonnie's Personality closely parallels mine (although she is a smidge more Popular Sanguine) and Jack, like Chuck, is predominately Perfect Melancholy (although his secondary Personality is clearly Peaceful Phlegmatic).

At the beginning of each day of our stay, Bonnie would tell Jack that she and I were leaving. He'd ask when we thought we'd be back, and Bonnie would give him some vague answer like "three hours." Five hours later, we would return with bags and bags of purchases. However, Jack would never respond with comments such as "Where have you been?" or "I have been waiting for you for hours" or "Why did you buy so much?"

He was not at all stressed that we were later than we said we'd be. I stayed in their home for three days. And at the end of my stay, I realized that not once had I gotten into trouble.

At home, I am always in trouble. I am always doing something wrong and always apologizing for it. Chuck doesn't mind if I take longer than I said I'd be, but he prefers that I call ahead of time and let him know of any change of plans. My stay with Bonnie and Jack made me realize that Chuck's secondary Personality was clearly not Peaceful Phlegmatic, because if it were, he (like Jack) would not care what time I got home. Instead, Chuck's secondary Personality would be better defined as Powerful Choleric.

Now, please don't get a wrong impression of Chuck—he doesn't yell, scream, beat me or throw things. It is not that Chuck disapproves of me as an overt form of punishment; it's just that I get a subtle sense that I have disappointed him again or that I am in the wrong. Because approval is so important to the Popular Sanguine, this is an effective means of encouraging us to get it right the next time.

A perfect example of this happened as I was writing this chapter. Chuck's sister was flying into Albuquerque for a visit. Before he left for work, we discussed whether or not I should take the time away from writing to join him in picking her up. Chuck mentioned that it would mean a lot to her if I did, and so, based on that comment, I made the decision to take the afternoon off.

Chuck's sister's plane was scheduled to arrive at 1:45 P.M. We live 35 minutes from the airport (if there is no traffic) and his office is on the way, so I figured that if I was on the road by 1:00 P.M., I'd be in great shape. I called Chuck a little before 1:00 P.M. to let him know that I was on my way. I did not tell him I needed to get gas or that I was planning to stop at the Starbuck's across from the gas station. Five minutes after leaving the house, I realized that I'd forgotten something important, so I turned around and went back to the house.

Thinking that I was still ahead of schedule, I went back home, unlocked the door, went into the house, turned off the security system, got what I needed, reset the alarm, closed the door and headed out again. Of course, I had neglected to update Chuck—and now I was late. So I made sure my radar detector was turned on and buzzed down the highway. I skipped getting gas (after all, we could take Chuck's car) and stopping at Starbucks (after all, I could get a café mocha at the airport).

I got to Chuck's office within a reasonable time, only to find that he was on the phone. So I went to get gas, and when I came back, he was ready. I was not in trouble, but I knew that I was late. If Chuck hadn't been on the phone when I had arrived—if he had been standing there waiting for me—he would have said something like, "See, this is why I thought we should meet at the airport." Then I would have been in trouble.

Did you notice anything wrong with my little story above? The next morning, before heading out the door to work, Chuck mentioned that I had forgotten to lock the front door the day before. He and his sister had arrived home before me and found that I had failed to lock the door. I had been in such a rush to get back on the road and not be late—and therefore not get in trouble—that I forgot to lock the door. So I got in trouble anyway. *Ugh!*

When I speak on this topic and I mention this "getting in trouble" idea, the Popular Sanguine women who are married to Powerful Choleric/Perfect Melancholy men can always relate. If Chuck's secondary Personality was Peaceful Phlegmatic, he would not care that much. And I would not be in trouble as much. Yet because I understand the way that Chuck is wired, I know that keeping things locked is important to him. Knowing that, I realize that locking up is something that I can do to show him I love him. Understanding the intricacies that his secondary Personality—Powerful Choleric—gives him helps me in my relationship with him.

Nichole sent me this note about the importance of understanding one's true secondary Personality:

> I am way Powerful Choleric (NTN), but I was told from someone whose opinion I respect that my secondary Personality was Popular Sanguine. Over and over again, this person told me that I was a Popular Sanguine and that I needed to embrace those characteristics. So I exhausted myself to try and fit into that

Personality box. I now realize that while I do have a smattering of Popular Sanguine traits, I am actually a Perfect Melancholy. It wasn't until I moved away and was on my own that I could really allow my Personality to come out! And I have felt such freedom from not trying to be someone I am not.

Grasping this deeper level of comprehension will help you in your personal interactions and in your own personal growth. It is important to understand these concepts and claim the secondary Personality that is truly yours.

Natural Combinations

Certain combinations of Personalities go together more naturally than others. The "Emotional Needs" chart on the following page illustrates some of the commonalties among the various combinations that make them naturally go together.

Popular Sanguine/Powerful Choleric

I mentioned that I am about equal parts Popular Sanguine/Powerful Choleric. This is a common Personality combination, as both the Popular Sanguine and the Powerful Choleric share complementary traits that make them a logical blend. Both are outgoing, optimistic and energized by people. The combination of these traits makes both the Popular Sanguine and the Powerful Choleric natural leaders. They are comfortable being out in front (and often uncomfortable stuck behind the scenes!) and people just naturally tend to want to follow them.

While having leadership abilities is a positive, those of us with this particular Personality combination need to be careful that we are not overpowering those around us. If this book were printed in color, I would use the color yellow to represent the Popular Sanguine and red to represent the Powerful Choleric. Both red and yellow are "warm" colors, and likewise both the Popular Sanguine and Powerful Choleric are hot (and, like hot air, they are on the top of the chart!). A person with this

Emotional Needs

POPULAR SANGUINE	POWERFUL CHOLERIC
Attention	Loyalty
Affection	Sense of Control
Approval	Credit for Good Work
Acceptance	Achievement
PEACEFUL PHLEGMATIC	**PERFECT MELANCHOLY**
Peace and Quiet	Sensitivity
Feeling of Self-Worth	Support
Lack of Stress	Space
Respect	Silence

combination of traits is upbeat and energetic, combining the fun-loving, charming nature of the Popular Sanguine and the drive of the Powerful Choleric. The Popular Sanguine side tones down the intensity of the Powerful Choleric side.

As Powerful Choleric/Popular Sanguines, we are often referred to as the Energizer Bunnies. We just keep going and going. These are great qualities, but if we are functioning in our weaknesses—or even simply working with those of different Personalities—we must be careful to not be too over the top. We are the turbo-charged Personality combo about whom others say, "Just watching you wears me out." We do wear others out—and we will also often get asked if we are ADHD, as all this energy makes it hard for us to sit still.

A note of clarification: When I present this material, I find that people often get confused about the idea of being "energized by people."

People whose presenting behaviors are clearly in the Popular Sanguine/ Powerful Choleric areas will come up to me and say, "I do not think I am that Personality mix, because while I like people, I also like to be alone." What "energized by people" means is that as long as there are people and activities around, we have energy. When the action stops, so does our energy level. Chuck says I have two speeds: on and off. This does not mean that I do not like to be alone—after a full day of teaching a seminar, there is nothing I like more than soaking in a hot bath. But if there is something else going on, I do not want to miss it.

I saw this typified one evening in Kathryn, who (like my Perfect Melancholy friend Georgia) is on our teaching team. We had worked hard all day, interacted with a lot of people, and were all tired. After our night session, Georgia was eager to get to bed. Kathryn, on the other hand, couldn't resist when a group of our attendees announced that they were going somewhere for pie and coffee. She jumped at the chance to be part of the crowd—and to have another audience!

Other than the obvious percentages on the Personality Profile, it is easy to determine whether a person is more Popular Sanguine or more Powerful Choleric by whether he or she is more people/relationship-oriented or more work/task-focused. If he or she is more work/task-focused, that person would be referred to as a Powerful Choleric/ Popular Sanguine, rather than the other way around.

Perfect Melancholy/Peaceful Phlegmatic

This is another logical combination often found in people. Both Perfect Melancholies and Peaceful Phlegmatics tend to be introverted, pessimistic (or "realistic," as Chuck likes to say) and energized by solitude. Each prefers to be behind the scenes. These are the ones who like to analyze what's happening in life. For this reason, they tend to be deeper than most other Personalities.

In the color wheel, these Personalities would be represented by the cool colors—blue for Perfect Melancholies and green for Peaceful Phlegmatics— as they are deep and calm, like a mountain lake. Their cooler nature often makes them easier to be around, since they are mellow and less demanding.

A person with this combination is someone who is likeable and accomplishes what needs to be done. The Peaceful Phlegmatic tones down what is often perceived as the persnickety nature of the Perfect Melancholy, and the Perfect Melancholy's focus on tasks keeps the Peaceful Phlegmatic moving.

When Craig, a Peaceful Phlegmatic/Perfect Melancholy combination, came to work for CLASS, he only planned to stay a year. By the time he left, he'd been with us for seven years! Craig ran our speaker services department. He was easygoing and likeable. The clients who called our office looking for speakers always praised Craig, as he was such a delight to work with. In the office, he fit in and did not seem to mind the predominantly female atmosphere. If something needed to be done that was outside of his job description—or even a distraction to it—Craig cheerfully jumped in and did it. Still, at the end of every day, Craig would clean off his desk, leaving everything neat and tidy. Craig's primary Peaceful Phlegmatic Personality made him a pleasure to be around, while his secondary Perfect Melancholy Personality made him efficient and productive on the job.

Just as the Popular Sanguine/Powerful Choleric needs to be careful that he or she does not overwhelm people by living in his or her extremes, the Perfect Melancholy/Peaceful Phlegmatic must take caution as well. Because those with this Personality combination fit in the low-key camp, they need to be careful that they are not so mellow that they slide into the classic couch-potato mode, never getting up and doing anything. Living in their strengths, the Perfect Melancholy/Peaceful Phlegmatics can accomplish a lot without offending anyone.

Powerful Choleric/Perfect Melancholy

I like to call those with the Powerful Choleric/Perfect Melancholy combination corporate America's favorite people. The common denominator for people with this combination is their work or task focus. They are decisive, goal-oriented and organized. When people have both their primary and secondary Personality in this production-based side of the chart, they are the worker bees of life. If you want something done, the person with this Personality combination is the one to do it.

My sister is like this. Once her children were raised and she began to work with me on the CLASS seminars, it made my life so much easier. She easily took over organizing and was not easily offended if someone was unhappy with her direction. With her on the team, there were so many things that I no longer had to worry about. Now, if someone comes to me with a problem, I just say, "Don't worry, Lauren will fix it." I can live happily as a Popular Sanguine when Lauren is there because I can trust her to get the job done (Powerful Choleric) and to get it done right (Perfect Melancholy).

Since both the primary and secondary Personalities of this person share the production factor in common, he or she will need to be careful that work does not become so important that people get squished in the process of reaching the goal. Jean, a Powerful Choleric/Perfect Melancholy combination, affirms this. She told me, "I always have to tell myself, 'People are more important than paperwork and goals.'" Even with a total goal-oriented mind-set, the Powerful Choleric/Perfect Melancholy must remember that other people and their cooperation are essential in reaching goals. So if you are a Powerful Choleric/Perfect Melancholy, be aware that you do not need to control or fix everything. Be sure to allow for grace, and liberally apply it to the things that aren't exactly the way you'd like them to be.

A note of clarification: Because both the Powerful Choleric and the Perfect Melancholy are organized, people are often confused as to which Personality they are. However, it is important to remember that both Personalities are well-organized—the difference is how and why they organize. Powerful Cholerics organize things quickly in their heads to aid in production—they believe things just work better and they can do their tasks faster if everything is organized. My sister, who is more Powerful Choleric than Perfect Melancholy, walks into a situation, quickly analyzes it, and then instantly knows what needs to be done to get the problem solved. Perfect Melancholies, on the other hand, organize for inner peace. They sleep better knowing that the bumps of their socks are facing the same direction in the drawer or, as is the case at my house, all the motorcycles are facing the same direction—left-leaning motorcycles in the front row and right-leaning in the back row (Chuck collects vintage motorcycles). Perfect Melancholies also need more time to analyze things and tend to organize on paper.

To determine if a person with this Powerful Choleric/Perfect Melancholy combination is more one Personality or the other, observe whether he or she is more outgoing or more introverted. If the person enjoys being a leader and likes to be the center of attention, the dominant Personality is probably Powerful Choleric. If this person would rather be in the background, the dominant Personality is probably Perfect Melancholy.

Peaceful Phlegmatic/Popular Sanguine

While the Powerful Choleric/Perfect Melancholy combination is corporate America's favorite person, the Peaceful Phlegmatic/Popular Sanguine is everyone's favorite person! People who have this Personality combination have the easygoing nature of the Peaceful Phlegmatic and the energy and excitement of the Popular Sanguine. Because they have the "play" and "people" elements in common, they are usually witty and fun to be with, and they seldom push for their way.

People with the Peaceful Phlegmatic/Popular Sanguine combination are not goal-oriented. They will probably never be CEO of a major corporation, but they do not care. In fact, they cannot comprehend why anyone would want that much stress. They are so universally liked that others want to help them. In fact, those with this combination often get ahead in life beyond the successes of the Powerful Choleric/Perfect Melancholy because people want to open doors for them.

Wendy is a Peaceful Phlegmatic/Popular Sanguine combination. She hardly ever gets upset. Everyone loves her, and she is such fun to be with that she gets invited to all the parties. People are always bringing Wendy gifts—they seem to want to shower her with presents "just because." When you are in her presence, you feel totally accepted and free to be yourself. Wendy is comfortable with herself, too—comfortable enough to laugh at herself. The Popular Sanguine part of her makes her fun, while the Peaceful Phlegmatic side brings a sense of calm to everyone. Wendy calmly goes through life having more fun than anyone else!

Again, you'll know if a person is more Peaceful Phlegmatic or more Popular Sanguine based on whether they are more outgoing or more introverted. Wendy would be described as Popular Sanguine/Peaceful Phlegmatic, as she is clearly more outgoing.

While people with this combination of traits sound wonderful, they have reasons to be cautious as well. Because they tend to focus on people and play, Peaceful Phlegmatic/Popular Sanguines often let projects go unfinished. The Popular Sanguine part of them starts projects with great enthusiasm, but the Peaceful Phlegmatic can then step in, easily setting the project aside and never getting back to it.

When I am speaking and teach on this concept, I say, "This is everyone's favorite person—unless he is your son-in-law. If your little princess has married a man who, in your view, lacks motivation and therefore does not earn enough to take care of your daughter, he would not be your favorite person." Society is more forgiving of women with this Personality pattern than they are of men. Regardless of gender, those with the Peaceful Phlegmatic/Popular Sanguine combination must be careful to work on motivation and achievement, lest they reach a mature age and realize that they have never really gotten their lives together.

The following "Natural Blends" chart depicts some of the characteristics of the natural Personality blends that we have just discussed. Notice that with each Personality combination, the Personality combination opposite on the chart will have completely opposite admonitions. For example, Popular Sanguine/Powerful Cholerics need to tone down and slow down (lest they become brassy and overbearing), while Perfect Melancholy/Peaceful Phlegmatics need to be careful not to be too sluggish. Similarly, Powerful Choleric/Perfect Melancholies need to be careful to not run over people in favor of the project, while Peaceful Phlegmatic/Popular Sanguines need to work on working!

Opposing Blends

Each of the combinations that we discussed in the first half of this chapter share common elements that make them work well together. Next,

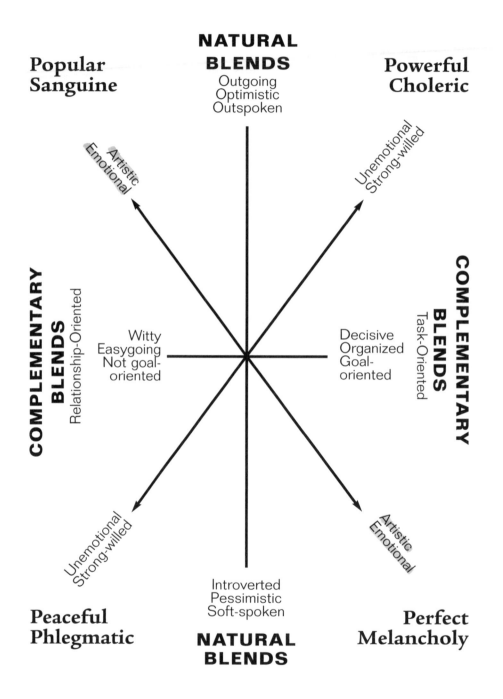

**Popular
Sanguine**

**NATURAL
BLENDS**
Outgoing
Optimistic
Outspoken

**Powerful
Choleric**

Artistic
Emotional

Unemotional
Strong-willed

**COMPLEMENTARY
BLENDS**
Relationship-Oriented

Witty
Easygoing
Not goal-
oriented

Decisive
Organized
Goal-
oriented

**COMPLEMENTARY
BLENDS**
Task-Oriented

Unemotional
Strong-willed

Artistic
Emotional

Introverted
Pessimistic
Soft-spoken

**Peaceful
Phlegmatic**

**NATURAL
BLENDS**

**Perfect
Melancholy**

we will look at combinations that are opposite from each other on the chart. As we study these opposing blends, it will be important to remember that none of these Personality combinations will be a *natural* blend. Instead, these combinations will occur as a result of people *learning* certain behaviors that allow them to function in their environment.

Sometimes, after reading a book, hearing a speaker, or taking the Personality Profile, people believe that they are a combination of either the Popular Sanguine/Perfect Melancholy or the Powerful Choleric/ Peaceful Phlegmatic. This is confusing to people because the two Personality types seem to be diametrically opposed. It is true—they are opposite Personalities, yet many people do seem to function as either Perfect Melancholy/Popular Sanguines or Powerful Choleric/Peaceful Phlegmatics. However in the decades of teaching these concepts, we have not found anyone who truly is a *natural* combination of these opposites.

Powerful Choleric/Perfect Melancholy

Organization

As I mentioned previously, both the Powerful Choleric and the Perfect Melancholy are organized, but the difference lies in their organizational styles and their motivations for being organized. Yes, the differences are subtle, but they are necessary to understand in order to accurately assess people's Personality types. For example, because I am a Popular Sanguine/Powerful Choleric, by nature I am not organized. However, I run a business, so I have had to learn how to get organized and make the best use of my time.

If I did not understand that both the Powerful Choleric and the Perfect Melancholy are organized, I might decide that I must have a lot of Perfect Melancholy traits in me. However, to determine whether this assessment was correct, I would have to look at my reasons and motives for being organized. Perfect Melancholies tend to organize systematically for the pure joy of knowing that their shirts are all facing the same way in the closet and that their life is in order. Powerful Cholerics, on the other hand, organize functionally and without much thought—and they only organize those things that are needed for them to function efficiently.

Organization for a Powerful Choleric is the result of practical neces-sity and training. It's not an inborn need, as it is with the Perfect Melancholy person. The key is to look at a person's natural self rather than their trained self. In my case, because I am organized only because I have to be in order to run a business, I would be more Powerful Choleric than Perfect Melancholy.

Popular Sanguine/Perfect Melancholy

Emotions

Both the Popular Sanguine and the Perfect Melancholy are emotional—the Popular Sanguine cries easily, as does the Perfect Melancholy. The difference is what moves these different Personality types to tears. Because Popular Sanguines want everyone to love them, they will cry if someone says mean or spiteful things to them. Since their emotions are close to the surface, they will also cry at touchy-feely things such as Hallmark commercials or even some McDonald's ads.

Perfect Melancholies, on the other hand, are moved by the deeper injustices in life. If a Popular Sanguine and a Perfect Melancholy were watching TV together and flipped to a documentary about starving peo-ple in a far-away country, the Popular Sanguine would react by saying, "Oh, yuck! Change the channel. I don't want to watch that!" However, the Perfect Melancholy would be touched—almost gripped—by the drama on the screen and may be moved to tears over the tragedy of suf-fering and loss of life.

Creativity

Both Popular Sanguines and Perfect Melancholies are also creative, but this artistic talent takes very different forms. Popular Sanguines are bursting with creative ideas (most of which they never act upon), will put a project together quickly, and will lose interest if it takes too long. Most Popular Sanguine women have closets or garages filled with partially completed craft projects in which they have lost interest. They may go through a macramé phase, a decoupage phase, a needlepoint phase and a stenciling phase, but they will never settle on anything in particular.

In comparison, Perfect Melancholies tend to gravitate toward one skill and work to master it. They may also have uncompleted projects, but these projects will be unfinished not from lack of interest but because of the Perfect Melancholy's need to have the time to make them perfect.

Music

Related to this discussion of the arts, both the Popular Sanguine and the Perfect Melancholy can also be musical. Again, the difference is in how this talent plays out. Popular Sanguines are more interested in performance, while Perfect Melancholies focus more on perfection.

I saw this play out one day when I was visiting my sister's house. My oldest nephew, Randy, is the pianist in the family, and when I arrived, he happened to be in the living room practicing his piano lesson. We heard him in the background playing and replaying each portion of the piece until he got it perfect. At the end of Randy's required practice time he left the room, and for the moment, everything was quiet.

A few minutes later, we heard the same song start up again, but this time it sounded different. Lauren and I looked questioningly at each other and tiptoed to the doorway to find my six-year-old nephew, Jonathan, sitting on the piano bench that his older brother had just vacated. Jonathan had not yet taken piano lessons, but he was naturally musical. He'd been watching his brother labor over the assignment, and when Randy left, he had jumped up to play the same song. The song wasn't perfect (although it was discernable), but Jonathan didn't seem to know or care.

We continued peeking through the door throughout Jonathan's entire performance. We practically burst with laughter when, upon completing the portion of the composition that he chose to play, he slipped off the bench and bowed to the empty living room. It was obvious that day that Randy wanted perfection but Jonathan wanted performance. Both boys continued to be active in music programs throughout school. Today, Randy is a professional musician. Jonathan is still passionate about music—but it's not his profession.

I shared this story about my nephews one time when I was speaking on the Personalities. When I was done, the gal who was singing at the event came up to me and said, "Now I understand why my singer friends get so upset if they miss a note. I always figured that the audience wouldn't know what note was supposed to be hit. Now I see that I am a Popular Sanguine, more concerned with the performance and the subsequent applause, while they are Perfect Melancholies, aiming for perfection."

I trust that like this Popular Sanguine singer, you have had some "a-ha!" moments regarding the Popular Sanguine/Perfect Melancholy combination.

Powerful Choleric/Peaceful Phlegmatic
Goal Orientation

The other common misunderstanding is with the combination of Powerful Choleric and Peaceful Phlegmatic. I usually find this supposed combination attributed to men by their wives, because while their husbands are the "boss" at work (Powerful Choleric), once they get home, they won't do a thing (Peaceful Phlegmatic). However, although on the surface these husbands may appear to be this combination, I have never found one who truly is.

What I usually find is that these men are Peaceful Phlegmatics with perhaps some Perfect Melancholy thrown in. Since our society typically doesn't honor gentle men, they have learned to put on a tough, macho, Powerful Choleric image. This alone can be confusing, but to make matters worse, most of these men have been in the work force for many years and have been *pushed* up the corporate ladder. Notice the emphasis here on the word "pushed." These men weren't chomping at the bit to be promoted, yet due to their steady nature and abilities that are typical of Peaceful Phlegmatics, they kept getting promoted—often right out of their comfort zone.

Along the line, many of these men were probably sent to sales training courses, Dale Carnegie workshops, and other management seminars. Through these training sessions, they *learned* to be the managers that they have become. They learned to discipline employees and terminate them if necessary. Even though these activities are totally out of Peaceful Phlegmatics' natural comfort level, as intelligent human beings they have adapted and filled the required job role. However, because management on such a scale is not natural or easy for them, they come home exhausted from struggling all day to be someone whom they are not.

Once these men are home, they settle into their La-Z-Boy, turn on the TV, and tune out the world. They don't want to be bothered by anyone or anything. Like the Peaceful Phlegmatic/Perfect Melancholy that they truly are, they need solitude to recharge their batteries. Meanwhile, the wife looks on, wondering how this man who runs a multimillion-dollar facility all day can be such a couch potato at home.

So these husbands are not Powerful Choleric/Peaceful Phlegmatics—rather, they are Peaceful Phlegmatics who have worn themselves out. They have learned to be tough and strong. It doesn't necessarily mean that they have any deep problems—it is usually just a misunderstanding of who Peaceful Phlegmatics and Powerful Cholerics really are.

Control

It may also be the case that the husbands in these situations are Powerful Cholerics who have simply learned to adopt Peaceful Phlegmatic behaviors to survive. This often occurs when both the husband and the wife are at least half Powerful Choleric. In cases such as these, the spouses have two choices: They can fight for control, or one of them can agree to be the dominant person in certain settings.

Most marriages don't start out with a clear understanding of these concepts, so people typically just fall into a pattern to avoid constant conflict. Since the woman is traditionally the homemaker and the man is traditionally the worker, the husband usually runs the business aspects of the family while the wife runs the family. This makes a lot of sense when you consider the fact that Powerful Cholerics have an unwritten rule: "If I can't win, I won't play the game." When the husband comes home from work, rather than fight his wife, he simply gives up, retreats into his own world, and appears to be a Peaceful Phlegmatic.

Leadership

Another instance of Personality confusion can occur when a Peaceful Phlegmatic thinks he is a Powerful Choleric, as happened with one pastor who wrote to our office. While the pastor knew that he had the peaceful traits of the Peaceful Phlegmatic, he was also the leader of a successful congregation. However, as we looked more deeply into his life, we discovered that he was, in fact, a Peaceful Phlegmatic/Perfect Melancholy. As a pastor, he had learned leadership skills that had not come naturally to him. By reading books, attending seminars, observing role models and, of course, seeking the guidance of the Holy Spirit, this pastor had become an effective leader. But that didn't mean he had become a Powerful Choleric— it just meant that he had developed skills not natural to his Personality.

While there are no absolutes, if a man is displaying the Peaceful Phlegmatic/Powerful Choleric combination, he is most likely a Peaceful Phlegmatic who has learned Powerful Choleric behaviors in order to survive in business. Such an individual has usually been in the same job for many years, growing and maturing within that position. In contrast, a true Powerful Choleric usually is in business for himself or has changed jobs frequently.

One of the benefits of understanding your Personality type is an awareness of both your natural areas of gifting and those that will need to be learned. I had to learn to be organized, yet that organization doesn't make me a Perfect Melancholy. I am merely a Popular Sanguine/ Powerful Choleric who has learned to overcome some of my weaknesses and has worked to obtain skills that are not natural to me. The pastor in the above story is not a Powerful Choleric. He is a Peaceful Phlegmatic/ Perfect Melancholy who has learned to be an effective leader by obtaining skills that are not natural to him.

Have these examples cleared up any confusion you might have had regarding your Personality or that of someone close to you? In most cases, a closer look at the motives behind certain behaviors will probably resolve the confusion. However, if the examples I have shared don't seem to ring true in your case, I encourage you to look deeper into what we call a "Personality mask."

Masking

Learned behaviors are a sign of growth and maturity. A learned behavior comes into being because at some point in people's lives, they realize that they have a need, and so they set out to meet it. They make a conscious choice to acquire a skill or behavior that would make them into a better person.

In contrast, a mask represents a behavior that people have unconsciously adopted for survival. Usually this occurs in childhood, often to make their parents happy or to make their parents like them better. The problem with Personality masks, however, is that they create an internal struggle. People may be aware of this internal battle, but since the mask is subconscious, they do not understand the source of the struggle or what to do about it. Ultimately, this causes fatigue, creates stress, and can lead to illnesses.

We often see people who live their lives with Personality masks and yet appear to be successful. So why is this a problem? Because it's not healthy for people to spend huge amounts of emotional energy trying to be someone whom they are not. And the older people get, the more difficult it is to keep the mask in place. Generally, around age 40, people who have adopted these Personality masks begin to get tired and develop stress-related illnesses. They know something is wrong, but they can't figure out what it is. Imagine the freedom for such people when they discover who they were meant to be and realize that they don't need to wear a mask anymore. I have been told by such individuals that they have always felt as if they have a split personality, like Jekyll and Hyde.

Popular Sanguine/Perfect Melancholy
(Real Personality: Popular Sanguine/Mask: Perfect Melancholy)

This is the most frequent masking situation I see. Because Popular Sanguines want to be loved and desperately seek approval, they are more likely to take on masks than any of the other Personalities. These inborn needs make Popular Sanguines the natural codependents of life. They subconsciously say, *If you will like me better this way, I will change.*

Typically, a Popular Sanguine woman will masquerade as a Perfect Melancholy. While she knows that she has both the strengths and weaknesses of the Popular Sanguine, when she takes the Personality Profile or reviews the chart showing the strengths and weaknesses of all the Personalities, she discovers that she has many of the Perfect Melancholy traits—in particular, she is "moody," "depressed" and "perfectionist." Yet these negative emotions are not coming from her true Personality. Her moodiness and depression come from her feeling that she never measures up and is not good enough—and the perfectionism comes from her trying to live up to that standard.

Parenting Mistakes

My friend Cindy is predominantly a Popular Sanguine. However, she grew up in a strict religious home, and her father, a Perfect Melancholy/ Powerful Choleric, was the pastor at their church. As a Popular Sanguine, Cindy wanted approval from her dad and for him to tell her that she was wonderful. Although it was unspoken, Cindy learned early on that the only way her father would affirm her was if she sat in the front pew in church, didn't wiggle, didn't talk, and basically behaved like a Perfect Melancholy. So without being aware of what she was doing, she began to adopt that Personality.

One day, Cindy's family was driving home from church and she and her sister were horsing around in the back seat. Her father turned around, pointed his finger at her, and said, "There is no place in the Christian life for frivolity." Cindy subconsciously grasped that not only did her father not like her the way she was, but also that God didn't like her either. So, to make herself acceptable, she began to take on more and more traits that we would ascribe to the Perfect Melancholy.

When I met Cindy as an adult, her profile showed her to be a Popular Sanguine/Perfect Melancholy. Yet while that was how she functioned, that was not the way that God had made her. Her true Personality had been masked in reaction to her environment. She didn't act out of her true Personality because she believed that she could not be herself and still be loved.

In Cindy's case, the Personality masking was a result of simple parenting mistakes. If someone had asked Cindy if she had been abused as a child, she would have said no, since she came from a "good Christian home" and her parents meant well. Her parents were not alcoholics, she was not molested, and no one beat her. Because the cause may be difficult to pinpoint—and the mistakes innocent in motive—women with this type of mask often have difficulty accepting that they are truly Popular Sanguines.

Sexual and Emotional Abuse

If innocent mistakes and minor emotional abuse can create a Perfect Melancholy mask in someone who is naturally a Popular Sanguine, you can imagine what more severe circumstances, such as incest, can bring about. In my experience, I have found that Popular Sanguine children are the ones who are most frequently molested, since their cute, perky and precocious nature gets them noticed—often by the wrong people. The perpetrator of the abuse usually makes them think they are special because they receive so much attention.

This was the case for my friend Dee Dee. If you met her, you might think she is a Perfect Melancholy. She is beautiful and always looks perfectly put together, and while she is confident, she doesn't push her way to the forefront. Yet she struggles with organization and is frequently overcommitted and late—all traits ascribed to the Popular Sanguine.

Dee Dee's stepfather began having sexual relations with her when she neared puberty. During her growing-up years, he was able to keep up the charade and continue the abuse by telling her that this was their "special" time. He put her on birth control pills (he told her it was for acne) and continued relations with her until she was out of the house and strong enough to put him off.

Dee Dee always felt that if she could just be good enough or quiet enough, her stepfather would not notice her. When she took the Personality Profile, she checked off both strengths and weaknesses in the Popular Sanguine category but only chose weaknesses in the Perfect Melancholy category, which was an indication to me that there was a problem—that a masking had taken place somewhere along the line. Today, even though Dee Dee knows that she is a Popular Sanguine and no longer struggles with depression or feelings of inadequacy, she still practices many of the habits that she adopted during her youth in order to survive.

Adapting to a Spouse

While a mask usually has its origins in childhood, the Popular Sanguine wearing a Perfect Melancholy mask can often begin wearing that mask as an adult—and often without realizing it. Most often, this happens when a Popular Sanguine marries a Powerful Choleric/Perfect Melancholy man.

Initially, the Powerful Choleric/Perfect Melancholy man was attracted to her bubbly personality and the fact that she was able to cheer him up. But after a few years of marriage, he soon tires of her constant talking and tardiness. He tries to tone her down and get her on a schedule. She wants to please him, so she tries to adopt the behaviors that she thinks will make him happy. Subconsciously, she feels that she cannot be loved and accepted the way she is. As a result, she withdraws, stops seeing her friends and tones down her Personality.

Without fun in her life, she becomes depressed. After years of this, she takes a Personality Profile and checks off some of the Popular Sanguine traits—especially the weaknesses, since her husband has made it very clear she has these—but she also checks "insecure," "depressed" and "moody" from the Perfect Melancholy column.

For the Popular Sanguine wearing a Perfect Melancholy mask of pain, the solution is often as simple as asking, When did the fun stop? For a woman in this place, just that question may bring tears to her eyes as she remembers what life was like when it was fun and she wasn't depressed all the time.

Depending on the depth of pain, the fix for bad parenting mistakes can be as simple as the woman realizing, *Dad doesn't live here. I am an adult. I do not have to live my life to make him happy.* If the mask is the result of years of sexual abuse, counseling may be needed for the woman to rediscover the happy little girl inside. If it is due to a marriage to a demanding man, the best-case scenario is if the husband sees what he has done, backs off, and begins to appreciate the girl with whom he fell in love. Unfortunately, short of a miracle, this last scenario is not likely to happen, so if this is your situation, look for ways to put fun back into your life. Go to lunch with your girlfriends, take tennis lessons, learn to rollerblade, or do whatever else will give you a healthy release in life. Without some healthy resolution, this can easily lead to an affair.

Perfect Melancholy/Popular Sanguine

(Real Personality: Perfect Melancholy/Mask: Popular Sanguine)

People who are really Perfect Melancholies but who think they are Popular Sanguines put on the mask of a clown because they think being funny will bring them popularity, or they do it to mask the pain of a bad situation at home. On the Personality Profile, these people usually check both the strengths and the weaknesses of the Perfect Melancholy, but seem to have only the strengths of the Popular Sanguine, like being sociable, funny and popular. These people haven't acquired the Popular Sanguine traits of being undisciplined, haphazard or messy.

Seeking Popularity

I have heard of situations in which a child's mother is very sick (perhaps even terminally ill) and the father, struggling to keep the family going, make his wife happy, and earn a living, tells his son to "go in there and cheer your mother up." When the boy enters the room, his mother smiles, and since he wants her to get well, he works hard to cheer her up. Maybe he learns funny routines or acts out scenes from TV shows. He learns to be a clown. Now, in his adult life, he thinks that he is funny and tries to cut up, but it doesn't ring true. He tells jokes or pokes fun at people. They chuckle politely at his humor but do not know how to react to him—often wondering whether he is for real.

The same masking can occur when a Perfect Melancholy has a Popular Sanguine sibling that everyone likes and praises—especially if a parent appears to favor the Popular Sanguine. The Perfect Melancholy sees that the sibling gets more praise and attention. Often in this case, a parent will make comments such as "Why can't you be more like your sister? You need to learn to lighten up!" So, working from this implicit rejection of who he or she is, that Perfect Melancholy child tries to copy the behaviors of the Popular Sanguine sibling. When people interact with this person when he or she is an adult, they see that this person's humor doesn't quite work. They do not know why, but they do not really want to be with this person.

Hiding Pain

Sometimes, the Popular Sanguine mask of a clown is used to hide pain. If life at home is a mess, the Perfect Melancholy wants to separate himself or herself from the chaos and pretend it doesn't matter. In this case, the Perfect Melancholy's secondary Personality is usually the Powerful Choleric, as he or she has the strength and drive to try to fix the problem.

Nancy, one of our Certified Personality Trainers, discovered that this was true in her life. Everyone who knows her today would ascribe to her the qualities of a Perfect Melancholy/Powerful Choleric, but as a child she was the class clown. Nancy's parents divorced before she was five years old, and her father was not an active part of her childhood. Her mother, an alcoholic, was at best a part-time parent. She told me:

> Without the benefit of my parents' nurturing, I became a class clown, comedian and drama queen throughout my early school and teenage years. I was very talkative, often interrupting the class, consistently vying for the attention of my teachers. I was starved for attention and approval, and if my entertaining personality didn't get them, I would misbehave to get what I needed. When playing with my friends, I would direct and star in the neighborhood plays, always being the heroine. I would make sure the parents of my friends came to watch our productions so that I could receive the praise I so craved. At home, my job was to entertain my depressed mother in hopes that I could cheer her up and keep her from drinking.

Nancy's form of survival in a dysfunctional home was to become the clown. As she has learned about the Personalities and how to accept who she really is, Nancy has become at peace with the way God made her. And though she can incorporate the learned strengths of the Popular Sanguine in her life, she doesn't live her life being a phony.

If you appear to have this Popular Sanguine/Perfect Melancholy Personality, usually the only thing you need to do is to accept and embrace the Perfect Melancholy that you are while maintaining some of the strengths you acquired when you were trying to be a Popular Sanguine. Once you feel free to be your Perfect Melancholy self, you will find that you feel more comfortable in your skin and that others are more comfortable around you.

Peaceful Phlegmatic/Powerful Choleric
(Real Personality: Peaceful Phlegmatic/Mask: Powerful Choleric)

A Peaceful Phlegmatic wearing a Powerful Choleric mask is more likely to be a male than a female, although it could be either. Such a masking usually occurs when a Powerful Choleric father attempts to make his quiet, passive son "more manly." Though the father often means to be encouraging, in reality he is conveying to the child that the son is not acceptable as he is. And so, the son tries to be what Dad wants him to be.

Another instance of such masking can take place when a Peaceful Phlegmatic has to take on a role of being the "man of the house" because his father is no longer there. This was the case with one man who attended our seminar who had qualities of both the Peaceful Phlegmatic and the Powerful Choleric. His parents had divorced when he was six years old, and with his father gone, his mother told him that he now had to be the man of the house. Basically, she expected him to be a Powerful Choleric, and she applauded him for taking care of her. A few years later, a new man of the house moved in, and the boy was relieved of his Powerful Choleric role. The new man captured the mother's attention, and the son felt lonely and rejected. However, after a few more years, the new man left, and his mother again moved her son back into the man-of-the-house role. This occurred several times in the boy's life until he grew up and was able to move out of the house.

It is no wonder that as an adult, this man saw himself as having the traits of a Peaceful Phlegmatic/Powerful Choleric. Once he recognized who he really was, it was as if a huge burden had been lifted from his shoulders. He was free to be himself—even though he had not even been aware that he had been trying to be someone he was not.

Powerful Choleric/Peaceful Phlegmatic

(Real Personality: Powerful Choleric/Mask: Peaceful Phlegmatic)

Because of the inherent strength of Powerful Cholerics, they are less likely to put on a mask. They are not as pliable as the other Personalities. However, if they do put on a mask, it is usually as a result of something in their lives being out of control. As mentioned previously, Powerful Cholerics have an unwritten rule: "If I can't win, I won't play the game." This mind-set causes them to subconsciously shut down if they see they cannot win, which results in their appearing to be Peaceful Phlegmatics.

I remember when my parents first started teaching this material and my father created the Personality Profile. His mother (my grandmother) took the Personality Profile and declared herself to be a Peaceful Phlegmatic—yet anyone who knew her described her as a Powerful Choleric. I remember how shocked my mother was at Grammie Littauer's proclamation: "Peaceful Phlegmatic? What about you do you think is Peaceful Phlegmatic?" Grammie said that she was a peacemaker, submissive and diplomatic—all qualities she possessed. But she was also controlling, could not rest, and when she walked into a room, all eyes were on her. We all saw her as a Powerful Choleric, but she saw herself as a Peaceful Phlegmatic.

Upon a closer look, it was easy to see when and why she had donned this mask. Both her parents were Powerful Cholerics. Her father was a Perfect Melancholy/Powerful Choleric and her mother was a Popular Sanguine/Powerful Choleric. Since both her parents shared the Powerful Choleric Personality, they enjoyed a good emotional arm wrestle, and my grandmother's childhood home was filled with constant bickering. She became the peacemaker. Later, she worked for her parents in the family business. They, in turn, decided whom she would marry, and later they used their purse strings to exercise control on her life choices. My great-grandparents were such a formidable force that my grandmother had no choice but to play Peaceful Phlegmatic, even though she had no clue about these concepts at that time.

When Grammie Littauer looked at herself, she truly saw a Peaceful Phlegmatic. Yet I've never met a more imposing presence. She had played her life out as a Peaceful Phlegmatic/Powerful Choleric, but when you looked deeper, you could see that the Peaceful Phlegmatic was just a mask she had put on to survive in her family.

Are You Wearing a Mask?

If your Personality Profile—or your general understanding of the subject—indicates that you have a Personality combination made up of any of these opposing Personality combinations, look deeper into your own life. Which feels true to you? Have any of these previous scenarios struck a chord for you? While you may be functioning fine with this split Personality today, you will be happier and healthier when you are free to be who God created you to be. Just don't throw out the baby with the bath water—keep some of those good qualities that you acquired (although now they'll be conscious, learned behaviors). You can grow and mature!

EMOTIONAL
NEEDS

Most of us grew up on what was called the Golden Rule: "In everything, do to others what you would have them do to you" (Matt. 7:12). While this is a great admonition in its original context (as the foundation of active goodness and mercy), it was never intended to be the foundation for our personal relationships. As we have already acknowledged, there are people out there who are different from us, and most of us live and work with those different people. Just as their Personalities are different, so are their emotional needs. Instead of doing unto others what we want, we need to give others what they want and need.

Think of someone with whom you'd like to have a better relationship. Maybe that person is your spouse, a friend, or a coworker. Whoever came to your mind, you can use the concepts of the Personalities to see immediate improvements in your relationship—even if that person never buys into this program. Once you can identify the Personality of the people with whom you live and work and adjust your expectations of them, you are ready for the really important stuff: meeting their emotional needs.

Since each Personality has distinct emotional needs, it will take a bit of effort to step outside of who you are and what you want in order to look at the other person and change your approach to them. But this is where real growth in relationships will take place. Once you "get it," you will find that you can apply these insights in all your interactions, not just with those with whom you are in a deeper relationship. Why not leave a smile on the face of the grocery store clerk you see every day? Or the UPS driver who visits your office? Or your child's teacher?

Even though you may not be conscious that you even have emotional needs, those needs are at the core of your being. They are not just wants or desires, but they are also hardwired into who you are. And if those needs are not met in healthy ways, you will seek to have them met in other ways.

As we review the emotional needs of each Personality, think of the people with whom you interact day in and day out. Also, think about your own Personality—both your primary Personality and your secondary one. What do you need? Are you getting those needs met in a healthy way? If not, what changes can you make in your life so that you will have those needs met?

Popular Sanguine
Attention · Affection · Approval · Acceptance

Those of us who have the Popular Sanguine Personality come hardwired with a need for attention, affection, approval and acceptance. We are the ones who are most likely to behave in such a way that we virtually demand others to give us what we want. This was the case for Cheri's daughter, Annemarie.

When Annemarie was about three years old, she brought me a picture that she'd just drawn. Having just read the latest child psychology books that warned about the evils of praise, I looked at her picture and said, "Wow! You used a lot of colors. How did you feel while you were drawing this?" She looked at me in utter disgust and walked away, muttering, "You were supposed to say it's beautiful!"

My Perfect Melancholy husband tries the same thing with me when I model a new outfit for him. He tries so hard to avoid the psychologically incorrect compliment, saying, "Your figure really complements the fabric . . . the dress is okay in and of itself, but it really is you that enhances the dress . . ." I stop him and say, "Really, it is fine to just say that I look fabulous!"

Attention

For us Popular Sanguines, one of our greatest fears is being normal and blending in. We like attention and we want to be noticed. That is why we dress the way we do and talk with loud voices. We want attention.

My mother tells me that as a child, when I would read a book (such as one of the Dr. Seuss books), I would always want to tell her about it. Of course, she practically knew the book by heart, but as a child, I did not understand that. I'd follow her around the house trying to tell her all about the book. Today, she tells me, "I could have read the book faster myself," but she knew that was not the point. The point was that I wanted—and needed—her attention. Because she realized this, she stopped what she was doing, looked me in the eye and asked me to tell her about the book—or whatever it was I wanted her to listen to at the moment. Once I'd gotten the attention I was after, I went on my merry way and she could go back to what she was doing.

If Popular Sanguines do not get attention in ways that are healthy, they will get it in other ways—perhaps even in destructive ways. Teachers often see this in their students. If they cannot get attention for being good, they will misbehave. Andrea, a Certified Personality Trainer, found that this was the case with one of her students. She told me this story:

> I had a student named Jasmine in my fourth grade class. She was bright in clothes and attitude, very loud, and as cute as she could be—all of which made it obvious that she was a Popular Sanguine. When things were going well at home, she made good grades, listened to my instructions, and was fun to be around. However, all this changed when things at home were not going well.
>
> When Jasmine's mom got a new boyfriend or was busy at work, I immediately knew. Jasmine would start spending her time throwing things across the room, yelling at me, or ruining

her desk by doing things like pouring a bottle of glue in her pencil tray. When I would call her mom, her mom was very snappy and usually told me it was my problem to deal with Jasmine and that she was busy at work.

I spent the year with a broken heart for this child. A few years later, I saw Jasmine in Wal-Mart and called her by name. She asked me how I remembered her name. My first thought was, *How could I forget?* A teacher rarely forgets a Popular Sanguine student. When you spend the year saying a child's name over and over, it is hard to forget what that child's name was!

If you have Popular Sanguines in your life, realize that they want you to notice them. Comment on their clothes, laugh at their jokes, and let them tell you the long version. If you make a habit of this, they will be very forgiving when you tell them you don't have time to listen to them due to a pressing deadline—they'll already know that you really do like them.

Affection and Approval

Popular Sanguines want to be loved. This is the root of their touchy-feely body language. If you do not hug them, they will reach out and hug you. If affection is not found in healthy realms, Popular Sanguines will find it elsewhere. It is not that they intentionally determine to make poor choices in order to fill this need, but because these emotional needs are hardwired, Popular Sanguines will subconsciously do what they can to get them met. Popular Sanguines will sell their souls for a cuddle.

This was the case for Nikki, and thousands of girls like her. Her childhood home was unstable, leaving her looking for affection. She was 15 when she found pleasure in the arms of a boy. By 16, she was pregnant. Once the boyfriend heard she was pregnant, he wanted nothing to do with her and severed all contact with her and the baby. With the hole in her heart that much bigger, she went back to finding affection in the only way she knew how: in the arms of boys. Nikki ended up pregnant again at age 19.

Nikki's story has a positive ending. She found her way to a maternity home that helped her get her GED and put her through a program that taught her computer skills. She has worked hard to get her life together and has found the strength to get a job, finish a year-long pharmaceutical tech program at a local college, and support her children on a single income.

A secondary aspect of affection is approval. Popular Sanguines do not want to do anything specific—like work—to get people's approval; they just want people to touch them, hug them and tell them they are wonderful.

Acceptance

Most of us who are Popular Sanguines have people in our lives who are always trying to fix us, shape us up and make us better. But instead of always having people make plans for our lives, what we really need is for them to accept us as we are. The interesting thing is that once people quit trying to remake us and give us the praise and approval we crave, we are much more likely to want to make them happy and to change. But first we need to feel accepted.

Looking back at her teenage years, Kathleen, a Certified Personality Trainer, realizes that back then her paycheck—a rarity in those days—bought her the acceptance with the "in crowd." She told me:

> As a teenager in the late '60s, very few girls had their own cars. But because my parents both worked and we lived outside of town, I had to have a car to drive back and forth to my job. I now realize that I was invited to run around with the "popular group" at just about the time I acquired that car.
>
> I worked at the local café each day after school until closing at 8 P.M. Then on Friday night, after work, I would go pick up all the girls. We had a great time, and I loved feeling accepted. Since nobody else contributed to the gas, I usually spent most of my weekly paycheck each Friday night as we drove up and down the streets, but it was so cool to be accepted into their group that I did not mind the cost.

Now that I understand the Personalities and the corresponding emotional needs, I realize that I got off easy just trading my weekly paycheck for acceptance. I know of some girls who dressed in brightly colored dresses and traded their dignity for attention and acceptance in the back seat of some boy's car each Friday night.

Powerful Choleric
Loyalty · Sense of Control · Credit for Good Work · Achievement

Those of us who have the Powerful Choleric Personality come hardwired with a need for loyalty from the troops in terms of support, control, credit, appreciation and achievement—since we have a mental to-do list longer than anyone else's!

Loyalty

Powerful Cholerics are natural leaders and will go to the wall for those who are on their team. However, because they are on the front lines, if they look back and see that anyone whom they thought was with them has backed off, they will feel betrayed and, as a result, may completely sever the relationship.

Depending on the level of maturity, Powerful Cholerics may attack, sever relationships, or extend grace. Immature Powerful Cholerics (those living in their weaknesses) who are betrayed will attack so-called team members or friends and attempt to destroy them. The knee-jerk reaction of most Powerful Cholerics is to go home—thinking it is the other person's loss. For high functioning Powerful Cholerics (those living in their strengths), when faced with a situation in which they feel betrayed, they will try to see the other's point of view—realizing that very few people are really out to get them. These Powerful Cholerics will offer grace and resolution.

Clayton is an example of the immature, betrayed Powerful Choleric. When his teenage children made mistakes, Clayton disowned them and kicked them out of the house—even though he had done many of the same things growing up. Whenever his wife, Gail, tries to defend or help them, he feels betrayed and then he verbally attacks her for being loyal to them.

Gail, on the other hand, is a Perfect Melancholy. As a result of the situation at home, she struggled with depression and was ultimately put on medication. When her attitude became more positive and she felt stronger, she stood up to Clayton. He did not know how to handle her lack of passivity and felt that he was losing control over her. So he attacked Gail and accused her of not loving him and of having an affair.

Over the years, Clayton has repeatedly told Gail that he is just the way he is and will never change. It is a shame to see someone destroy relationships rather than restore them. But this can happen when an immature Powerful Choleric perceives disloyalty.

How can you show your loyalty to the Powerful Cholerics in your life? Remember, Powerful Cholerics' focus is external, and they see the big picture. Because of their need to see things grow and progress, the best way to show them loyalty is to give them your active support.

We had a neighbor who would come over to visit my husband because he liked to have a verbal arm wrestle. While he was a Powerful Choleric, his secondary Personality was Perfect Melancholy, and he couldn't multitask. He could either talk or work, but not both. Since his goal in dropping by was verbal sparring, he talked. I watched as he followed my husband around the yard, talking as my husband raked leaves. It never occurred to him to pick up a rake and talk while they worked in the yard. While my husband enjoyed the rapid exchange of ideas, he dreaded seeing this neighbor heading down the sidewalk.

To a Powerful Choleric, physical action is the best indication of loyal support. It drives Powerful Cholerics crazy when other people don't seem to see what needs to be done. So if you are in a relationship with a Powerful Choleric, roll up your sleeves and get to work!

Sense of Control

Control is one of the biggest issues for a Powerful Choleric. This innate need for control is clear even when they are children. My Powerful Choleric sister's nursery school teacher told my mother, "I never have to worry if I have to miss a day. I know Lauren can take over for me."

Certainly, young Powerful Cholerics need a sense of control in their lives. Take Garrett, who even at two years of age needed to be in control

of something. However, because he was the youngest of five boys, his natural ability to take charge was often stifled under the weight of bigger brothers. His mother reports:

> Our older boys were already teens by the time Garrett was two years old, making for an interesting dilemma when everyone had to ride in the same van. Already having raised two sons with Powerful Choleric in their Personalities, I knew I had to give this "Little General" something to control before he started to take control of his world in inappropriate ways. So I put him in charge of the seat-belt brigade. It was Garrett's job to check each one of his brother's seat belts to make sure it was fastened before I put the van in gear. He pulled on each seat belt, getting an unhappy growl out of each brother. When satisfied that all was as it should be, he buckled himself in his car seat and gave me the sign that I could go. By giving him an important job, he had a sense of control over his brothers, who were all bigger and more powerful than he was.

If you have a Powerful Choleric in your life, especially a child, look for healthy ways that he or she can have a sense of control. Look for appropriate things that he or she can be in charge of.

Powerful Cholerics have a built-in need to be right. When they are right, they lord it over others, as it makes them feel powerful—and thus, gives them control. Over the years that I have spent teaching seminars, the Powerful Cholerics are the only ones who regularly come up to challenge my message or ask me if I have thought of a particular perspective. Understanding that these individuals are Powerful Cholerics who need control, I ask them what they know, and thus give them an opportunity to share their expertise with me. Powerful Cholerics like a good emotional arm wrestle. If you are not aware of this in your interactions with them, they will wrestle you to the ground, leaving you wounded and them triumphant—and in control.

Mature Powerful Cholerics will find worthy opponents of an equal mind-set for their verbal sparring, while Powerful Cholerics living in

their weaknesses will look for people of lesser strength, whom they can beat up on.

Credit for Good Work

Because Powerful Cholerics are the worker bees of life, they will work harder, longer and faster than anyone else. They are willing to do it all, but they need acknowledgment for all the work they do (even if it made more work for others!). They like top billing and will be wounded if their work goes unnoticed.

A friend of mine was in charge of her daughter's fourth-grade play. One of the dads offered to build the background sets. Knowing that he was good with things like this, she took him up on his offer. He built wonderful backgrounds and the play was a great success. However, when my friend looked at the programs, she noticed that this man's name had been left off the "special thanks" list. Feeling horrible about this oversight, she tried to apologize to this hard-working dad. He was polite but cold toward her efforts to make things better. Later in the year, she asked this man if he would again be willing to help with the outdoor carnival. He refused.

Powerful Cholerics need recognition for their efforts, and if they don't get it, they may not be willing to put you on their to-do lists a second time. Even Powerful Choleric children want credit for all the work they do. Christy Largent, one of our Certified Personality Trainers, shared this story with me:

> One Friday night, my niece, Aubrey, aged five, spent the night with us. On Saturday morning, we got up and I helped her make her bed in the guestroom. We got the comforter all fluffed and the pillows just perfectly in place. The minute we finished making the bed, she ran full speed into the kitchen where my husband Tom was making breakfast for us. "Tom, Tom," she said excitedly, "come look at my work!"

Out of the mouths of babes! Isn't this what all Powerful Cholerics are screaming for on the inside? After they get older than age five or so, they can't politely say it out loud, but inside they are screaming, "Come look at my work!"

One of the best ways to improve your relationship with a Powerful Choleric is to say something such as "I do not know how you do all you do" or "This place would fall apart if it weren't for you." You will visibly see them perk up with the pleasure such comments give them.

Achievement

As water is to fish, so achievement is to a Powerful Choleric. Powerful Cholerics cannot live without achievement in their life. At the end of a day, Powerful Cholerics will recite their accomplishments, either in their head for a self-pat on the back, or to the people around them so that they can receive that needed "Way to go!"

While writing this book, I still had to live my everyday life. I still had my day-to-day responsibilities. I had interruptions just like everyone does. As I was writing this section, I became very snappish. I had many things on my plate that needed to be done immediately, but I knew that if I did not work on the book, I would not finish it by the deadline. I was feeling stressed and torn. I really wanted to work on the book, but I had to finish these other items before I could get to writing. Finally, I was able to get all of those other tasks completed and get back to writing this chapter. Even though I teach this stuff, I was amazed at how my disposition improved when my mental to-do list had some items checked off.

The previous week I had had a similar kind of day. At the end of the day, I was so happy with myself—and all I had accomplished—that I sent my friends and those who have been helping me on this book the following e-mail:

Subject: A Choleric Kind of Day

Omigosh! Have I had a banner Choleric day. My oven got fixed this morning, and then the water truck came and filled the cistern with 3,500 gallons of water. Then pump guys came and worked all afternoon to get water to the little house—and were successful. The tow truck driver came and got the red TR7 and took it to the mechanic. He is bringing the dead, dead blue TR7 home.

I have sent the lease to my new tenants in Carlsbad. I've talked to the bank about funding to buy the five acres adjacent to our property. I have worked on finalizing the job descriptions for the office staff—and have them almost all complete and agreed upon. I have been e-mailing back and forth on GCWC stuff and have made huge progress. And I just finished up the covers for the CLASS Communicators Club. What a day!

Now I just have to wait for the blue TR7 to come home, figure out what to cook for dinner and then go to the grocery store—even though right now there is a big thunderstorm with hail that has my dog hiding in the closet. All this would be great if my goal for the day wasn't to work on *Wired That Way*. But that was my goal. I hope to get to it soon.

Appropriately, I got many "Way to go!" responses and was able to continue to make good progress on the book.

In addition to hearing Powerful Cholerics talk about all that they've done, it is not uncommon to hear them complain about not having time to waste. They have the same 24 hours as everyone else, but their to-do list contains more than is humanly possible for anyone to achieve. Because they frequently push themselves to exhaustion, Powerful Cholerics often explode at their families, friends and coworkers. They assume that the reason they could not do all that they set out to do was because of all these interruptions. As a result, Powerful Cholerics often need a reality check to bring their goals back in line with reasonable limits.

Perfect Melancholy
Sensitivity · Support · Space · Silence

Those who have the Perfect Melancholy Personality come hardwired with a need for those around them to be sensitive to their feelings. They have a deep need to be understood and supported, but they also need space to recharge their batteries and space to feel their pain. Their head rattles when there is too much noise. Perfect Melancholies must have quiet time in order to feel at peace with themselves and the world around them.

Sensitivity

When Chuck is feeling down (and it's really obvious with Perfect Melancholies when this is because a black cloud travels with them), my natural reaction is to try to cheer him up. That is what I want others to do for me. I want them to fix my problems and make them better—buy me ice cream and make me smile! But because I understand my husband's Personality, I know that is not what he needs.

One day, many years ago, I came home from work and immediately sensed that all was not well. A large black cloud seemed to fill the living room. When I saw Chuck, I asked what was wrong. "Nothing," he replied. Being fluent in "Perfect Melancholy," I knew that this meant something was definitely wrong.

So I stepped outside my natural response and applied what I teach: I realized that Chuck needed sensitivity (he needed me to hurt when he hurt and cry when he cried), I slowed down, sat down, and focused on him. I quieted down and started speaking in softer tones. I again asked him what was wrong. Once he could tell that I really cared, as opposed to just breezing through and asking a rhetorical "How are you?" he shared what had him down. "I've been transferred to Mission Valley," he said.

At this point in our lives, Chuck worked in Oceanside, a Marine-base town, for the San Diego County Social Services. He worked in a temporary, modular unit and had an old metal desk. The environment was such that he had installed a lock on his desk drawer to secure his valuables, including a headset telephone that was his personal property. In contrast, Mission Valley had high-rise, glass office buildings, a restaurant row and two malls containing both a Nordstrom's and a Neiman Marcus.

Understanding this background information, my natural reaction would have been to try to cheer him up: "That is great! You've always hated Oceanside. I'll take the train down to Mission Valley and meet you for dinner. We can do the theater." I knew that this was the wrong reaction, but I wasn't sure what the right reaction was. So I took a deep breath and asked, "What do you need from me right now?"

I was surprised when Chuck said, "Don't tell me that it is going to be all right. Don't try to fix it." Again, I took a breath and tried to be sensitive to where he was coming from. Chuck had just completed graduate school. This was his first job. He had been at this job for two months, and now they were transferring him. I thought back farther. Chuck's parents were separated, and he had lived with his dad. One day, he had come home from high school to find his father dead on the sofa. Chuck had been married briefly before we met, and his wife had left him and remarried as soon as the divorce papers were signed. I put two and two together and softly said, "I bet you feel really rejected right now." He replied affirmatively, and we then had a positive, adult conversation.

The reality is that everything I might have said to try to cheer up my husband would have been right, but the timing would have been wrong. Chuck needed me to be sensitive to how he was feeling. If you have a Perfect Melancholy in your life and you know he or she is having a tough time, think through that person's thoughts and feelings before you respond. With the Perfect Melancholy, timing is everything. Think before you speak, and only speak what is appropriate at the time. When the Perfect Melancholy does open up and share how he or she is feeling, you may be tempted to bark back, "That is the most ridiculous thing I have ever heard!" But this will only cause that person to retreat further and clam up the next time you ask him or her what is wrong.

If you are the Perfect Melancholy and your friend, coworker or mate is trying to be helpful by asking what is wrong, answer honestly. Popular Sanguines and Powerful Cholerics living in their strengths will understand and adjust their approach so that you will know they care. However, someone who does not understand the Personalities—or is living in his or her weaknesses—will give up and not even bother to ask you the next time.

Support

Think of the Perfect Melancholy as a bridge. Without the supports underneath it, the bridge would fall down. In the same way, without the support of people who care, Perfect Melancholy individuals feel let down. And then they fall apart.

I learned a great lesson from an aunt of mine whose husband, my uncle, is in a high-profile position and used to having things his way. Although my aunt has also made a name for herself, she told me, "When I am with him, I view my job as holding the spotlight on him."

I like the visual those words created and I have adopted that approach when I am with Chuck—both personally and publicly. It is not that he wants to be in the spotlight, it is just that with our Personality mix, it would be easy for me to always be center stage and easy for him to always slip into the background. I have plenty of attention when we are not together, so when we are together, I work to support him. I focus on what is going on in his life. If we are in public, I quietly steer the conversation away from me and toward topics related to his areas of expertise—letting people know how accomplished he is and how proud I am of him.

Space

After attending Personality Training, Andrea found out that one of the emotional needs of Perfect Melancholies is space. When she thought about the layout of her house, she realized that her Perfect Melancholy husband did not have a space that was all his. So, she decided to move her projects and the children's things from the office they all shared to somewhere else in the house. She decided that this was a small sacrifice that she was willing to make for her husband. When she offered the office space to him, she immediately saw the relief on his face. Just the thought of having space to himself that he could organize, sit in alone and decorate as he chose turned him into a different and more relaxed person.

David is a Perfect Melancholy who fulfills his need for space in a totally different way. He is a busy politician who works with people all the time. His days are filled with decision-making, talking to the media and his own constituents, and attending social functions. So it came as no surprise to his wife, who understands the Personalities, that each weekend there was nothing he loved more than riding his fast, red

Italian motorcycle for hours in the countryside. He returns home happy, recharged and energized.

Is there a Perfect Melancholy in your life who needs space? Is there something you can do to help him or her have that space? Or are you the Perfect Melancholy? Are there some changes that you can make in your life so that you can have the space you need?

Silence

Being a Popular Sanguine, Theresa enjoyed listening to her favorite radio programs and chatting with her neighbors while she worked in her front garden. She was enjoying her existence until one day, Phil, her Perfect Melancholy computer programmer husband, came home and announced that he had made arrangements to work from home. Now, as he spent each day in the house with Theresa, he could not believe how noisy his wife was.

He soon put a stop to the loud radio by going out and buying Theresa a set of wireless stereo headphones. He accused her of "monstering" the neighbors and told her to back off. He even asked if she could do the vacuuming while he was out so that he could avoid the noise. He purchased some earplugs to wear while he was working, because he couldn't even stand the noise coming from the computer! Yes, silence is a definite need that must be met for the Perfect Melancholy individual.

When Kathleen began teaching financial seminars, she didn't realize that it was a way to meet her needs—and her husband's. As a Popular Sanguine, she loved the attention, approval, acceptance and appreciation that she received from the audiences. She found that she loved being center stage and having all the participants appreciate her as the expert! Kathleen said, "I developed 'new best friends' at almost every class. It often happened that participants hugged me on their way out. *And I got paid for doing this!* What a deal!"

Kathleen was really loving this newfound role, but then she discovered another benefit: When she got home, she was exhausted and even her mouth was tired. As a result, she was not motor mouth with her husband, and they began enjoying quiet evenings together. Karen writes:

Now that I understand my husband's need for silence, I am no longer crushed when he doesn't ask about the details of my day. In the past, I was shocked and dismayed that when he asked how my class was and I responded, "Great," his response was, "That's good." How could he not want to know the details of a great class? It's because he had dealt with people all day and was in need of silent support. All he wanted was for us to sit together and watch a Discovery channel program about Mayan Ruins. Now I am okay with that. If my day has been just too great not to share, after I rest a bit, I call a Sanguine friend!

Peaceful Phlegmatic
Peace and Quiet · Feeling of Self-Worth · Lack of Stress · Respect

Those who have the Peaceful Phlegmatic Personality come hardwired with a need for peaceful, quiet surroundings, a feeling of self-worth, and a lifestyle that minimizes stress and maximizes respect.

Peace and Quiet

For Marilyn, the Personalities were simply an interesting study and a way that she could use labels to describe a specific set of traits. It was not until she went to our training to become a Certified Personality Trainer that she realized the Personalities go way beyond a label and a study—they are really all about relationships! And nowhere was this clearer to her than in her relationship with her daughter. I'll let Marilyn share her story:

From birth, our daughter Meredith has been very laid-back and easygoing—what I now know to be a Peaceful Phlegmatic Personality. As a baby, she would sit for what my Popular Sanguine Personality perceived as an unusually long period of time just looking around. When I put her in the car seat, she did not fuss. She just looked out the window and commented on the trees or whatever else she saw. Meredith never complained about anything.

Meredith is now a junior in high school. Because it was important for me to be popular, I have always tried to push her to have friends come over for the weekend. I would start in the middle of the week, trying to make her plan her weekend and invite friends to spend the night. I was always trying to get her to smile, laugh and act interested. She would finally acquiesce and have some kids over. Every time they left, she said, "What's the use in having friends over? They just hang out with you and don't pay any attention to me."

I have known about the Personalities for years, but it wasn't until I attended the Personality Training that I began to understand that she was right. I absolutely loved having all these kids in my house. I found them very entertaining. After Meredith's friends left, I'd tell her how she should have acted, what she should have done, and so forth.

When I got home from the Personality Training conference, I sat down with Meredith and asked her to forgive me. I told her that I now realized that I had been trying to arrange her life and circumstances to fit her life into how I had enjoyed my teenage years. And things truly did start to change. One morning on our way to school after a few weeks had passed, Meredith looked over at me and said, "Mama, thank you for giving me my life back." I was overwhelmed. She told me how she was so appreciative that I was giving her space and down time.

Before this epiphany, I had just thought—and, I am ashamed to admit, *told* her many times—that she was just lazy. Now I understood that she *needs* quiet and rest, especially after a long, fast-paced, hard week at school. I see that she has to expend so much energy to get everything done that she really needs peace and quiet so that she can unwind.

When I finally truly understood that Meredith actually enjoyed being alone, I stopped arranging sleepovers. This was difficult for me, because I never wanted time alone as a teenager and still do not need it very much. But now I let Meredith decide when she wants company.

Feeling of Self-Worth

If you are living or working with a Peaceful Phlegmatic and you do not share this Personality, the following illustration may help you understand why a feeling of self-worth is so important for that person.

Picture four children in a family, each having one of the four differing Personalities. The Popular Sanguine child goes to school. When he comes home, he announces (as my nephew once did), "I am the most popular kid in my class. In my school, they will not have a party without checking with me first, because they know that if I can't come, it will not be any fun!" Now, for a child like that, his parents must give him the attention and approval that Popular Sanguines need. They need to tell him, "Everybody does love you—you *are* the most popular kid in school."

Then you have the Powerful Choleric child. She comes home from school and says, "Guess what, Mom? The teacher made me the room monitor!" What should Mom say? "They picked the right one. You have great leadership potential. You will probably be president of the United States some day."

The Perfect Melancholy child is, of course, the "perfect" child. He makes his bed before he goes to school in the morning (like my little brother, Fred, always did) and then goes off to school, where his teacher says, "My job as a teacher would be so much easier if all my students were just like you." The Perfect Melancholy child comes home and does his homework like he is supposed to. His mom says, "You are the perfect child—I wish all my children were just like you."

Then you have the Peaceful Phlegmatic child. She did not make her bed before she left for school, didn't clean up her toys, and didn't get voted anything at school. She comes home and heads straight for the refrigerator, and then the television. You have to nag her to do her homework. This child is likely to grow up to be the person who has fallen through the cracks her entire life. For this type of child, her parents will need to instill in her a sense of self-worth—otherwise she may fail to receive this in her life. She will need to feel like her parents value her, not for what she does or for what she produces, but simply because of who she is.

Lack of Stress

When Cheri was a brand-new teacher, she took three of her high school students out for ice cream as a thank-you for having helped her in the classroom. Although all three students clearly stated what they wanted, one girl was given the wrong flavor. The other two shook their heads knowingly and said, "This always happens to Susan."

Cheri asked Susan what she'd ordered, intending to get her what she had wanted in the first place. And as a Popular Sanguine/Powerful Choleric, she didn't hear Susan quietly beg, "Don't! Don't! It doesn't matter!" Cheri walked up to the cash register, returned the incorrect scoop of ice cream and requested the correct flavor.

Feeling triumphant, Cheri brought the right ice cream to Susan. But Cheri's action had brought Peaceful Phlegmatic Susan to a state of complete anxiety—almost panic. She kept saying, "I would have eaten it. It didn't matter." She was miserable during the drive back to school. Cheri could tell that Susan really would have preferred to eat the wrong ice cream than "cause trouble" by asking for what she actually wanted.

Respect

Peaceful Phlegmatics are the middle-of-the-road people. In school, they did not get great awards for being good, nor were they bad. Because of this, Peaceful Phlegmatics need respect more than the other Personalities. The hardest thing about giving the Peaceful Phlegmatic respect is that the other Personalities—especially the Powerful Cholerics—view respect as connected to production or works. But the Peaceful Phlegmatics need respect just because of who they are.

So how can those of us who are more driven show respect to the Peaceful Phlegmatic? By setting aside our agenda and doing something that we know is important to that person. This might mean simply sitting on the sofa with the Peaceful Phlegmatic—without multitasking—and watching a ballgame in which we have no interest. It could mean carving time out of our schedule to sit and watch a movie. It is not complicated, but for those of us who are not Peaceful Phlegmatics, we need to be reminded to do this. Let me illustrate.

My friend Melody's primary Personality is Peaceful Phlegmatic. We used to be neighbors in California, and even though it has been years since we lived near each other, we have stayed in touch. When she and her husband bought a new house in Reno, I offered to come help her decorate and get settled. I accepted a speaking engagement in the area that paid my airfare but little else. This was an important fact, as I had told Melody that I was really making the trip just for her, rather than squeezing her into a nonstop speaking tour.

I was able to stay with Melody for three days. During that time, we unpacked all her kitchen boxes, arranged her cabinets, created artistic displays in the space above the cabinets, and shopped for decorative and organizational items that were needed to finish up the room. Years later, she told me that everything was still exactly where I had put it. Melody knew that I had a very full schedule, and the fact that I took time out just for her showed her that she was *valued*.

Listen to the Peaceful Phlegmatics in your life. What have they been quietly asking you to do? Make it a priority. Peaceful Phlegmatics are not demanding, so you may have to do a bit of sleuthing to figure out what they need and want. But when you cheerfully do what is important to them, they will feel valued and respected by you. And you do not need to acquiesce to their wishes often—even just once a month will let them know you care.

Recognizing and Fulfilling Emotional Needs

As you read the descriptions of the various emotional needs that go with each Personality, I trust that you found yourself nodding as you grasped the emotional needs of your Personality. The explanations and stories that were included with each description were chosen to not only help you figure out your own core needs, but also to help you in your relationship with others.

Recognizing the Emotional Needs of Others

The next time you are in an interaction with someone and you sense static, instead of giving that person a piece of your mind, do the mature thing: Stop and think back to the emotional needs chart (maybe even copy it and post it on your bathroom mirror or on the wall next to your computer), and ask yourself, *What can I give this person right now that will help reduce the static?* Pick one or two of the emotional needs and fill them. At first, this may feel wrong—maybe even manipulative—but do it anyway.

It is amazing how fast a static-filled relationship will become clear when you give to others what *they need* instead of what you want to give them: anger, condemnation, a bony finger in the face or, at the very least, a dirty look. Filling appropriate emotional needs is one of the most powerful tools that you can have in your "fix a relationship with a friend" toolkit.

Recognizing Our Own Emotional Needs

When you understand the way that you are wired, you can begin to understand and meet the emotional needs that are built in to each Personality. Just as air, food and water are essential to your physical well-being, these needs are essential to your emotional wellness. And remember, these are not wants—they are *needs*.

As previously mentioned, our Personalities come with their own unique set of needs that make us predisposed toward certain behaviors. When these emotional needs are not met in the proper way, we are more likely to do whatever it takes to ease the pain or the craving that occurs because of these unfulfilled needs. However, by understanding the whys of our behavior—our core emotional needs—we can exchange a destructive behavior for a healthy behavior, which will result in us having our true emotional needs met.

The "Emotional Wellness Checklist" on the following page lists some classic behaviors that should be red flags to indicate that some emotional needs are going unfulfilled:

This list is not to say that only the specified Personalities have the noted tendencies—it's just that some behaviors are more of an issue in some Personalities than in others. When our emotional needs are not being met, an internal panic starts, which propels us into behaviors that may be harmful to us. Right or wrong, we tend to hook on to behaviors

Emotional Wellness Checklist

POPULAR SANGUINE Excessive/compulsive talking Using sex as a replacement for affection Overextended—too many activities Eating (especially sweets) to medicate pain	**POWERFUL CHOLERIC** Overstepping boundaries/ usurping authority Arguing every point, never wrong Needing credit for everything they do Having fits of rage
PEACEFUL PHLEGMATIC Compulsive lying Checked out ("Lights on, nobody home") Physical illness or pain Becomes passive—easily bullied or abused	**PERFECT MELANCHOLY** Obsessive worry or fear Overly sensitive Reclusive behavior Eating disorders, such as anorexia and bulimia

that make us feel like we are breathing again, when in reality some of these behaviors are leeching the life from us. In many circles, this is referred to as dysfunctional behavior.

By addressing our emotional needs, we can calm the internal panic. This calm, or peace, is essential to healthy living. Why? Because it's almost impossible to work on personal strengths and weaknesses (self-improvement/behavior modification) until we have first met our emotional needs. Since we are usually a blend of Personalities, knowing our secondary Personality is also very important, because these secondary emotional needs have to be met right along with our primary emotional needs. For example, as a Popular Sanguine/Powerful Choleric, my need to be in control may be as strong as my need for approval. Both needs are important to me.

The Importance of Recognizing Emotional Needs

When we don't recognize our emotional needs, the result is disaster. Let me share Cassandra's story with you to illustrate this point. Cassandra grew up the younger of two girls, five years apart. Her older sister was a Perfect Melancholy and was a good fit for her Perfect Melancholy mother. Cassandra came wired as a Powerful Choleric/Popular Sanguine, which didn't suit her mother's style at all. She was often told to "sit still" and "don't be so loud" and asked, "Why can't you play quietly like your sister?" Over time, Cassandra figured out that in order to get the attention, approval and acceptance she craved, she needed to squish her Popular Sanguine side and become a Perfect Melancholy to please her mother. Over time, this became a way of life for Cassandra—and resulted in a squished Personality. Cassandra says:

> As an adult, I gave up and settled for being a secondhand Perfect Melancholy, even though I was not aware of what I was doing. While I accepted this mentally, my body and spirit were unhappy with this decision. High blood pressure started to be a problem for me. I used eating sweets to help medicate the problem. After the death of my father, I grieved not just for the loss of my dad but also for the loss of the one person I was most like in my family—the person who met my emotional needs. I knew that I was never going to receive the same acceptance from my mother as I had from my father.

Cassandra's Popular Sanguine side withered when her emotional needs weren't met. As Cassandra learned more about the Personalities, she started to notice which of the emotional needs felt good to her. Sitting still and becoming quiet (the Perfect Melancholy needs of sensitivity, space and silence) did not feel good. The more she tried to make these feel good to her and meet her needs, the smaller and more worthless she felt.

One day, Cassandra's mother heard that she was helping a friend harvest crops. Cassandra liked the idea of playing farmer. But Cassandra's mother was aghast at the temporary job she had taken to help a friend. She didn't think that it was a ladylike job or appropriate for her daughter. In desperation (and total confusion), Cassandra's mother looked at her and said, "You are such a maverick!" Cassandra was thrilled at this remark. For the first time, her mother had seen her for who she really was. Finally, Cassandra released her Popular Sanguine side, letting it bounce back into health.

It feels good when we wear the skin of our own Personality—when, like Goldie Locks in the house of the Three Bears, we try out different things to find out which one just feels right. It is important to know who we are so that we can feed our souls the proper nutrients—or, as I like to say, fill our emotional needs. Look for moments that reveal the true Personality that is you.

"Stealing" Emotional Needs from Others

As we become aware of each Personality's emotional needs and how to best fill those needs for others, we can monitor our own emotional health by watching our behaviors. "Stealing" our emotional needs from others is an indicator that all is not well in our lives. Let me use a story to explain what I mean.

Kathryn is a Powerful Choleric. Her early childhood was filled with tragedy, which led to trauma in her life. As a result, her emotional need for control was pinched off, creating an internal panic. To compensate, being bossy became second nature to her. She told everyone what to do and wagged her finger in everyone's face. The adults in her life tried to correct her behavior, but no one understood her emotional need to have a sense of control in her life. So the behavior continued.

As an adult she constantly overstepped her bounds, resulting in her being removed from various committees and clubs. Because her motives were usually good, it was hard for her to see the error of her ways. In despair, she prayed for help. Soon, she found the information about the Personalities and started applying this knowledge to her life. Slowly, her emotional health returned. She discovered something amazing about her soul functions: They bounce back if given a chance!

Now when Kathryn catches herself wagging her bony finger in

someone's face or too frequently showing off her hard work to others to receive a "Way to go!" she steps back and takes a look at what is going on in her life. She asks herself, *Am I overextended? Are there circumstances out of my control?* By using her emotional needs as a checklist, Kathryn has learned to correct her course before her behaviors become destructive.

You can do the same. When you become aware that these Personality extremes are manifesting in your life, allow that to be a red flag for you, telling you something needs adjustment. Then look at your life to see where the issues are coming from and which of your emotional needs are not being met. Once you see where the problem lies, you can take steps to correct the problem.

Earlier, I mentioned feeling frustrated while writing this book. The symptoms were short-lived and did not escalate to the level of rage. However, I was certainly snappish—which is a red flag for me. What was wrong? Which of my primary or secondary Personality's emotional needs were not being met? Accomplishment! As soon as I was able to check some things off my mental list as completed, the snappishness left and I could return to my happy, productive self.

Taking Responsibility for Our Well-Being

It's vital that we take responsibility for our well-being—that we take stock of our lives to see whether our needs are being met. If we don't, we abdicate that responsibility to those around us. And when we leave our emotional health in the care of those around us, we run the risk of becoming victims.

Sandy believes that had she understood her Personality and used that knowledge to take control of her own emotional health, she would not have suffered the abuse she did as a child. This is her story:

Growing up, I never had the affection from my dad that I needed. Since I was not the boy that he had wanted, I was of little value to him. All through my childhood, I faced this kind of rejection. By the time I was a teenager, I was very bruised.

One day, in high school, there was a boy in my math class who thought I was the greatest thing. He admired me because I was smart (my dad always pointed out how much smarter my brother was, even though I outranked him in my class) and told me all the time how beautiful I was. Even though I cared little for the kind of person this boy was (he flunked out of classes and was a troublemaker), he gave me attention and made me feel good about myself—something my Popular Sanguine Personality needed. So I hung around him. Within six months, the relationship became like a drug to me. I could not get enough of him or the affection I was receiving. Despite what I knew as a good church girl, I had sex with him. I wanted affection so badly that I went against what I knew to be right.

This continued for about six months until I had some positive role models in my youth group rise up and show me that I did not need this kind of person in my life. Some women started to mentor me and show me positive attention, and I was able to break the relationship off after youth camp one summer. I did not have sex again until I was married, but I don't think that would be true if I had not finally had my need for affection met in some positive ways.

Sandy's story is like that of so many men and women. Yet she was blessed that she did not suffer more dire consequences as a result of meeting her needs in unhealthy ways. Not every similar story has such a happy ending.

Use the knowledge of Personality needs to take control of your own emotional health. By taking the time to check how your emotional needs are being managed, you have the potential to live emotionally healthy and happy lives.

CHAPTER 6

MARRIAGE

Every relationship takes work: two best friends from high school, an employer and a long-time employee, a husband and a wife—all have to invest in their relationship to make it last over the years. Nearly everyone who has been involved in any type of long-term relationship can cite numerous rough spots when either party could have walked away or quit, but instead chose to work through the differences.

Yet most of us do not view marriage the same way. We expect the blush of love to cover over the differences in marriage—differences that we'd accept and expect in any other relationship. While every relationship takes work, nearly every relationship can work, especially when both parties are willing to make the effort that is required to make that happen. Even if only one party is willing to make changes, remarkable improvement can be made.

It is a fact that when it comes to relationships, most of us are attracted to people who are opposite from us. When we look at marriage, I believe this is how God intended it to be. When functioning in our strengths, the varied skills, emotions and viewpoints that a husband and wife bring into marriage create balance and perspective. The two truly do become one, with a complete complement of abilities. In areas in which I am strong or gifted, my husband is weak or less gifted; likewise, in areas in which he excels, I need help. When we understand each other, our varied abilities and opposing strengths and weaknesses, we can take advantage of those differences. Together, we can bring about personal growth and balance in one another. Without such an understanding of our Personalities and how we can complement each other, we would switch from "attract" mode to "attack" mode!

Opposites Attract

Since I had an understanding of the Personalities from childhood, I fully understood the idea that opposites attract. When I attended seminars and conferences at which my mother was teaching the concepts of the Personalities, I often heard people ask, "What Personality type should I marry if I want to be happy?" Her tongue-in-cheek reply was, "If you want to be happy, don't marry anybody!"

Having seen the struggles in my own parents' marriage of opposites, and after hearing many distressful questions from those who were in similar situations, I decided to date men who were just like me. I dated men who were strong self-starters, often outgoing salesmen or driven entrepreneurs. They were usually older and financially solid (or at least they appeared to be) and almost always Powerful Cholerics—some with Popular Sanguine traits and some with Perfect Melancholy traits. Yet while my dating life netted me many good times and some nice jewelry, I never fell in love with any of these men. Until I met Chuck.

Chuck did not fit my profile. Despite my best efforts to date men who were more like me, Chuck's Personality was opposite from mine. Chuck was only three years older than I was; he was 27, and I was 24. He had a degree in art (motion picture production), and when we met he was making movies for the Air Force. With no business background and no entrepreneurial drive, Chuck was an artist at heart.

We got married five months after we met. So much for trying to disprove that opposites attract!

In looking back at the 23 years of our marriage, I am so grateful that I understood our Personalities. When Chuck and I function in our weaknesses, my Popular Sanguine part and his Perfect Melancholy part are often at odds, while our mutual Powerful Choleric parts battle for control. But when we understand each other's Personality and live in our strengths, my Popular Sanguine cheers him up and his Perfect Melancholy provides grounding in my life. Our shared Powerful Choleric means that we each want to "go" and "do," and we share who is in charge of what based on our individual giftings, available time and priorities. We have learned to make our marriage work—and it does take work!

VALENTINE'S DAY EXPECTATIONS
SHERYL VASSO, CPT

One of my female students was newly married and all excited about celebrating Valentine's Day with her husband for the first time. A week before Valentine's Day, she was sharing with me how excited she was, because her husband had prepared a special surprise for her for Valentine's Day. She could hardly contain herself, and as in typical Popular Sanguine manner, she was enthusiastically preparing for the evening by purchasing a flashy dress that she described as having various shades of pink and red and sequins—with shoes to match! I told her that I could hardly wait until next week to hear about her evening.

The following week, my Popular Sanguine student returned to class with her enthusiasm greatly deflated. When I inquired about her Valentine's surprise, she said, "It was awful!"

Now, while I am predominantly Perfect Melancholy and my student is Popular Sanguine, I was not sure what Personality type her husband was. But I quickly concluded that he was a Perfect Melancholy when my student shared what happened on Valentine's Day.

The surprise that her husband prepared for her was a lovely, romantic, candlelit dinner at home for just the two of them! As she told me about the night, I responded with "oohs" and "aahs," thinking how romantic and private such an evening would be. My student did not enjoy the romantic solitude, and I couldn't understand why. After all, I would have loved to have a Valentine's dinner like that! So I asked her, did she have to prepare the dinner? No! Clean up the dinner? No! Her husband did it all!

"So, why, then," I asked her, "are you upset?" She said, "No one got to see my new dress and shoes! I wanted to be out for the evening celebrating like most other people and then come home for the romantic solitude!

If you are currently single and the "Which Personality should I marry if I want to be happy?" question struck a chord with you, pay special attention here—especially if you are thinking of entering into a second or third marriage or if you are older than 25 and have never been married.

This is relevant because if you are young and entering into your first marriage, no matter how many books you read or how determined you are, you will probably marry for love ("He makes my tummy feel funny"). However, if you are older, you have probably seen many of your friends go through difficult marriages and terrible divorces and have vowed not to make the same mistakes. If you are considering a second or third marriage, it is usually due to the fact that your previous marriage(s) did not work. In either case, you are more likely to make an intellectually based decision. If you were married previously and the marriage didn't work, the fact that your spouse was opposite from you probably played a big part in the "irreconcilable differences." As a result, you now look for someone who is either more like you or different from the last person—which essentially gives you the same outcome.

I find that when I talk to couples at my conferences, virtually the only time I find that the husband and wife really do have a very similar Personality mix is when it is a second or third marriage (for at least one of them) or when they married late in life. We are naturally attracted to those who are opposite from us.

But if you are looking and want to make an intellectually based choice rather than an emotionally based decision, here's what you need to do: Marry someone with whom you have "one square in common."

One Square in Common

While every marriage takes work, certain combinations tend to work more easily, while others take more work. I have found that the marriages that take the least amount of work are those that have what I call one square in common. Remember that each square in the Personality chart (see page 16) represents one of the four Personalities. While we are naturally attracted to someone whose Personality is opposite from ours, the marriages in which the partners share an overlapping square usually work more easily and take less work. The common square gives both parties something in common.

Sharing the Popular Sanguine Square

My friend Melody is a Peaceful Phlegmatic with some Popular Sanguine. Her husband is a Powerful Choleric/Popular Sanguine combination. Together, they share the Popular Sanguine square. When Melody asked me to explain how this plays out in their marriage, I told her that because they both share the optimistic, fun-loving outlook of the Pop-ular Sanguine, it is unlikely that they will have any serious marriage problems. Having fun together allows them to overlook many other prob-lems. However, since neither of them has any real quantity of the Perfect Melancholy, they may never get their finances in order. I painted the following scenario of a day in their marriage:

> You have a bad day at work. You come in and look at Mark with those big eyes and say, "Mark, I've had a bad day. Let's go out to dinner and see a funny movie. I need to be cheered up." Knowing that finances have been a problem area, you two have worked to create a budget and are trying to stick to it. So Mark says, "We can't. It is not in our budget." You say, "But I really need to go out. We have credit cards. Let's go." Being a Popular Sanguine himself, Mark doesn't want to see you unhappy, so he agrees. Some form of this scenario repeats itself frequently over the years, and while you may not be horribly in debt, you are unlikely to ever get ahead.

Melody looked at me wide-eyed. My creative scenario had been exactly right! I told her that the good thing about their combination is that they will never really care about financial success, as the comfort of a huge savings account is not an issue to them. (Of course, when it comes to the in-laws, that's a whole other story!)

When we lived near Mark and Melody, we always had a good time with them. They either came to our house for dinner or we went out to dinner. After an evening with Mark and Melody, we always commented on what fun we had with them. With both of them being partially Popular Sanguine, they lifted our spirits. Couples with the Popular Sanguine square in common are lots of fun. You don't want to have a party without them!

Sharing the Perfect Choleric Square

Let's take Chuck and me as the example here. As I've mentioned, I am about half Popular Sanguine and half Powerful Choleric, and Chuck is mostly Perfect Melancholy with some Powerful Choleric. We are opposites in that I am Popular Sanguine and he is Perfect Melancholy, but we both share Powerful Choleric traits. The benefit of this to us is that neither of us ever really wants to rest. On any given weekend, we both have more to accomplish than is humanly possible. We both have our mental lists, and we view the weekend as an opportunity to accomplish the things that we cannot get done during the work week. With the Powerful Choleric square in common, our marriage is one of action. We view vacations as opportunities for seeing and doing new things, not for resting.

Sharing the Perfect Melancholy Square

Chuck and I used to know a couple who shared the Perfect Melancholy square in common. They lived next door to us in our neighborhood right before they bought their dream house. The wife was a Powerful Choleric/ Perfect Melancholy, while the husband was a Perfect Melancholy/ Peaceful Phlegmatic.

In contrast to the couples with the Popular Sanguine square in common, those who share the Perfect Melancholy trait are the picture of success. They are usually well-educated, drive the right cars, and have large homes. They have retirement funds and their futures are fully mapped out.

When we use go to this couple's home for a social event, we always had a lovely time. When we left, Chuck and I would say to each other, "That was nice." And it was. We didn't leave bursting with excitement, slapping our knees, or talking about what a blast it was. The Perfect Melancholy home isn't that type. Couples who share the Perfect Melancholy square are pleasant and enjoyable, but "fun" and "exciting" are not the first words you would use to describe them.

Sharing the Peaceful Phlegmatic Square

My friend Brenda is a Peaceful Phlegmatic who married a man who was also about 50 percent Peaceful Phlegmatic. In their home, comfort is a priority. They value harmony and stability. If a guest drops by unannounced, they do not panic and frantically throw things into the closet in an attempt to make a good impression—the house looks the way it looks whether they know people are coming or not. They are very content with each other and with their life and do not feel a compulsion to conquer anything.

The household that shares the Peaceful Phlegmatic square in common will be a very comfortable home. When both parties in a marriage share that comfortable quality, everyone relaxes with them. The couple with the Peaceful Phlegmatic square in common may find that they have many projects that are unfinished, but like the Popular Sanguine marriage, they won't mind.

The following "Marital Balance Sheet" chart illustrates the assets and liabilities of each "one square in common" type of marriage.

Marital Balance Sheet

POPULAR SANGUINE THE "FUN" MARRIAGE		POWERFUL CHOLERIC THE "ACTIVE" MARRIAGE	
Assets	**Liabilities**	**Assets**	**Liabilities**
Spontaneous	Lack of plans and goals	Goal-oriented	Struggle for control
Exciting	Unstable	Clear boundaries	Overcommitted and late
Enthusiastic	Flirtatious	High accomplishments	No time for relationship
Keep marriage fresh	Messy	Respect each other	Two careers pulling on marriage
Flexible	No one listens	High energy	
Compromising	Relationship remains superficial	Championing causes	Marriage a low priority
Forgiving	Fail to put down roots	Firm parents	
Play with children	Blurred generational boundaries	Quick sex	Blurring of personal and professional boundaries
Creative sex	Financial matters lack budgeting, accounting and retirement planning		Shouting contests
			Fear of sharing

PEACEFUL PHLEGMATIC THE "RELAXED" MARRIAGE		PERFECT MELANCHOLY THE "ORGANIZED" MARRIAGE	
Assets	**Liabilities**	**Assets**	**Liabilities**
Stable	Low accomplishment	Neat home	Critical
Agreeable	Lack of planning	Long-range plans	Danger of mid-life crisis
Content	Kids can take over	Financial order	Depressed and brooding
Low pressure	Dull	Punctual	
Satisfied	Control is passive-aggressive	Value education	Keep record of wrongs
Modest		Remember important dates	Reinforce each other's negativity
Lack of direction	Lack of communication	Committed to each other	Stuck in routines
Patient with children	Loss of individual identity	Loving and protective with children	May be unfaithful
Special-event sex	Blurred generational boundaries	Romantic sex	Repeat maladaptive behaviors
	Fear of conflict		High expectations place heavy burden on relationships

No Squares in Common

Marriages with one square in common work the easiest because of the common traits they share. Marriages in which one spouse is a Popular Sanguine/Peaceful Phlegmatic and the other is a Powerful Choleric/Perfect Melancholy have a similar advantage: Each is somewhat outgoing/optimistic and somewhat introverted/pessimistic, and so they share these qualities in common. However, this combination is likely to require more work than those with one square in common.

I find the marriage that takes the most work and the most adjustments is the one in which one spouse is Popular Sanguine/Powerful Choleric and the other is Peaceful Phlegmatic/Perfect Melancholy. Look again at the "Marital Balance Sheet" chart. The top two squares represent the outgoing, optimistic person (the one who is energized by people). When both of these Personalities are combined in one person, you get someone who is supercharged, high-strung and overwhelming to others. The bottom two squares are the more pessimistic and reclusive people: They are drained by people and recharged by solitude. When both of these Personalities are found in one person, that person can easily slip into being the true couch potato—someone who is hard to motivate or get moving.

When these two people marry, not only are they opposites, but they also do not share any part of a square in common! The marriage can work, but both parties will have to be willing to put forth extra effort to understand each other's Personality and corresponding emotional needs.

Many years ago, I had an employee named Janis. When a mutual friend referred Janis to me, she described Janis as being my "clone." We ended up working together for many years, and she even lived with us for a while before she got married. Janis, who was about an even Popular Sanguine/Powerful Choleric, married Boyd, a Perfect Melancholy/Peaceful Phlegmatic who worked in his family's business. For those of us who worked with Janis, it was difficult to watch her adjust to their first year of marriage.

Janis and Boyd went to the same church that Chuck and I attended. One Sunday after services, a group of us were scheduled to go out to lunch for a birthday party. On Friday, Janis and I had discussed the party and what gift we were purchasing. I knew that she was planning to go and had the gifts all wrapped, but when the lunchtime came, Janis and Boyd never showed up. The party went on without them, but I knew that Janis hated to miss a party. On Monday, I asked her what had happened. She looked down and sadly said, "Boyd didn't feel like going."

Janis had to learn to do things on her own—which was not what she had expected in marriage. After Janis had been married a few months, I asked her if she'd like to go on a trip with me. My father had two frequent-flier tickets that were going to expire at the end of the year, so he had offered them to me. I wanted to visit my aging but favorite relative, Aunt Jean, but Chuck was in graduate school at the time and could not get away.

When I asked Janis if she'd like to go with me, she answered, "Yes, yes!" as she jumped up and down. Travel was an adventure to her, while Boyd did not see a need to go anywhere, since he lived in paradise and could surf every day. I warned Janis that we might not do anything but sit on Aunt Jean's persimmon couch, and that she needed to be okay with just doing that. She said that was fine—she just wanted to go.

We did sit on the persimmon couch, and we did drag the aluminum Christmas tree up from the basement and decorate it for Aunt Jean. And we did go to Sturbridge Village. It was not a dream vacation, but it was a memorable trip for Janis.

If Janis was excited about sitting on Aunt Jean's persimmon couch in the middle of Massachusetts, you can imagine how excited she was when Boyd's company sent them to New York City for the annual trade show. Boyd was a carbon copy of his father, and the two of them had worked the trade show booth for years. You can imagine how things lit up when Janis worked the booth. Her adrenaline was pumping just because she was in New York City, but then, all day long she got to talk to people!

At the end of the day, Janis was all wound up. She wanted to go to a show, tour the Statue of Liberty, and ride the subway. She wanted to go and do. But Boyd and his dad were tired. They'd been with people all day long and needed solitude and space. When Janis offered exciting options for the evening, they yawned and suggested that they have pizza delivered to their room while they watched a movie—hardly the New York nightlife that Janis had envisioned. It was a tough adjustment.

Janis and Boyd have had to work on their marriage. But because they love each other, are both Christians, and understand the Personalities, they have been committed to their marriage and have made it work. At the time of this writing, they have been married for 17 years and have three children.

RECONCILABLE DIFFERENCES
SHERRI VILLARREAL, CPT

I am so thankful for Dan, my precious Peaceful Phlegmatic husband of 33 years. However, that wasn't always the case. The first 17 years of our marriage were a constant battle. Being a Popular Sanguine, I was fun-loving and spontaneous; he was reserved and reclusive. I was energized by people and parties; he was drained by them. I loved being the "life of the party"; he was embarrassed and suspicious of my flirtatious nature. These are just a few brief examples of how incompatible we were.

Despite our vast differences, we had two beautiful daughters and built a lovely home together, and he developed a successful career in law enforcement. Deep down, we really loved each other, but it seemed to each of us that marrying someone so different from ourselves had been a terrible mistake. On the advice of a secular counselor, we decided that our differences were irreconcilable and that it was time to end the marriage.

About that time, I heard Florence Littauer speaking on Focus on the Family. I was so intrigued by her story that I immediately bought her book Personality Plus, and for the first time I began to understand that both Dan and I were unique creations of God. What a relief to know that there were others like me (and him) and that there was hope for us to learn to live in our strengths and minimize our weaknesses. We decided that we had too much invested to just throw it all away, and we committed to putting our hearts and souls into healing our family.

The journey during these past 15 years has been nothing short of miraculous. With the tools provided to us through the study of the

Continued on next page

Continued from previous page

Personalities, and with the prayerful guidance of the Holy Spirit, we each went on a personal mission to become all that God intended us to be. Our failing marriage was healed, and we now have the most incredible relationship.

We have learned to appreciate our differences, and because we are a blend of all four Personalities (Dan is Peaceful Phlegmatic/Perfect Melancholy and I am Popular Sanguine/Powerful Choleric), we feel that we make the best possible team. As we have matured, God has helped temper our weaknesses and has taught us to operate more consistently in our strengths—so much so that three years ago, we quit our respective jobs and started our own private consulting business. We loved working and traveling together, and soon after, we bought property in the mountains and worked side by side for six months to build a lovely little home near the lake. We also buy and rehab income property now. We are basically together 24/7, putting our heads together and delegating responsibility according to our Personality strengths. We are constantly delighted (and we're in our 50s!) to find so many untapped talents and abilities that we might never have explored had we not learned about our Personalities—and about how to maximize our potential.

We are living proof that God knew just what He was doing when He allowed opposites to attract—He intended for people to complement each other's strengths and compensate for one another's weaknesses. The possibilities are truly limitless when we make the decision that settling for mediocrity in our relationships, or in our life, is no longer an option.

We now have the honor, as Certified Personality Trainers, to share these concepts with others who are struggling in various areas of their lives. Coupled with prayer and the healing power of the Holy Spirit, the Personality Profile has been the single most practical tool that we have used in ministry because of its life-changing potential. I am so thankful to the ministry of Fred, Florence and Marita Littauer. Our goal is to perpetuate their teaching and continue reaching others with the message of hope and healing that not only saved our marriage, but also changed our lives.

After years of Christmas-card-only contact, I called Janis to ask her permission to share her story in this book. Of course, being a Popular Sanguine, she gave me carte blanche. But she said, "I have to tell you the rest of the story!"

Due to the responsibilities of motherhood, Janis has not been to her husband's industry trade show in 10 years. After this long hiatus, she went again this year. She said, "We have each grown so much, and Boyd now understands what I need. As a surprise for me, he bought me a tour package that included several different options for the four evenings we were in New York. He said that I could pick and choose what I wanted to do and he would do them with me."

I had to ask, "Did you do them all?"

"No," she said. "I did two and by the third night I was so tired that I just wanted to eat dinner in the hotel." So now he is willing to go out and she is willing to stay in!

Yes, every relationship can work, but every relationship takes work!

Emotional Needs in Marriage

Understanding the emotional needs that are a part of each Personality is essential in a marriage relationship. However, many couples do not even know about the Personalities, let alone how to appropriate their value. Without understanding how to meet a spouse's emotional needs—difficult even when spouses share a common Personality—it is no wonder that so many marriages fail. Subconsciously, most of us tend to apply the ingrained golden rule to our relationships, giving others what we want. Without even thinking about it—and with no malicious intent—we withhold from our spouse the exact thing they need.

Just like meeting anyone's emotional needs, meeting the emotional needs of our spouse will require caring enough about him or her and our relationship to step outside of what is easy and comfortable for us, thinking through his or her emotional needs and then behaving and reacting in an appropriate way. To do this, we will have to learn how to love differently from the way we need to be loved.

Here is how these differences tend to be played out in a marriage of opposites.

Popular Sanguine/Perfect Melancholy Marriage

Popular Sanguine Needs

You already know about emotional needs and understand that the Popular Sanguine needs attention and approval while the Perfect Melancholy's goal is perfection. So, in a marriage between a Popular Sanguine and a Perfect Melancholy, what do Popular Sanguines need to do in order to get the attention and approval they desire from their spouse? They will need to be perfect. Of course, they can never be perfect enough for the Perfect Melancholy to praise them—the Perfect Melancholies will feel that if they offer the praise the Popular Sanguines need, the Popular Sanguines might think that what they did was good enough, when it could have been better.

With their emotional needs unmet, Popular Sanguines are set up to get their needs met somewhere else. They may become louder or even more outgoing in their quest for attention. Since this is a behavior that Perfect Melancholies dislike, the gap widens as the Perfect Melancholies continue to withhold approval. Some Popular Sanguines may go to further extremes by changing jobs or having an affair. The latter disaster occurs when the Popular Sanguine has been starved for attention. The first person of the opposite sex who offers any type of approval—"you look nice today" or "you are lots of fun"—begins to fill a big void in the Popular Sanguine that should have been filled by his or her spouse. Before long, the Popular Sanguine is in an affair that he or she never intended to be in.

To prevent this, the Perfect Melancholy spouse must realize that much of the undesirable behavior of the Popular Sanguine would be minimized by a healthy and frequent dose of praise. The Perfect Melancholy spouse must realize that rather than the praise causing the Popular Sanguine to believe his or her behavior is acceptable, it will spur him or her on to try even harder to make the Perfect Melancholy spouse happy. Popular Sanguines will have their needs met and their

ENGAGED BY SPREADSHEET
WENDY STEWART HAMILTON

Nothing prepared me for my engagement to my Perfect Melancholy husband, Mike. Oh, I knew it was coming. The numerous hints of, "If I were . . . not that I am right now . . . to ask you, what would you say?" inquiries led me to believe that at some point, my prince would come to his senses and get the words out. Then I could officially plan for our wedding—which in his thinking would be about eight months away. Eight months to plan a wedding is not much time for a Powerful Choleric/Popular Sanguine woman. I'd been making lists and checking them twice, sketching out dress designs, seating arrangements, working menus, designing our invitations, and drawing the heart-shaped key for our invitations long before I had even been asked for my hand in marriage.

The day of the proposal finally came, but it was not as I had envisioned. My thinking was that we would recapture the scene of our first date with a walk along the Bay at Corpus Christi after having delicious gourmet fare at The Republic of Texas, the acclaimed restaurant at the top of the Omni. I had envisioned our eyes catching over brandied-brazen oysters and filet mignon and seeing sparkling love reflected in our crystal goblets by candlelight. I thought it would be wonderful to walk to the Rose Garden at Heritage Park and stop under the trellis—that's when he would kneel down, slip a ring on my hand and ask me to marry him. Well, that wasn't to be.

The proposal I received felt more like I was in a business meeting, finalizing terms of the biggest deal of Mike's life. Instead of dinner and a romantic stroll, we were sitting in my small, two-bedroom apartment. Mike pulled out a spreadsheet, in which he had divided 20 GIA Certified diamonds according to the 5 Cs: Color, Cut, Clarity, Carat and Cost.

I can still hear him now: "These are my top three choices. This one here is larger, but it has a slight inclusion that affects the overall shine. Here is the illustrated graph of where the inclusion is; note that when the light comes in this way at the top from an angle, this inclusion doesn't allow it to bounce off here, here and here. I liked this one; it is flawless and the right size, but the cost was off the charts. And it's not really worth it, considering the size of the stone. Well, this one is the one that

Continued on next page

Continued from previous page

I picked because using all five of these criteria it came out on top as the best one. It is perfect in color, with a slight blue haze that doesn't distract. The cut is a radiant one—a lot like the princess cut you like, but with more of a face for it to reflect and give that flash and sparkle you like. The clarity is flawless. The size is perfectly 3/4 of a carat, and it is overall a good deal."

Mike then just sat there and stared at me, his eyes shining. I sat there and stared at five printouts of diamonds, trying to make sense of what was happening. I could see his optimistic attitude begin to fail as his brain working frantically over the planned steps he had made. Surely, he thought, I asked her enough in the past to know that she would say yes, so why is she not saying yes? Did she not like my stone? I knew I should have gone bigger.

Meanwhile, my brain was trying to find some sort of balance between the Rose Garden dream and the Spreadsheet reality. I was confused. Was Mike actually asking me to marry him, or was this another preview to a proposal? Finally, I choked out, "Are you asking me to marry you? Are you for real?"

Had I understood the Personalities at the time, I would have known to keep the "for real" part to myself. My future hubby was now flustered. He had planned this proposal down to the least little highlighted column on his spreadsheets. "Yeah," he finally said. "I thought you wanted to marry me?" (The last part was more of a question than a statement.) I could see that Mike was now on the verge of taking his briefcase and running.

I knew then that this was **the** proposal, though it was not even close to how I had dreamed it would be. Nonetheless, this was his unique and special proposal for me. I eagerly accepted and in a few weeks, over dinner, he placed the actual ring, more beautiful than I could imagine, on my finger. He then proceeded to go through how he designed the ring: "The ring is set in platinum, the most durable of all substances for setting rings in. The center stone is the one that came through the filtering processes with flying colors. As you can see, it is perfect and sparkles just as you like it. It looks like a full carat, but it is actually slightly over 3/4 of a

Continued on next page

Continued from previous page

carat—around the ballpark of .857 of a carat. Underneath this center stone is a channel that has alternating diamonds and peridots. Since we are getting married in August and my birthday is in August, you shouldn't have any trouble remembering when our anniversary is. We are getting married on the tenth, and there are a total of 10 stones in the ring."

I stared at Mike and then at the ring, the beauty of which only a Perfect Melancholy could take the time, work and effort to produce. In that moment, I realized that while his proposal had lacked the flair that I thought I needed, it gave me a lasting beauty and sparkle. And even when we have been married for 50 years, I will remember just how much he cared, then and now, and how much he wanted to make sure that everything was what I truly desired—that everything was perfect.

offensive behavior will be reduced—replaced by increasingly improved performance. Everyone wins with an understanding of the Personalities.

Perfect Melancholy Needs

For Perfect Melancholies, the most important needs in marriage are sensitivity and space. Perfect Melancholies need their Popular Sanguine spouse to hurt when they hurt and cry when they cry. They also need time to themselves. Perfect Melancholies recharge their batteries with solitude.

Without understanding the Personalities and the accompanying emotional needs, the Popular Sanguine will never give the Perfect Melancholy what he or she needs. Again, we all naturally give what we want to be given. To a Popular Sanguine, silence is dead air—and dead air is bad!

When Chuck and I would drive down the road after we were first married, I always tried to keep up a lively banter. When I thought about why I had to do this, I discovered a typical Popular Sanguine surface reason: I did not want the strangers driving by to look in our car and see both of us just staring out the window with a blank or disgruntled look on our faces. Whenever I passed people and saw this look on their faces, I would always satirically say, "Boy, they look like they are having fun!" I didn't want anyone to look into our car and say that about us—so I talked. But I have had to learn that Chuck does not share my need for constant activity and noise. As a Perfect Melancholy, he actually likes the quiet.

As a marriage therapist, Chuck has often seen situations like our own: the talkative Popular Sanguine spouse married to the quiet, reclusive Perfect Melancholy. As I mentioned, Chuck finds that in order to foster harmony in those marriages, he has to tell the Popular Sanguine to learn to "play the silence." Chuck tells me that this also means that the Popular Sanguine needs to listen to more of the classical stations. Just as Beethoven placed moments of silence in his works, we need to learn that what we have to say has more impact when we know the times we should remain silent.

Now when we go somewhere in the car, I bring books and mail order catalogs, look out the windows, or sleep—activities that "play the silence." If I have something that Chuck and I need to discuss, I ask, "Is this a good time?" Usually he says yes, but occasionally, he says no. In either case, I abide by his wishes. When I have been "good" by being quiet, I often point out (with a big smile) that I have been playing the silence, and ask if he has noticed. Because he understands me, he knows the Popular Sanguine's need for approval and gives me the appropriate praise for my silence.

Perfect Melancholies also need sensitivity. Remember, much like those in the military, they operate on a "need to know" basis. Unlike their Popular Sanguine spouse who is constantly spewing out whatever thought enters his or her head, the Perfect Melancholies are private people. They tend to hold their thoughts inside and do not disclose intimate information about themselves unless they sense that they will receive a favorable hearing. However, while they do not often share their thoughts, they believe that a sensitive and caring partner will intuitively know what they are feeling and act accordingly.

If the Perfect Melancholy is married to a surface Popular Sanguine, there is little hope of this ever happening. Instead, what typically happens is that the Popular Sanguine knows something is wrong, but misreads the nonverbal clues. As a result, the Popular Sanguine spouse will quip "What's wrong?" in a tone that clearly tells the Perfect Melancholy spouse that he or she doesn't have much time and doesn't really care. The Perfect Melancholy, feeling hurt and having not received the comfort and compassion he or she was seeking, will simply respond, "Nothing."

When I share this scenario at my seminars, I ask the Popular Sanguines in the room if they can tell when their Perfect Melancholy spouse is having a bad day. They always reply in the affirmative. Next I ask how they respond—what they try to do to help their spouse. I always get one of two answers: "try to fix it" or "try to cheer them up." To which I ask, "How often does it work?" As if they'd been rehearsing for a choral speaking part, they shout in unison, "Never!"

Without having their emotional needs met, the Perfect Melancholy will subconsciously look elsewhere to find comfort and understanding. We have all seen cases in which a quiet, brooding, attractive Perfect Melancholy male is married to a cute, bouncy, cheerleader-type Popular Sanguine woman. On the outside, observers think it is good that he has someone to pick him up and that they make such a handsome couple. Then one day, he leaves her (and all the social standing or prestige they may have acquired in the church or community) for another woman— often a woman who has none of his wife's physical attributes.

When we see this happen, we cannot help but question, "Why? How? What does he see in her?" Usually it boils down to the simple fact that the new woman has time for him and she listens. The Perfect Melancholy's wife long ago gave up trying to cheer him up and has set herself up in a variety of activities that bring her the praise she needs, leaving little time to make him a priority.

Powerful Choleric/Peaceful Phlegmatic Marriage

Powerful Choleric Needs

As we've discussed, Powerful Cholerics need appreciation and accomplishment. They need to accomplish tasks for their own self-worth and identity. At the end of the day, Powerful Cholerics go through their mental checklist to ensure that they have accomplished more than anyone else they know. Assuming they have, they can sleep well. And while they do typically accomplish more than anyone else, they also need others to appreciate them for all they do.

Given what you already understand, you can imagine what happens when a Powerful Choleric is married to a Peaceful Phlegmatic. Production, or accomplishment, does not carry the same value to Peaceful Phlegmatics, because they value peace, harmony and stability. They like taking vacations without a schedule and enjoy the luxury of lying on a beach, doing nothing but reading a good book. Knowing this, how do Peaceful Phlegmatics feel about everything their Powerful Choleric spouses produce? How do they feel about their spouse's whirlwind of activity?

When I ask my audiences, "What do Peaceful Phlegmatics wish their Powerful Choleric spouse would do?" the answer is always the same: rest or sit down. When I ask, "How does all this activity make the Peaceful Phlegmatic feel?" the standard response is "tired" or "worthless." Peaceful Phlegmatics who do not understand the Personalities will never acknowledge their Powerful Choleric spouses accomplishments in a positive way because all these accomplishments will make them feel worse about themselves. They will just wish that their Powerful Choleric spouses would slow down.

Powerful Cholerics will often react by thinking that if they do more, their spouses will have to notice. So they tend to become workaholics in hopes of being recognized. The professional world usually does notice the good workers—in fact, the working world counts on these Powerful Cholerics to carry far more than their share of the load. And because work is often the place where they get this needed appreciation, it makes it easier and easier for them to spend more and more time there—ever widening the gap between themselves and their spouse.

So, what's a Peaceful Phlegmatic to do? First, realize that withholding needed appreciation will only cause Powerful Cholerics to work harder and do more. The Powerful Choleric isn't looking for competition, just compliments. Like the Perfect Melancholy, the Peaceful Phlegmatic also needs to learn that compliments cost nothing. They need to make an effort to notice and comment favorably on both the big and small projects that the Powerful Choleric does. This will go a long way toward the Powerful Choleric's shortening up his or her to-do list and being willing to do some of the things that are important to the Peaceful Phlegmatic.

Peaceful Phlegmatic Needs

The Peaceful Phlegmatic needs respect and a feeling of self-worth. Unfortunately, because Powerful Cholerics respect production, achievement and accomplishments, without an understanding of the Personalities, the Peaceful Phlegmatic will never produce enough to gain the respect of the Powerful Choleric. In turn, the Powerful Choleric will naturally hold back respect, waiting for the Peaceful Phlegmatic to accomplish something he or she values, basing the approval on tasks and production. In many cases, the Powerful Choleric will consider the Peaceful Phlegmatic to be in a production deficit. Even if that "do nothing" spouse suddenly got active today, he or she could never make up for years of having lived on the sidelines.

In our current society, accomplishment and earnings are valued over patience and traditional values such as simplicity and gentleness. Because of this, the Peaceful Phlegmatic Personality is not reinforced in our current society. A Peaceful Phlegmatic man once said, "I would rather be happy than successful." Without missing a beat, his Powerful Choleric wife said, "If I am successful, I will be happy!"

As I mentioned in the last chapter, Peaceful Phlegmatic children are the ones who often simply slip through the cracks. So you see how it is that they often grow up to be adults who need respect and a feeling of self-worth, not for what they do, but just for who they are. This is a difficult concept for the Powerful Cholerics to grasp, since their values are based on production. I remember a Powerful Choleric woman asking me at a seminar, "How do I give my Peaceful Phlegmatic husband respect and a feeling of self-worth when he doesn't do anything?" Therein lies the problem. The Powerful Choleric cannot see that his or her spouse may be worthy of respect and a feeling of self-worth unless he or she produces something of worth *in the Powerful Choleric's eyes.*

SAFE HAVEN
NANCY AUCLAIR, CPT

After teaching a workshop on the Personalities at my church, a very Powerful Choleric woman in her late 30s came to me in tears. She told me that she now realized she had not made it safe for her husband to communicate his feelings, his opinions, or even his disagreements with her.

Because I was teaching on the Personalities in a church setting, I had been pounding home the fact that we are commanded to love others as ourselves, and that by understanding our spouse's Personality and needs, we can learn to respond to his or her Personality rather than reacting out of our own. I explained that Powerful Cholerics are often partnered with Peaceful Phlegmatics and that they have a responsibility to not overwhelm their spouses with their power, for if they do, their spouses will not feel comfortable communicating. I spoke specifically about the Powerful Choleric tendency to contradict and correct or to control by threat of anger. When Powerful Cholerics do contradict, control and threaten anger, Peaceful Phlegmatics, who go along to get along, will cease communicating for fear of conflict, disagreement or outburst.

This message had struck a chord with this woman, who had been struggling in her marriage. After hearing the teaching, she realized that she had not made it safe for her husband to speak, and she came to tell me that the trouble in her marriage was her fault, as she had acted out of all of her Powerful Choleric tendencies. Together with this woman's sister, we prayed that she would go home and apologize to her husband, asking him to forgive her and inviting him to talk to her whenever he disagreed. She shared during that prayer that God had spoken to her about the fact that her husband would always agree with her, say yes to doing something or going somewhere, and then be angry about it. He needed to be able to say no. She couldn't wait to go talk to her husband, but I cautioned her that since he was a Peaceful Phlegmatic, she should not expect him to get emotional or even to acknowledge that there was anything to forgive.

The next day at church, this woman was smiling from ear to ear. I couldn't wait to hear how things had gone with her husband. She said

Continued on next page

Continued from previous page

that he listened and that they had a great evening, He did not show any emotion, but because she was prepared, she was okay with that.

God had a plan for this woman the day of the workshop: that she would embrace the understanding of the Personalities as a tool for building a better marriage. It took a few months to undo the years of damage in the relationship, but her husband now attends church with her, and she says that their communication continues to improve as she allows him to be who God created him to be and chooses to respond into his Personality.

The Powerful Choleric is as far from the Peaceful Phlegmatic as the East is from the West. Given this, the Powerful Choleric needs to think "Japanese." In Japan, questions are often phrased to allow for a positive response. You do not go into a store and ask, "Do you have any bananas?" forcing the proprietor to say, "No." Instead, you would ask, "Do you not have any bananas today?" allowing the shopkeeper to say yes in either case—"Yes, I do have bananas" or "Yes, you are correct; I do not have bananas today." Powerful Cholerics seek to establish absolutes, while Peaceful Phlegmatics prefer to see infinite variations of shades of gray.

Peaceful Phlegmatics will feel respected and valued when the Powerful Cholerics in their life notice what is important to them and cheerfully make suggestions and engage in that activity, even if it is only taking a break to watch a movie or having a picnic in a park. Doing things that are important to Peaceful Phlegmatics, without prodding and without making them feel guilty, goes a long way toward meeting their needs of respect and self-worth.

Making a Difference in Your Marriage

After reading through this chapter, I trust that you have gained insights into your marriage—or your future marriage. Once you have this insight and apply it, you truly will see almost overnight improvements in your marriage relationship. Even if only one party in the marriage understands these concepts, amazing changes can take place when that person cares enough to take the first step and make a difference.

Even though I grew up understanding the Personalities, Chuck had no real knowledge of them when we got married. With only one of us understanding and employing the tools of the Personalities, our relationship was still positively impacted. Now Chuck uses these concepts daily, both in his job in health-care management and in his practice as a marriage and family therapist. If you need to see a professional counselor like Chuck, or someone else trained in these concepts, please get the help. But better yet, if you apply these truths now, you may never need a therapist!

CHAPTER 7

PARENTING

Florence Littauer with Kathryn Robbins

===

"Was she born that way?" asked a frustrated mother at the first break in one of our seminars. "She's just nothing like the rest of us. She'd rather play in her food than eat it, and no matter how I try to teach her to draw, she will not color within the lines."

By "the rest of us," this Perfect Melancholy mother meant herself and the child's Peaceful Phlegmatic father. Somehow, they had produced this happy-go-lucky child who didn't take life seriously. This mother was on a campaign to wipe the mischief out of this Popular Sanguine child and turn her into the perfect child that this Perfect Melancholy mother deserved. The thought that this child was actually wired differently had never occurred to her.

In 2000, geneticists announced the completion of a study to show what traits people inherited. Eye color, hair color and body shape had been accepted for years as being inherited. But the most exciting discovery was the fact that children do inherit their Personality. They *are* wired that way! The great physician Hippocrates pronounced this fact centuries ago, but now finally there was academic proof.

What does this mean to us as parents? First, we need to determine the Personality of each child and then train him or her accordingly.

Scripture tells us in Proverbs 22:6, "Train a child in the way he should go, and when he is old he will not turn from it." While this directive is often interpreted as a challenge to raise our children in the Christian faith, it is also a mandate to us as parents to understand, and then appropriately nurture, their God-given Personality.

Recently, I had the opportunity to attend a party for my granddaughter's third birthday at her nursery school. Her mother, Kristy, and I arrived carrying cupcakes, drinks and napkins adorned with little Tinkerbells. Her peers were out on the playground, so we watched them through the window. We knew our little Lianna Marita was a Powerful Choleric, as she was already pointing at her mother in a commanding way by the time she was six months old.

Lianna is taller than most of her classmates, and while she is slim, she is definitely sturdy and in control. As we watched, the teacher told the children to get in line to come in from recess. Lianna immediately grabbed the hand of a fragile-looking little girl with wispy light-red hair. She pulled her along, marched her into the classroom and seated her at one of the tables. That done, she made her way to her place at another table. I leaned over to her and said, "That was so good of you to be nice to that little girl." Lianna said matter-of-factly, "She needs help," as if to say, "It's all in a day's work."

Lianna then told the group to sit down so that they could eat. A little Peaceful Phlegmatic boy sat down at his place and folded his hands in front of him. Another Powerful Choleric child called out, "Do what she says!" I noticed a Perfect Melancholy girl straighten the napkins, since some of the Tinkerbells were upside down.

As they were all getting settled, a Perfect Melancholy little boy let out a deep sob and continued to cry with loud bursts of emotional pain. "Is he sick?" I asked the Powerful Choleric teacher. "No, he cries all the time," she said. "We've just learned to ignore him and move on."

At that point, the fragile girl with the wispy hair jumped up on her chair, put her hands up in the air and yelled, "Look at me! Look at me!" Full of Popular Sanguine joy and exuberance she almost fell off the chair, but the teacher grabbed her and plunked her back down into her seat.

Kristy and I observed in amusement as the Powerful Cholerics told the others to eat up and get on with it, the Perfect Melancholies tidied up, the sad little Perfect Melancholy boy moaned, the Peaceful Phlegmatics quietly ate and waited for instructions, and the Popular Sanguine girl cried out, "Look at me!" What an array of three-year-old personalities. Yes, they all come prepackaged—they are wired that way!

Now that you know your Personality, you can begin to think through the Personality of your children, your grandchildren, or your pupils. Once you identify the Personality, the next step is to use what you have learned. Move the information from the pages to practical use. Raising children is a learning experience for all of us, but when we are willing to use our knowledge to meet our children's emotional needs, we can have positive relationships with these little ones who are so often completely different from us.

What Kind of Parent Are You?

Many times, we may find that we get along with one child but not with another, and have no idea why there is a problem. Frequently, the problem is just a Personality clash. Our Personality sets the tone for how we approach parenting. So let's take a look at what each Personality's parenting style looks like and then how that style responds and reacts to the different Personalities of our children.

The Popular Sanguine Parent

Popular Sanguine parents love to play and have fun. They may grow older and wiser, but they never outgrow the delight of childhood. At birthday parties, we might not know who likes the party more—the Popular Sanguine parent or the child. In such situations, the children can become the audience for the Popular Sanguine mother or father, which can be a problem if the children get tired of the Popular Sanguine parent "stealing" their friends when they bring them home.

Kathryn once told me that her second son, Ryan, wouldn't bring his new girlfriend over to the house to hang out. When Kathryn asked why,

Ryan told her, "I want my girlfriends to like me more than you. So, when I'm sure my relationship is tight, I'll bring her over."

One of the most desperate problems that Popular Sanguines have is their inability to tell time. This causes them to guess and, since they are poor estimators, often results in them being late in bringing their children to school or forgetting to pick them up. If the child is also a Popular Sanguine, this won't be a problem, because they will find new best friends while they wait—until the school officials lock up and leave them on the curb. Then the drama begins! Remember, Popular Sanguines need and love attention, so with a real reason to draw attention to themselves, the tears start flowing. Perfect strangers see these children crying and make plans to get them home, all the while rehearsing the speech they are going to give these negligent parents.

My Popular Sanguine brother, a Chaplain in the U.S. Air Force, came home from a six-month tour of duty in Taiwan. His wife and six children met him at the airport, had an exciting reunion, got the luggage, and went home. After unpacking the station wagon and beginning dinner preparations, someone asked, "Where's Jimmy?" The conversation stopped. No one knew. They scoured the house, but couldn't find him. "We must have left him at the airport!" someone cried. They all piled back into the car and headed to the airport, where they found Jimmy, happily riding the escalators. When they asked if he had been afraid, he replied, "No, I had fun, and I knew you'd come back.

Popular Sanguine children will take their parents' tardiness in stride. But not all children will react in the same way. Take Powerful Cholerics, whose parting words to this errant parent will be, "Don't be late this time!" And when that parent is late, again, they will point that bony finger and demand to know why—just once—that parent can't get there on time.

Perfect Melancholy children will worry that something has happened to their parent and start building tragic scenarios in their mind, only to be crushed later to find out that their parent had forgotten them. My son Fred could put on a pained and pitiful look with little effort, so after I had been late in picking him up from school several times, he tearfully turned me into the principal. The principal promptly

Popular Sanguine Parent

WITH POPULAR SANGUINE CHILD	WITH POWERFUL CHOLERIC CHILD
Strengths They share a zest for life, sense of humor and optimism that can bind them together. **Pitfalls to Avoid** Because organization is not a strength for either child or parent, parent must make an extra effort to instill a sense of discipline and responsibility. Parent must be careful not to compete for the spotlight with the Popular Sanguine children—particularly around their friends during teen years.	**Strengths** Parents and children share an optimistic outlook, and a Popular Sanguine Parent is a good "cheerleader" for a Powerful Choleric child who thrives on praise for achievements. **Pitfalls to Avoid** These children will fight to get their way, and a Popular Sanguine parent may give in just to avoid conflict. Being a parent means you will not always be liked by your headstrong, Powerful Choleric, children but if boundaries aren't established and enforced, your roles as parent/child may actually be reversed.
WITH PEACEFUL PHLEGMATIC CHILD	**WITH PERFECT MELANCHOLY CHILD**
Strengths You share a relaxed attitude and an appreciation of wit. **Pitfalls to Avoid** Don't expect your Peaceful Phlegmatic children to express excitement over the things you think are fun. Encourage them, but in a loving, quiet way, for they will likely retreat if pushed. You both need to work on organization, so demonstrate self-discipline in your own life.	**Strengths** You share a creative spirit and artistic nature. Although you are very different in Personality, you can share a very complementary relationship if you work at understanding one another. **Pitfalls to Avoid** Don't expect these children to be as demonstrative and bubbly as you. Be quiet and take time to listen to them. Offer lots of positive reinforcement for accomplishments. Encourage them in their pursuits, and provide private space and silence for refueling. Respect their need to be prompt, to stick to routines and schedules.

wrote me a threatening letter and suggested that I curb some of my civic activities so that I could get to the school on time.

But for Peaceful Phlegmatic children, let us thank the Lord! They won't go to the principal, throw a tantrum or have a meltdown. They will just sit and wait. They won't even tell you what a bad mother you are—unless they need a favor.

The Powerful Choleric Parent

Because Powerful Choleric parents instantly become commander and chief in any situation, being in charge of the family comes naturally for them. If Powerful Choleric parents are living in their weaknesses, they might squash their children in the process of getting the job done. If they choose to use their strengths, however, these Powerful Cholerics can give a deep sense of security to their children because they know how to take care of business and can be trusted. Cheri shares this story:

> I was a teenager working at the clinical lab of a major medical center near my home when a mother brought in a little five-year-old boy to have blood drawn. He was clearly scared. After handing me the paperwork for processing, the mother sat down next to her son, looked him in the eye and said, "In a few minutes, they're going to draw your blood. That means they're going to take a sharp needle and stick it a little way into your arm." At this point, I could see her son shrink back in fear. "Yes," she continued, "it will hurt, but not too much. You may choose to cry, or you may choose not to—it's okay either way."
>
> When I heard this, I was stunned. Pretty much every parent I'd encountered in my two years working at the lab had typically lied to their children, assuring them it wouldn't hurt and then demanding that they not cry when the unexpected pain began!
>
> "But," this mother continued dramatically, "what you really want to do is watch the syringe above the needle. Because after the pain, you'll get to see your blood!"
>
> At this point, I thought this woman was stark-raving mad. I knew from experience that when children see the blood in the

syringe, they go ballistic, often requiring two or three people to hold them still!

Her son looked uncertainly at her, but he seemed strangely calm. In a few minutes, the three of us went into a small room with the phlebotomist. Sure enough, the boy winced when the needle went in, and he began to cry a bit. But when he saw the brilliant red blood begin to fill the syringe, his tears stopped immediately. He gasped and, with a look of awe, pointed to the syringe and said, "Mama, look! Look! My blood! It's my blood!"

When it was all over and the two of them left, I could still hear him talking excitedly about seeing his blood, all the way to the elevator.

Keep in mind that the goal of Powerful Choleric parents is to "just do it." They often make play feel like work, because work is play to Powerful Cholerics. Because of this, the tone in the Powerful Choleric home is usually businesslike and fast paced—unless someone stages an insurrection.

HOME SWEET HOME
KAREN R. KILBY, CPT

David and I had been empty-nesters for a long time. But then, we started considering sharing a home in Texas with our son, Michael, and his new bride, Erin. No longer would it be just our 10-year-old grandson, Tyler, staying with us on the weekends—we would have a full house! I knew that it would be extremely important to find a home that could accommodate all of us.

We needed a home that not only would give each of us elbowroom and privacy, but also one that would allow for the differences in our Personalities. I knew that my husband, with his strong, take-charge Powerful Choleric Personality, would want to be in control. Michael, with his easygoing Peaceful Phlegmatic nature, would find it difficult to give

Continued on next page

Continued from previous page

up some of his independence. Erin, with her outgoing, fun-loving Popular Sanguine Personality, would be anxious to make it work and keep everyone happy. As for me, I knew that with my Perfect Melancholy nature, I would want everything perfectly in place. We were all hoping it would be a win-win situation as we helped each other out financially.

"You actually enjoy living with your in-laws?" friends would later say when they learned that we all lived together. "I couldn't share my home with my daughter-in-law if my life depended on it!" People just couldn't believe it could work. What they didn't know was that Erin and I had been "forewarned and forearmed," which gave us an advantage. My excitement over what I had learned as a Certified Personality Trainer was contagious, and Erin was eager to absorb as much as she could. Now we had an opportunity to put it into practice in our onsite laboratory.

Erin and I knew that we had something in common, as we shared the Powerful Choleric square, but we also realized that we could either complement each other or be at war over the differences of my neatnik personality and her carefree nature. Rather than being offended by our differences, we determined to understand and appreciate them in each other.

The kitchen was one area that could have been a potential war zone for two women with totally opposite operational modes. We determined to take turns cooking and cleaning, allowing each other the freedom and space each of us needed. With this arrangement, we were able to share each other's creative culinary skills and enjoy many family meals together.

Respecting our individual space was key to living together harmoniously. Erin knew that order was paramount to my well-being, and I knew that she needed to have the freedom to allow her things to be in disarray. So giving Erin and Michael privacy in their upstairs quarters suited us both. She was able to be herself—and I discovered that "out of sight, out of mind" really can work for a Perfect Melancholy!

Now that we are no longer living in the same house, Erin and I look forward to enjoying each other's company whenever we can. I truly believe that we would not care for each other as much as we do if we had not shared a home and had the opportunity to discover each other in the process.

Powerful Choleric Parent

WITH POPULAR SANGUINE CHILD	WITH POWERFUL CHOLERIC CHILD
Strengths You share an optimistic outlook and enjoy people as you are both outgoing. Your Popular Sanguine children will likely follow your leadership if offered plenty of praise. **Pitfalls to Avoid** Don't expect your Popular Sanguine children to have the same intense drive for accomplishment you have. Allow plenty of time for fun, or your children may seek to find fun outside the home in unacceptable ways.	**Strengths** Both are self-motivated, outgoing people who share a love of accomplishment. **Pitfalls to Avoid** If your goals and likes are very different, conflict is inevitable unless you appreciate your differences and truly listen to each other's viewpoints. Establish ground rules for dealing with conflict, which may require that you both have a "cooling down period" before any discussion. Teach the art of compromise by developing the ability to do so in yourself.
WITH PEACEFUL PHLEGMATIC CHILD	**WITH PERFECT MELANCHOLY CHILD**
Strengths There can be a natural balance in these relationships with children willingly following the parent's lead. Your natural ability to organize is a skill that children can model. **Pitfalls to Avoid** Although it might seem easier, don't do everything for these children or make all their decisions for them. If the Powerful Choleric parent doesn't foster responsibility, children may never "grow up" and assume responsibility for their lives. Use kind words to motivate them. Help them get organized, but don't do the work for them. Create an area in which they can relax and have "downtime."	**Strengths** Your ability to motivate others can bring out the best in these creative children if you take a quiet, positive, encouraging approach. **Pitfalls to Avoid** Don't insist on quick, decisive action from these children. Give them time to mull things over. Allow them to express themselves without being judged, ask for their opinions and then listen before offering your own advice.

Parenting a Powerful Choleric child can also be difficult. Suzy, a Certified Personality Trainer, writes this about her Powerful Choleric daughter:

> My 12-year-old daughter, Lauren, is sandwiched between her two brothers. Since her Powerful Choleric Personality thrives on control, she constantly tries to usurp my authority by chiming in her ideas for discipline when I'm trying to deal with her brothers' misbehavior. I tell my daughter, "When I need your help, I'll let you know."
>
> "Well, what you're doing with them isn't working," she will quip in reply. She watches me like a hawk, and if I'm inconsistent or try to let something slide in their behavior, she's all over it.
>
> When she gets disciplined, however, it's a different story. When I sent her to bed one time for disrespectful behavior, the next morning she told me about a dream she had: "I dreamed that I had the whole world and I was holding it in my hand, and then you came and ripped it away from me." Now that's an honest dream, because we constantly battle for control of the house.

The Perfect Melancholy Parent

The Perfect Melancholy parent is what all the others wish they could be: clean, neat, organized, on time, detail-conscious, talented, dedicated, musical, artistic, sensitive, sincere and steadfast. This is great, unless the Perfect Melancholy's child is *not* clean, neat, organized, on time, detail-conscious, talented, dedicated, sensitive, sincere or steadfast. Coming under the critical eye of the Perfect Melancholy parent can be painful.

To Perfect Melancholy parents, raising children is serious business, and they will dedicate their lives to raising perfect children. Of course, since we do not live in a perfect world, not all children respond the way that these perfect parents would like. Lynn is one example of a Perfect Melancholy mom who tried to be the perfect parent. She shared the following experience with her daughter:

Four-year-old Sheridan ripped open the package of Resurrection Eggs, a gift from her godmother. Each egg contained a token that symbolized an aspect of the biblical narrative from Good Friday to Easter Sunday. She especially loved the little donkey, which represented the animal Jesus rode into Jerusalem when the people waved palm branches and shouted, "Hosanna! Jesus is coming!"

Sheridan, being the fun-loving little Popular Sanguine that she is, wanted simply to play and fabricate her own assorted versions of the Easter story. She was having a wonderful time. I, on the other hand, a studious Perfect Melancholy, saw this as a wonderful teaching opportunity. I decided to read a few detailed biblical passages associated with each toy symbol and then quiz Sheridan on what she'd just heard. Unfortunately, she kept fidgeting and handling the toys, preferring to continue inventing storylines and having fun.

Whenever I asked her a question, Sheridan seemed completely preoccupied. She either didn't respond or did so inaccurately. After repeating the questions numerous times, I finally gave up, totally exasperated. But rather than vent at Sheridan while discussing the Bible (which certainly seemed inappropriate), I suggested we take a walk. I thought that I could blow off steam and she could expend some of her boundless energy.

Despite the scenery change, in no time at all, I—being the perfectionist that I am—began drilling her again. This time, she cooperated and began responding accurately, so I pressed on and asked her about her favorite part of the story: "Sheridan, what did the people shout when Jesus rode into Jerusalem on the donkey?" She enthusiastically shouted in reply, "O Susannah! Jesus is coming!"

I burst out laughing and gave her a big squeeze. How I adored this happy, carefree little child. At that moment, it was if God were saying, "Lynn, lighten up. It's important to study and to get to know Me through My Word, but you can also have fun. Don't take everything so seriously."

I was amazed! Sheridan *had* paid attention after all, and she had basically understood the story, even though I had interrupted

Perfect Melancholy Parent

WITH POPULAR SANGUINE CHILD	WITH POWERFUL CHOLERIC CHILD
Strengths Perfect Melancholy parents can help Popular Sanguine Children develop needed organizational skills, and children can inject humor and fun into the home. **Pitfalls to Avoid** Recognize that your Personalities are quite opposite! If you don't let these children have fun at home, they'll find it elsewhere. Whereas you are naturally organized, Popular Sanguines are not, so help them develop discipline without nitpicking or criticizing. Instead, reward jobs well done with praise and opportunities for creative fun. Allow some messiness in a designated area. Encourage participation in the arts, but don't expect your Popular Sanguine children to master each skill perfectly. Allow them to learn just for the joy of learning, not to be perfect.	**Strengths** These two share a natural ability to organize and keep to a schedule. **Pitfalls to Avoid** You want these children on your side! Powerful Choleric children want to get credit for their hard work, so don't reserve your praise for only tasks done "perfectly" or you'll have an adversarial relationship. Be flexible and offer them choices whenever possible so they feel that they have a sense of control in their lives.
WITH PEACEFUL PHLEGMATIC CHILD	**WITH PERFECT MELANCHOLY CHILD**
Strengths These two can enjoy sharing a quiet, low-key atmosphere. **Pitfalls to Avoid** These children need a great deal of encouragement, which Perfect Melancholy parents are not used to offering. Remember to take time to guide them while offering lots of praise, encouraging them to reach their potential. Don't let them "slip through the cracks" or be forgotten just because they are quiet.	**Strengths** Both enjoy order, neatness, sticking to a schedule, and often a deep appreciation of the arts. **Pitfalls to Avoid** Recognize that just because you have definite ideas about the right way to do things, your children may have equally definite ideas, which may or may not reconcile with your own. Encourage your children in artistic pursuits of their own choosing, not only in the areas in which you want them to excel. Don't take normal rebellion personally, or you may both end up withdrawing from each other. Help these children learn to express feelings by developing your own ability to do so. They have a deep need to be understood.

her play. She had even understood the most important part—shouting praises to Jesus! I learned that as a Perfect Melancholy parent, not only should I try my best to teach Sheridan, but I should also let her absorb truths in her own Popular Sanguine time and way. Just because she is playing doesn't mean she isn't listening. And just because I'm teaching doesn't mean I can't learn to play!

The Peaceful Phlegmatic Parent

Peaceful Phlegmatic parents are low-key, relaxed and patient. They don't fight and argue. Their sympathetic nature makes them agreeable and easygoing parents that everyone likes. Kathryn shares the following story about her dad:

> My Peaceful Phlegmatic father's calm demeanor never wavered, even when I received all *F*s on my report card in seventh grade. My father never raised his voice. He sat looking sad, his blue eyes speaking volumes. Then came the words I dreaded to hear: "I can't believe a child of mine would want this to be her report card." The pain of his disappointment dripped from every word. At that moment, I would have rather been punished than have to sit and see how my actions hurt my father. "Dad, I'm so sorry!" I cried. "I promise, I'll do better. I promise!"
>
> Being a Powerful Choleric child, I needed a goal to help get me motivated. My father gave me one: For every *A,* he would pay me $5.00; every *B* was worth $3.00; a *C* grade was neutral; a *D* would cost me $3.00, and for every *F,* I would pay him $5.00. My father knew how to motivate me without yelling, hitting or name-calling. His gentle strength put me back on the right path. Little did he know that he would take a huge financial hit when the next report card came!

Although Peaceful Phlegmatic parents are easygoing, some children will find them an easy target and try to get away with murder. Being too laid back and always accepting a stance of peace can often create a much bigger problem than if these parents had just dealt with the situation to

Peaceful Phlegmatic Parent

WITH POPULAR SANGUINE CHILD	WITH POWERFUL CHOLERIC CHILD
Strengths Both possess a good sense of humor and enjoy a good time. Parents are delighted by entertaining children and children enjoy the appreciation. **Pitfalls to Avoid** Because neither parent possess natural organization skills, parents must develop these skills first, in order to model them for the children. Develop a set of guidelines for discipline and stick to it, or the Popular Sanguine children may charm their way out of deserved consequences and shirk responsibility.	**Strengths** These two Personalities can complement each other, but only if the naturally reticent parent establishes control from the very beginning and relinquish areas of control only when the child has matured to appropriately handle them! **Pitfalls to Avoid** Establish appropriate guidelines for discipline and stick to them. You'll do your Powerful Choleric children no favors by letting them run the household. Offer them plenty of choices whenever possible so that they are able to exert some control over their lives. Praise them and give them credit for accomplishments.
WITH PEACEFUL PHLEGMATIC CHILD	WITH PERFECT MELANCHOLY CHILD
Strengths Peaceful Phlegmatic can enjoy a relaxed, easygoing relationship. **Pitfalls to Avoid** Avoid falling into a rut of non-communication. You must put energy into these relationships or they might become non-existent. Parents must develop self-discipline to model to children. Motivate your children, help them set goals and develop steps to meet them. Praise them often.	**Strengths** Neither needs a lot of "chatter," so these two Personalities can enjoy just "being" in each other's company. **Pitfalls to Avoid** This combination can result in a severe lack of communication if the naturally quiet parent fails to "draw out" the naturally withdrawn child. The children, feeling misunderstood, may withdraw further, while discouraged parents may give up trying to communicate.

begin with. Cassandra, a Certified Personality Trainer, explains how this happened to a friend of hers:

> A friend's husband went away for several months on business, leaving her at home with their two grade-school children. My friend is a Popular Sanguine/Peaceful Phlegmatic, while her husband is a Peaceful Phlegmatic/Perfect Melancholy. In true Peaceful Phlegmatic style, he has learned to be a Powerful Choleric in business. He is the anchor of the family and the final arbiter of family disputes.
>
> When I went to visit my friend after her husband had been gone for a month, one of her children, a Powerful Choleric, was giving her instructions even before they left for school. When we went to pick the kids up after school, this child began again as soon as she got into the car. When my friend left the car to go back into the school to pick up some papers she needed, the daughter began to tell me how her mother was always late and needed to be told what to do—or else she would forget. This child felt that she had to remind her mother what to do all the time!
>
> This was an up-close and personal lesson for me on how a Powerful Choleric child will become a powerful controller when there's a void to fill. True to the nature of a Powerful Choleric, they will take over if the leadership is weak.

For Peaceful Phlegmatic parents that have boundaries, the peace and quiet they are seeking comes more quickly. Kathryn's father was this type of parent. While her Powerful Choleric mother was the taskmaster around the house, her Peaceful Phlegmatic father was the ever-patient nurturer. Kathryn and her siblings could easily send their mother over the edge, but their Peaceful Phlegmatic father allowed much more tomfoolery before they crossed the line with him.

Kathryn remembers, "One day my little brother and I did manage to cross it! We were pinching each other in the back seat of the car, giggling and bouncing around. Our dad matter-of-factly said, 'Knock it off back there. I can't drive with the two of you jumping around.' In true kid fashion we figured, *So what?* Once again, Dad told us to settle down; once again we didn't. Without another word, our dad reached back and disciplined us on the spot! We were stunned—usually our dad would put up with us for a lot longer than that. We had crossed the line! But Dad didn't yell or remind us forever about our behavior. When it was over, it was over!"

What Kind of Child Do You Have?

Understanding our Personality and that of our children will help us develop our children's strengths and minimize their weaknesses. This will allow our children to become more capable and confident individuals who are ready to embrace the challenges and opportunities ahead. Now that we have looked at how our Personalities affect our approach to parenting, let's focus on some of the aspects of our children's Personalities.

The Popular Sanguine Child

Popular Sanguine children are bright-eyed, talkative, energetic, light-hearted and funny. They love people and enjoy laughter. Popular Sanguine children are also a little scatterbrained and have a hard time being organized or remembering instructions. Work *is* a four-letter word for them. It takes a ton of praise to keep Popular Sanguines on task, because if it's not fun, they don't want to do it. Claire remembers:

> When I was a child, I was forced to take piano lessons. Not just any old piano lessons, but piano lessons from the *best* teacher in all of Southern California. *All* of her students took gold and silver medals at the Bach festivals and other competitions . . . all, that is, except for me. Although I practiced an hour every day, I hated the stress of performances. I always froze up and made mistakes.
>
> I begged my teacher to allow me to play ragtime and other fun pieces, but she gave me nothing but Bach, Mozart, Chopin and the like. My mother constantly told me, "You could become a concert pianist!" But she seemed oblivious to the fact that I didn't *want* to become a concert pianist! After 13 years of expen-

sive lessons, I was a technically accurate pianist, but I hated play-ing. I quit altogether when I left for college, and now I rarely play.

As a Popular Sanguine, I found that solo performances of classical music did not meet my Personality needs. I should have been trained to accompany singers so that my music would have had a social function. I could have toured with our school's choir instead of attending those much-hated Bach festivals.

The Powerful Choleric Child

Powerful Cholerics are born leaders who are strong in every way. If you have a Powerful Choleric child, you have probably already noticed that this child wants to take control of everything: you, the kids at school, your other children. If Power Choleric children think they can get away with it, they will take on any authority that stands in the way of their getting what they want. They are out to win, and if they can't win, they won't play the game. Even as small children, they are workers who love to be challenged. In fact, if these children aren't challenged, all their energy turns to anger.

Andrea, another of our Certified Personality Trainers, relates the fol-lowing story:

Life had become busier than usual for our family, and I started noticing that Allison, my Powerful Choleric child, was throwing numerous temper tantrums. I soon became so worn out and weary of these fits that I began praying about it. God answered my prayers by revealing to me that I was not properly meeting Allison's needs.

Because our lives had become busier and different from the way they normally were, Allison was feeling that things were out of her control. This is very unsettling for a Powerful Choleric child. So my husband and I decided to give her control over a few things so that she could feel more comfortable again.

We let Allison choose who got what color cup at supper, which car seat she wanted to ride in, and what shoes she wanted to wear with her outfits. Just letting her control these small things cut the number of tantrums in half. Life was more pleasant for everyone!

The Perfect Melancholy Child

Perfect Melancholy children are truly "perfect"—the children everyone else wishes they had. They are studious, orderly and quiet. They follow the rules and work well alone. The deep, passionate nature of the Perfect Melancholy lends itself well to the arts: music, drama, painting, photography, and so forth. Perfect Melancholies usually have talent beyond the norm.

Perfect Melancholy children often prefer to be alone because they can't handle too much noise and confusion. Because of this, forcing them to be social is more wounding to them than beneficial. And because Perfect Melancholies have a deep need for everything to be, well, perfect, as parents we need to be careful when giving them "helpful hints."

Perhaps the most important aspect of Perfect Melancholies that parents need to know about is this: Just because they don't look happy does not mean that they think they are unhappy. They just have a different definition of happiness. Cheri tells this story about one of her students:

> Chris was a classic Perfect Melancholy, careful and sensitive to the core. His mother was on the ditzy side of Popular Sanguine—she was oblivious to her son's deep nature and was always trying to get him to cheer up. One day while she was sitting next to me in the lunch area, Chris walked by. Impulsively, she reached out and pinched him in the rear. Chris whipped around, his face red, and protested, "Mom!" I could tell that he was deeply embarrassed that she had done something so familiar in front of me and all the other students. Ignoring his plea for respect, his mother simply said, "I gave birth to you, so I can pinch you any time I want."

The Peaceful Phlegmatic Child

Peaceful Phlegmatic children are the easiest children to raise because they always want to stay out of trouble. They are quiet, often shy, and usually have a dry sense of humor. They are easy to get along with and will do whatever is asked of them—unless that request bumps up against their will of iron. Of the four basic Personalities, the Peaceful Phlegmatic has the strongest will.

One of the only problems that parents of Peaceful Phlegmatic children encounter is getting them to move—off the couch or out the door. Work is something they might think of doing—later. Many parents of Peaceful Phlegmatics think they have failed because these children have no burning desire to do anything. Sitting around is just fine for them. And if their parents in frustration get up and do their work for them, these children will let them. Cheri proves this point with this story of her son:

> My son was about seven years old when my brother's family came over for a day of just hanging out together. About midmorning, my son, who was lounging on the couch near me, said, "Mom, may I please have a drink of water?" Out of habit, I got up from my seat in the family room and headed for the kitchen. My sister-in-law looked at him and asked "Aren't you perfectly capable of getting it yourself?" To which he responded, "Yes, but I've become accustomed to having my mother get it for me." I decided then and there that any child who could use the phrase "I've become accustomed" could start getting his own drinks of water!
>
> Because Peaceful Phlegmatic children are easygoing and charming, many parents cater to them without even realizing it. Jonathon, my son, has always been so polite. Unlike his demanding, finger-in-your-face Powerful Choleric sister, it truly is a pleasure taking care of him! But when Karen brought my attention to what I was doing—serving a child who was perfectly capable of taking care of his own needs—I was forced to recognize how much I was doing for him and how little I was teaching him and expecting of him.

The hardest part of parenting a Peaceful Phlegmatic child is motivating that child. Popular Sanguine parents will try to get this child to be up and attending every social function there is. Powerful Choleric parents will have a list of chores that need to be done before the child can enjoy any relaxation. Perfect Melancholy parents will try to get this peaceful child to see the importance of doing the job right the first time. Peaceful Phlegmatic parents will, for the most part, not demand too

Emotional Needs

POPULAR SANGUINE	POWERFUL CHOLERIC
Attention	Loyalty
Affection	Sense of Control
Approval	Credit for Good Work
Acceptance	Achievement
PEACEFUL PHLEGMATIC	**PERFECT MELANCHOLY**
Peace and Quiet	Sensitivity
Feeling of Self-Worth	Support
Lack of Stress	Space
Respect	Silence

much involvement from this child, so peace will remain in the house.

Many times, fear of the unknown is a major factor why Peaceful Phlegmatic children tend to procrastinate. What little energy they have is used up in the emotional turmoil of making a decision. When this happens, their tendency is to shut down. So as a parent of a Peaceful Phlegmatic child, it is wise to just quiet down and listen to that child's fears, and then address those fears in a low-key, gentle manner. Giving just a few choices and a deadline by which the choices should be made works well for most Peaceful Phlegmatics. Demanding, yelling, name-calling and the like should never be used to motivate these gentle children. Remember, they have a will of iron. They can outlast you, even if it is to their own detriment!

Understanding Your Child's Emotional Needs

The popularity of television shows such as *Super Nanny* indicates that today many people need help in parenting their children. Most of us hope that our families are not in that bad of shape, but we all have our fair share of static situations. This is where understanding emotional needs can make a night-and-day difference in raising our children. Taking another look at the "Emotional Needs" chart (from chapter 4) can help us consider these needs in light of improving our parenting skills.

Our emotional needs start the moment we are born. The earlier emotional needs are met, the better it is for everyone involved.

Popular Sanguine
Attention · Affection · Approval · Acceptance As Is

Our bright-eyed Popular Sanguine babies completely steal our hearts with their first smile. By the time we figure out that they are high maintenance, we are too attached to ever think of life without them. Popular Sanguine children love to laugh and have fun. They enjoy being with people—the more the merrier (and less is never more for the Popular Sanguine).

If you are a Popular Sanguine or Peaceful Phlegmatic parent, chances are you will enjoy the antics of this precocious child. But the Powerful Choleric or Perfect Melancholy parent will have a much harder time dealing with the weaknesses of the Popular Sanguine child.

Popular Sanguine children want to be loved more than anything else in life, so they are willing to remake themselves in order to get that love, even if it means denying their true Personalities. What they really need from us is acceptance "as is"—instead of us always attempting to fix them.

Kathryn tells this story about her son:

Our oldest son, Eric, is a Popular Sanguine/Powerful Choleric. You could tell from the first few days he came into the world that he had a mind of his own. If he wasn't smiling and cooing at you, he was screaming. When I stopped nursing him to burp him—because he was so colicky—he would become stiff as a board and scream as if someone were slowly ripping his arms off. As he grew older, if he didn't like the plan I had made for the day, he would just not do it! By the time he reached junior high school, we were at war.

When I was introduced to the information about the Personalities, I started to apply it to my parenting techniques. This was easier said than done—by that time we had developed bad habits, and habits of any kind create needs of their own. It took me several years before I caught on to the value of understanding the emotional needs of each of my children, but when I got it, I used it.

I was given an opportunity to catch an emotional need with Eric when he planned to be part of a mission trip with our church. The night before he left, he had 15 of his closest friends over to celebrate his departure. He would not be back for a whole week. At 3 A.M., I had had it with all the noise, so I told all of Eric's friends to go home because he needed to be up and out the door by 6 A.M.

Eric had washed a load of clothes, but failed to put them in the dryer because he fell asleep in a chair in the living room. When 5:30 A.M. came, he wasn't ready. My husband started to get angry, but I decided to try my hand at meeting Eric's emotional need of "acceptance as is." I kept my mouth shut and helped him pack his wet clothes in his suitcase. We were now late, and Eric was still looking for the bottom of his zip-off style pant legs. With wet clothes in his suitcase and pant legs in hand, he headed for the car.

My husband dropped us off at the airport to sit in line. As we waited in the line, I thought to myself, *If he doesn't have his passport, I'll fail this test of "acceptance as is," because I'll kill him*! It took all the willpower I could muster not to tell Eric to get his act together—not to make him feel rejected and worthless—but I did it!

Eric did have his passport, and he finished checking in before my husband was back from parking the car. We hugged and kissed, prayed for his safety, and sent him on his missions trip.

How many times do our Popular Sanguine children not want to come home and share their excitement for life because we parents can't see past the haphazard way they live it?

Powerful Choleric

Loyalty · Sense of Control · Credit for Hard Work · Accomplishment

If you are the parent of a Powerful Choleric child—bless you! These little generals were born to lead, but since good leadership is learned, your job as a parent is to teach them.

At a very early age, these little ones want to do everything by themselves. We need to take the time to let them do it, for every time we tell them, "No, you're too little" or "It will be too hard for you," we are telling them that they are worthless and stupid. Of course, this isn't what we mean, but that is how they will feel. Of all the Personalities, Powerful Cholerics need to try and fail or try and succeed on their own. What they need from us is support and loyalty. Just point them in the right direction and they will get there.

One point to keep in mind is that Powerful Cholerics think the rules *do not* pertain to them. Because they know how it should be done, they think they are exempt from such constraints. Stand your ground when your little general steps over the line. Tell them that because they are smart and brave, you can see leadership abilities in them, but all good leaders must first be good followers. This means following the rules.

Claire (bless her heart) has firsthand knowledge of how powerful these children can be:

> When our daughter was 12, she threw a knock-down, drag-out hissy fit about piano lessons. Through torrents of tears, Ashley sobbed about the agony of being forced to take the lessons. Since my childhood experiences with piano had been so negative, I found myself sympathizing with her—until she played one card too many. With heaving gasps and sighs, she dramatically proclaimed, "Practicing piano takes so much of my time and energy that *I don't even know who I am anymore!*" Trying to control my laughter, I told her to take some time to calm down and that we'd discuss the topic later.
>
> To get a good handle on the whole piano scenario, I began

sitting in on her lessons. Was that ever a revelation! At the beginning of the first lesson I sat through, Ashley started to tell her teacher that she didn't have any time to practice this week. "Wait," I interrupted, "you had *plenty* of time. You told me every day that you were doing what your teacher had assigned." It quickly became clear that Ashley had been lying to her teacher and to us, trying to get away with as little as possible while loudly proclaiming her martyrdom. She had even refused to play any of the songs the teacher suggested for an upcoming recital and, thus, had gotten out of the recital altogether!

I sat down and had a no-nonsense talk with Ashley, during which I let her know that piano was not an option. She *would* take piano lessons, and she *would* practice piano at least 30 minutes each day. I committed to attending *every* piano lesson for the coming year. Of course, Ashley hated the talk. She said that she was living in a dictatorship, to which we responded that while we tried to make it benevolent, our home is indeed a dictatorship. She tried every complaint and jab in the book, but we did not budge.

Over the next six months, I did attend every single piano lesson. As the teacher and I got on the same page, the excuses from Ashley quickly disappeared. My husband recorded some of her best pieces and embellished them with other instruments on the computer. Ashley loved hearing herself sound "so good."

Not too long ago, Ashley came home from a piano lesson and declared, "I *love* piano! I can't wait to play! It's so much fun!" Then she stopped, stared at me and said, "Not a word from you! I know what you're thinking. Don't say, 'I told you so!'" To which I responded innocently, "Who, me?!"

Control is a huge issue for Powerful Choleric children. They can't wait to become adults, and if they can call the shots, they feel they are one step closer to being one. So give them enough challenges to let them know that they are still children and need your help sometimes. Help them understand that being a kid is okay. These Powerful

Choleric children may wear you out, but think how proud you will be of all their accomplishments when they achieve their goal: adulthood.

Perfect Melancholy
Sensitivity to Their Feelings · Support When Down · Space · Silence

Perfect Melancholy children are typically quiet and sensitive individuals who have a deep need to be understood and supported. They need space to re-energize and process feelings of pain in order to feel at peace with themselves and others around them. Because of this, parents with opposite Personalities often find it hard to relate to their Perfect Melancholy children.

My son, Fred, is a Perfect Melancholy. Often times, the things that I think are funny he feels are tragic. I need an appreciative audience; he groans at my dramatic humor. If I didn't understand the Personalities, he and I would have no natural meeting of the minds. I have to realize that my fast pace overwhelms him.

When Fred was in his early teens, he once asked if his friend Michael could come over after school. Always liking a party, I encouraged him to bring his friends home. Then Fred stated, "When Michael's mother comes to pick him up, would you please go to your room and shut the door?"

"What's wrong with me?" I said. "I'll be good!"

Fred looked at me with somber eyes and shook his head. "You'd just be too much for her," he said.

"Me, be too much?" I cried. "I'll be quiet. I'll stand in the corner and pretend I'm a tree." I snapped into tree position.

"That's what I don't like about you," Fred sighed. "You think you're funny."

At this point, I had two choices: I could get mad at my son's honesty or go to my room and shut the door. Gratefully, I did the latter. That night, Fred thanked me for making it easier for him.

You may think that I gave in to a bossy child, but Fred was never bossy—instead, he was always pleading with me not to embarrass him. By my going to my room that day and not embarrassing him in front of his friend, I met his need for sensitivity. (If he had been a Powerful Choleric, pointing his finger at me and barking an order for me to go to my room, there would have quickly been an understanding of who was in charge!)

Kathryn's fourth son, Brett, is also a Perfect Melancholy. Being the low man on the totem pole in the family, often his needs for silence and space were not met. One Sunday afternoon, everyone in the family decided to take a Personality Profile as a family activity. As they worked through the Profile and talked, they all realized that Brett was often depressed and moody because they had not understood his needs.

So they developed a plan to meet Brett's needs. They gave him a room of his own. No one was allowed to go into that room unless he or she knocked, and nothing was to be borrowed without permission. Brett had some rules he needed to follow also. If someone did knock on his door, he had to answer instead of sitting silently and hoping the intruder would go away. He had to think of the needs of others before he just said no to a request. With this new space and silence, the weight of the world was lifted off Brett's shoulders. Today, he is a contented, though quiet, Perfect Melancholy artist.

Peaceful Phlegmatic
Feeling of Worth · Peace and Quiet · Lack of Stress · Self-Respect

Peaceful Phlegmatic children are born with a deep need for peaceful and quiet surroundings. They need nurturing to help them develop feelings of self-worth and importance as individuals. They also thrive best in a lifestyle that minimizes stress.

Cheri's years of teaching have given her valuable insights into children with this type of Personality. She relates the following story:

> In my first year of teaching, the mother of one of my Peaceful Phlegmatic students came to me, greatly distressed because her son wanted to be in my drama group. "I don't think it's a good idea," she said in a tone of great confidentiality, "because of his . . . you know . . . his . . ."
> "His lisp?" I said.

"Yes," she breathed painfully. "I don't want him to be the object of ridicule."

Since Matt had not shown the slightest concern about his own lisp, I was fairly certain that it was she whom she was actually concerned about. I assured her that I would do everything within my power to make sure that her son's strengths were maximized and his weaknesses minimized. I delivered on this promise by making Matt the star of our first play.

When this mother got wind of this, she hurried in to meet with me, again very privately, to express her concerns about what this kind of exposure would do to her son. "Don't worry," I said. "Nobody in the audience will notice anything other than Matt's superb command of his role." She looked startled at this remark.

You see, I had cast Matt as a snake and directed him to over-exaggerate his lisp for dramatic effect. Throwing himself into the role, Matt completely stole the show. Everyone congratulated him on his projection, delivery, timing and expressiveness. Even his mother commented to me, "I didn't know he had it in him!" To which I thought, *How sad for him . . . and how sad for you.*

Peaceful Phlegmatic children need to be reassured by their parents that they are an important part of the family. Kathryn's third son, Drew, is a Peaceful Phlegmatic. When he was 10 years old, Kathryn and her husband, Steve, found out that she was pregnant with their fifth child. Soon after, Drew quietly came to Kathryn and stated that he was worried about becoming a middle child. When asked why, Drew said, "Well, they say they have emotional problems." Kathryn states:

This was my clue that this gentle child was looking for a sense of self and to see if there was a place of significance for him in our family. I asked Drew to think of things that are in the middle—like the cream in Oreo cookies! In fact, I said, the middle is so good that they make Oreos with "double stuff."

Thinking of more middle things, I asked him, "If you were

shooting at a target, where would you aim?"

"At the bulls-eye!" he exclaimed.

"Well," I said, "from now on we will think of you as our 'bulls-eye guy.' God has made you to be the special person for the important job of being the middle of our family."

A look of pride replaced the look of panicked concern that had been evident only moments before. And as it turns out, the only problem we have had with Drew is getting him to take the trash out.

In addition, Peaceful Phlegmatic children have a deep need for privacy. This can create problems for the Popular Sanguine parents, who will want to share every detail of that child's life with others. Barbara, one of our Certified Personality Trainers, tells how this played out in her relationship with her daughter:

I am mostly Popular Sanguine (with some Powerful Choleric), while my daughter is mostly Peaceful Phlegmatic. When she was about 15, she commented, "Mom, I decided I'm going to go to the mall and have a custom T-shirt made for myself. It will read, *Hi! My name is Aimee Flowers. If you want to know anything else, just ask my Mom.*"

I had recently begun learning about the Personalities and was working at integrating the knowledge into my life. Knowing that Aimee was a Peaceful Phlegmatic, I understood that there was an important message underlying this humorous statement. I realized that my daughter was telling me something important about our relationship. I needed to respect her privacy and stop sharing everything I knew about her to anyone who would listen.

Although it has been a struggle, I have learned to edit my sharing as a mark of respect to her. As she has grown into adulthood, becoming a wife and mother herself, this single change in my behavior has helped us build a stronger mother-daughter relationship.

How many of our quiet Peaceful Phlegmatics fall through the cracks because we don't value their gentle strength?

Setting Our Children Free to Be Who They Are

God has made us all different on purpose. When we try to change our children instead of helping them to live in the strength of their Personality, we basically say to them, "Excuse me, but I think God made a mistake when He created you. See, I have a better plan—you need to be just like me, because I was created properly." We don't think that's what we are doing, but that's how it feels to them. Instead, let's take the time to listen, so we can understand what makes our children tick.

Ask your children how they feel about things: their school, their teachers, their siblings—even how they feel about *you*. Then listen. What do you hear? Do they talk about having fun? Do they go around telling everybody what to do? Do they fret about things not being perfect? Or do they take most of life easy?

Once we understand our children's Personality, we can then meet their emotional needs. And when we understand and meet the emotional needs of our own Personality *and* those of our children, the results are amazing! We experience a freedom and an openness in our relationships on a level we never dreamed possible.

CHAPTER 8

COMMUNICATION

As we have seen, our Personality impacts virtually every aspect of our lives—including our communication with other people. Every day, we communicate with others. It may be the people at work, the teller at the bank, the server at the restaurant, or our very own family members at home. As we communicate with these varied people—through both the spoken and written word—we invariably will have miscommunications with them.

Understanding the influence of the Personalities on communication will not prevent all these problems, but it will help to greatly minimize them. When a communication problem does exist, the concepts in this chapter will help you find the root of the misunderstanding and know how to work to correct it.

The Personality Languages

We can learn to communicate in the Personality languages of others. If I speak Greek and you speak French, I can learn French (or you can learn Greek) so that we can communicate in something other than sign language or gestures. In the same way, if I speak Sanguinese and you speak Cholericese, we can also learn each other's languages to better communicate.

Chuck and I had been married about three years when our communication differences became clear. Because of our opposite Personalities, we even used a totally different vocabulary. My words were colorful, exciting and extreme, while Chuck employed the "need to know" rule. If you didn't need to know something, Chuck wouldn't talk about it.

One weekend, I had cooked Chuck a special breakfast. This was not just Pop Tarts and Tang—I went all out. I prepared bacon and eggs and had strawberries, freshly squeezed orange juice, and ground coffee for him. I served it in the dining room on the good china and used coordinating linens. I set this extraordinary breakfast in front of Chuck, and he began to eat it. I asked him how his breakfast was and he answered, "Fine."

Fine?! I thought to myself. *I make this great meal and all he can say is that it is "fine"?* Chuck was communicating to me out of his Personality, and I was hearing him from mine.

I survey audiences when I speak and often find that those who have the Popular Sanguine Personality universally view the word "fine" as a negative. I ask them, "On a scale of 1 to 10, with 10 being the best, where is the word 'fine'?" They always shout out answers ranging from 1 to 3. One person in a hotel management group in Australia said, "minus 2!" To those of us who are the Popular Sanguines, the word "fine" is not a compliment. However, the Perfect Melancholy sees things differently.

Shortly after our breakfast experience, I was on one of my frequent speaking trips. I called home as I always do and asked Chuck how his day was. He responded with his predictable, "Fine." Without thinking, I asked him what was wrong. "Nothing," he replied, "I said it was fine. You need to learn that, for me, fine is as good as it ever gets."

If I had to face a life of just fine, I'd commit suicide. To me, a life of fine is not worth living. But to a Perfect Melancholy, fine is as good as it ever gets. Like fine china, fine sterling, fine crystal—fine is the best there is!

For Chuck and I to communicate (and, ultimately, stay married), we needed to learn to speak each other's Personality language. For example, Chuck has learned to use superlatives when speaking with me. If I have a new dress and I ask him how I look, he now says things like "terrific," "fabulous," "wonderful," "amazing!" He has learned that "fine" is not an acceptable answer! Likewise, when I ask Chuck about something in his life and he says it is fine, I have learned to say "great," and move on to the next subject.

On that day when I served Chuck the lavish breakfast and all he said was "fine," I quipped, "Wrong answer," picked up his plate and took it back to the kitchen. I then turned around, brought it back, placed it in front of him, and asked, "Chuck, how's your breakfast?" With a big smile on his face, he said, "This is the best breakfast I have ever had in my entire life!" I replied, "Good. Now you can have breakfast tomorrow."

As this mode of communication has become standard at our house, we can now joke together about Chuck's penchant for saying "fine." One day I got home from a trip while Chuck was still at work. When I walked in, I saw a greeting card on the table. I picked up the card, which featured a scruffy cat-like drawing on the front. In a small handwriting-like font it read, "You ask me how I feel . . ." Inside were two small words: "Fine, thanks." Beneath it, Chuck had written, "Sometimes 'fine' is as good as it's going to get."

Because we understand each other's Personality and care enough about our relationship to make the extra effort to communicate, we can laugh about things that would otherwise be problematic.

What Is Your Personality's Communication Style?

As you have learned, each of us has a primary Personality, and most of us have a strong secondary Personality. Prepackaged as part of that Personality is a built-in communication style. The Popular Sanguine can talk incessantly whether or not anyone is interested. The Powerful Choleric is good at quick commands, keeping conversation to "just the facts, ma'am, just the facts." The Perfect Melancholy is better at listening than talking, sharing only on a "need to know" basis. The Peaceful Phlegmatic is a listener, almost preferring to stay uninvolved—seemingly fearful of entering into conversation; yet in a time of stress, the Peaceful Phlegmatic is the one to talk to, as just the sound of his or her voice is calming.

When it comes to communication, each Personality has a number of strengths, but also a number of areas in which improvement is needed. In the following section, we will take a look at each Personality's unique areas of strength and weakness and then determine how we can best modify our approach to communicate more effectively with people whose Personality does not match our own.

The Popular Sanguine

Janis, a Popular Sanguine, is often the life of the party. When she and her husband, Boyd, go to social events together, she is immediately drawn into a circle of friends where she holds court all evening. Meanwhile, Boyd settles into a comfortable chair and has a meaningful conversation with one or two people.

When they get home, Janis is exhilarated, but Boyd is unhappy. She has had a great evening that has nourished her emotional needs, while he has felt ignored, left out and excluded. When she suggests that he should have joined in, he says, "I tried. No one heard me."

What does this story tell us? Janis's inherent strengths have some companion weaknesses that all Popular Sanguines need to work on in order to communicate effectively. Let's examine some of these weaknesses to determine how Popular Sanguines can best learn how to communicate with the other Personalities.

Limit Conversation

Popular Sanguines need to learn to limit their conversation and allow others the opportunity to talk—even if what they have to say is more interesting and entertaining (in their minds). Someone who talks constantly eventually becomes a bore. Popular Sanguines need to work on speaking only when they have something to say that people *need* to know, or that is vital to the situation. Like the little boy who cried wolf, Popular Sanguines who are always talking will not be heard when they actually have something important to say.

Whenever I am with a Popular Sanguine who has not worked to overcome this communication obstacle, I am reminded of a principle that I learned from my mother many years ago: If I am in the midst of a story or conversation and it was interrupted, I should just let it drop. If someone was really interested in hearing what I had to say, that person would remember and urge me to continue. If no one does, I can safely assume that my audience was not all that interested anyway. This is a painful lesson for all of us who are Popular Sanguines.

I remember being on a road trip with a group of women, many of whom were Popular Sanguines. One woman in particular, Patti, constantly battled for the "audience." While the stories she told were hilarious, she talked incessantly. If we stopped the car to use the bathroom, Patti would continue the story into the stall. When we got out of the car to look at the view, she would keep talking. When we returned to the car, Patti would pick the story right back up again. After an hour of this, as funny as her stories were, we all grew weary and longed for a few moments of silence.

All of us who are Popular Sanguines need to remember to limit our conversation. We need to be careful about overwhelming others with our words, and allow them to speak up and share their experiences with us.

Tone Down Voice

Remember that one of the traits of the Popular Sanguine is a loud voice. This is a great asset if the person is a public speaker in a room without a microphone. However, in most settings the loud volume is distracting, irritating and even obnoxious to others. In working with groups of people on this subject, the most frequent advice that is given to Popular Sanguines is to tone down their voice.

To help me remember this, each year I make 1 Peter 3:4 as my New Year's resolution: "Be known for the beauty that comes from within, the unfading beauty of a gentle and quiet spirit, which is so precious to God" (*NLT*). I use the same resolution each year, as I have never mastered

GUY DE MAUPASSANT

"Conversation . . . is the art of never appearing a bore, of knowing how to say everything interestingly, to entertain with no matter what, to be charming with nothing at all."

it. But each year I work at it. And I am getting better and better at acquiring the lasting charm of a gentle and quiet spirit.

I mentioned previously how Chuck habitually wants me to speak more quietly. Chuck and I have developed a code. When we are out in the public—or even at home—and I am wound up, he simply and quietly says, "FM." This is a reminder that I need to tone down and talk like an FM Deejay. One night when Chuck and I were listening to a new FM station in town, he said, "Ah, that is what a real FM deejay should sound like . . . like she is in bed." I paid attention to that deejay. Now when I come home from a trip and am a bit wound up, I practice my FM deejay voice by reading street signs and billboards in that low-key, sultry voice. While I can never really talk like that, it does help me tone down my voice.

Learn to Listen

Most Popular Sanguines think that to listen means to be quiet. However, in reality, when Popular Sanguines are listening, most likely what they are doing is working on their next lines.

I once heard that the reason people do not remember names is because they do not care enough to listen in the first place. I was sure this was not the case for me, so I set out to disprove the theory. I decided that when I met someone new, I would repeat her or her name within the first few minutes of conversation. I might say something like, "Really, Kathy, how did that happen?" Unfortunately, I discovered that the theory was true! More often than not, when I attempted to use that person's name, I could not remember it! This was not because of bad memory—it was because of poor listening.

To train myself to listen better, I humiliated myself several times by saying, "I'm sorry, what did you say your name was again?" It only took a few embarrassing repeats of that episode before I learned to listen better. Once I truly listened, I found that I was excellent at remembering names.

James 1:19 is a good verse for all Popular Sanguines—wise words that will help us improve our communication skills: "Everyone should be quick to listen, slow to speak and slow to become angry."

Stay on Track

A hallmark of the Popular Sanguine's communication style is jumping from one topic to another, often without finishing any of them. In Popular Sanguine to Popular Sanguine conversation, this is apt to be the sign of two people having a great time together.

Recently, my friend Dianne and I stole a few hours away from our over-full lives and went out to dinner together. We were both in a hurry and had other things we had to get done before the evening was over. We talked quickly throughout the mealtime. We quickly hugged good-bye as we dashed back to our respective cars. What a fun time we had together! We each agreed we needed to do that more often. As I drove on to my next responsibility, I realized that I was not sure that we ever finished one complete conversation. We jumped from topic to topic as one idea spurred another.

For us, this was a great evening that was representative of how most of our visits go. But for the other Personality types, this flitting conversation style can be frustrating to the listener. So if you are a Popular Sanguine, work to stay on track.

The Powerful Choleric

Since the ultimate goal for Powerful Cholerics is production and accomplishment, their communication style tends to be brief and to the point. They often bark out commands with little thought for other's feelings. While this approach is practical and keeps distractions to a minimum, Powerful Cholerics have to remember that communication is more than just relaying the facts.

Be Interested in Others

Because Powerful Cholerics are focused on production, people often get in the way. Additionally, the brisk manner of many Powerful Cholerics makes others afraid to even approach them. So one way Powerful Cholerics can improve communications is by being interested in others.

This can be done in several ways. One way is to listen to others' complete sentences—and even their entire stories. Those who are Powerful

Cholerics are usually quick thinkers, often knowing what other people are trying to say long before it's been said. Because Powerful Cholerics are always looking for the bottom line, they have a tendency to cut off other people's sentences and terminate the story, saying something like, "Yeah, yeah, I got it." In a fast-paced business setting, this style of communication serves as an effective way to relay information to coworkers and employees. But for the rest of the world, the "get to the point" approach of the Powerful Choleric shuts people down and limits future communication.

Many years ago, my sister, Lauren, and her husband were looking to buy their first house. After a full day of touring many strange and unacceptable houses, my Popular Sanguine/Powerful Choleric mother wanted to share the story with my Powerful Choleric/Perfect Melancholy father. As she went into detailed descriptions of each house, my father's patience wore thin.

"Did they buy a house?" he finally interrupted her.

"No," my mother replied, "but—"

"Fine," he said, again cutting her off. "I do not need to hear about all the houses they did not buy." With her balloon burst, my mother discontinued her conversation about the houses.

While it is true that my father did not need to know about all those houses, a pattern of disinterest such as this eventually closes the door to any communication, frivolous or functional. So even if you have already heard the entire story before, being interested in what others have to say encourages open communication.

Cultivate Small Talk

The old cliché about stopping to smell the roses is good advice for Powerful Cholerics. Because their work focus takes up all their time and energy, Powerful Cholerics don't typically take the time they should to invest in others. Because of this, they have limited ability to converse on topics of interest to others and often find small talk to be a waste of time.

A friend told me how disappointed she was that her father's focus on his work was so consuming that there was little else they could talk about. Her father had been a tennis pro in his younger years, and she had been taking tennis lessons—yet he showed no interest in joining her on the court. He was an excellent cook, and she was known for her gourmet skills, but at this stage of his life, for him, cooking consisted of providing nourishment rather than making an exciting discovery. Over the years, their communication had dwindled to perfunctory telephone calls and birthday cards.

Powerful Cholerics need to broaden their areas of interest in order to communicate with the other Personalities. This might include watching a bit more TV (especially the news), taking up a sport, or spending more time outdoors—anything that will expose them to something different.

If you are a Powerful Choleric, broaden your horizons. You'll find that you not only have more interests, but that you are also more approachable.

Ask Rather Than Demand

Remember the magic words "please" and "thank you" that you were taught as a child? In the bottom line communication style of the Powerful Choleric, these niceties are frequently ignored. However, by not using the word "please," the words of a Powerful Choleric often become a command that removes the "opt out" option for others. This builds resentment in people toward the Powerful Choleric.

When I teach the Personalities, I sometimes divide attendees into small groups and then have the groups list what they would change in the other Personalities. The most common wish for change in Powerful Cholerics is that they would ask for the things they need instead of commanding or demanding them. We all know how Powerful Cholerics can be about issuing commands without even realizing it!

Take Cheri, who purchased a backpack for her son at the start of the school year that began falling apart within the first week. Metal bars protruded from the top, seams ripped, zippers stopped zipping, and, ultimately, both straps broke free. Six weeks into the school year, she took the flawed backpack to the register at the store, looking for a refund. "I'll ask," the cashier said doubtfully, "but I don't think we can give you a refund because it's been more than 30 days." Dismayed that such an obviously defective item might not be accepted back, Cheri blurted out, "Oh,

I'm sure you can!" She spoke to the manager, who agreed to the return, but the cashier was noticeably unfriendly during the rest of the transaction. Cheri's attempts at humor brought not even the slightest smile.

Cheri told me, "It wasn't until I reflected on *how* I'd said, 'Oh, I'm sure you can!' that I realized the problem. While all I'd intended to convey was confidence, once again I'd gone overboard and communicated anger and dominance. I got my refund, but it was months before I got a smile from that particular cashier. Even then, it was a guarded one!"

Powerful Cholerics often believe that the time, effort and energy it takes to relate to people don't help the bottom line. However, if they truly want to be more productive, they will recognize that the nonproductive time it takes to ask questions, to listen and to say a heart-felt thank-you will make them more productive in the long run.

When communicating with others, those of us who are Powerful Cholerics need to remember the magic words and be especially careful of our tone of voice. I am always surprised when the words I thought I had said in a lovely and gracious tone are received as if they are a harsh barb. A good verse for the Powerful Choleric to memorize is Proverbs 16:24: "Kind words are like honey—enjoyable and healthful" (*TLB*).

The Perfect Melancholy

For those of us who are Perfect Melancholies, we need to remember that the title "Perfect" does not mean that we are perfect, but rather that we like perfection. While there are many aspects of this Personality that are perfect, which others would do well to emulate, there are still some areas in which the Perfect Melancholy *can* improve—especially in the area of communication.

Lighten Up

The Perfect Melancholy is the opposite of the Popular Sanguine. While the Popular Sanguine needs to learn to listen, listening is one of the strengths of the Perfect Melancholy. The Popular Sanguine is naturally funny, while the Perfect Melancholy has to work to add humor to his or her communication—to lighten up.

My Perfect Melancholy friend Marilyn told me that in her early years of speaking, she thought that she did not have a sense of humor. She has since found this is not true at all. I'll let her tell her story about how she found her sense of humor:

> After the death of our son Nathan, my husband, Glen, and I were really struggling in our marriage. As I trudged home each night from teaching at the school Nathan had attended, I often thought, *I could probably make it through this day okay if I just didn't have to deal with that man* [meaning my husband] *when I got home.* I'm sure Glen was thinking the same about me.
>
> As time went on, our relationship worsened to the point where we were barely speaking. One night Glen got between the TV set and me. He sat right in front of me, looked me square in the eye, and said, "I don't care what you do. I'm not leaving!" Well, I don't know about you, but at that point, that wasn't really good news to me!
>
> Whenever I share this story, my honesty about my feelings always gets a laugh. I have found that the story provides a light spot in a heavy subject.

Perfect Melancholies have a wonderful sense of humor. They will not use this humor to entertain (they would consider that frivolous), but their subtle humor will shine through naturally in their conversations. Their light touch will come through as they share true stories about their life and their family.

If you are a Perfect Melancholy, speak honestly about how you deal with life. Don't force it, and don't make up stories. Just be yourself. Another way to add a light touch is through the use of jokes and funny quips. Oddly enough, most joke tellers tend to be Perfect Melancholies, not Popular Sanguines. Why? Because Popular Sanguines can't remember the punch lines! Jay Leno is a Perfect Melancholy. He plans, rehearses and rerehearses the delivery of his comedy routine.

Enter into the Conversation

Since Perfect Melancholies are natural listeners, not talkers, they must work to participate in the conversation. It is very easy for Perfect Melancholies to feel hurt that no one cares enough to ask what they think or how they are feeling. While it is true that those of us who are not naturally sensitive and caring, like the Perfect Melancholy, need to learn to be more sensitive, Perfect Melancholies also need to take the responsibility to enter into the conversation themselves.

Think Positively

The term "Perfect" is ascribed to the Melancholy Personality because these individuals desire perfection in themselves and expect it from others. This natural tendency also allows them to see all the flaws in people, programs and plans—which makes them prone to being critical.

If you are a Perfect Melancholy, you need to work on thinking positively. It does not come naturally. Memorize Ephesians 4:29: "Do not let any unwholesome talk come out of your mouths, but only what is helpful for building others up according to their needs, that it may benefit those who listen." Work on offering praise and encouragement to others, rather than criticism. Make an effort to watch for opportunities to build up others and give unqualified praise. If you criticize or withhold praise, you're discouraging other Personalities from even trying to do better. Let me illustrate.

Linda once met a young woman who had just moved to a new home several weeks before her husband could join her. She didn't even attempt to unpack her husband's boxes. "I couldn't do it right for him anyway," she said. Married less than a year, her Perfect Melancholy husband had already trained her to not do kind things for him—for fear she would not do it right.

Many Perfect Melancholies feel that endorsing what they feel is substandard behavior in others will signal that a particular behavior or work level is acceptable, when really a change should be made. However, if you are a Perfect Melancholy, you need to realize that people are more likely to change or improve with positive reinforcement than with criticism.

For example, my Perfect Melancholy husband, Chuck, has learned the value of frequent accolades. He likes me to cook breakfast for him every morning, and I do so without complaint or hostility. Each morning I serve him waffles or pancakes (real, homemade ones), bacon and coffee. Sometimes I get distracted and slightly burn the waffles. Occasionally I run out of bacon. But Chuck never criticizes my cooking. Even on the "less good" days, he goes out of his way to thank me. If I am still sitting at the table when he gets up to go to work, he comes over to me, kisses me, rubs my back and says over and over, "Good Rabbit, good Rabbit" ("Rabbit" is my nickname from childhood, and I collect bunnies). If I finish first and am already doing the dishes, Chuck comes over to the sink and does the same thing. His adulation encourages me to keep making him breakfast every day—which is important to him.

The Peaceful Phlegmatic

While the Peaceful Phlegmatic and the Powerful Choleric are opposite Personalities, they do share something in common: neither is excessively expressive. Powerful Cholerics communicate in a brief, sometimes rude, manner. Peaceful Phlegmatics are hesitant to communicate at all, especially with those they do not know well. They are very likeable people, content and lacking in any obvious flaws in most aspects of life. Yet despite their lack of faults, Peaceful Phlegmatics have areas in which they, too, can improve their communication style.

Get Enthused

One of the easiest ways for Peaceful Phlegmatics to improve their communication style is for them to get excited about something. Because Peaceful Phlegmatics are naturally low key and tend to measure all of life in energy expenditure, they need to work to be expressive—especially when someone gives them a gift or makes a kind gesture.

If you are a Peaceful Phlegmatic, learn to be effusive. Muster up all the superlatives you can think of. Why? Because if other people feel discouraged by your lack of interest, they will eventually discontinue their interaction with you.

I used to write promotional copy for new books. I would interview the author and then scan the book to find a current news angle or emotional hook that would make radio stations want to feature an on-air interview with the author. While I got quite good at writing catchy ads, grammar was never my forte. However, providentially, Melissa, a Peaceful Phlegmatic high school student who was currently enrolled in English classes, worked in our office as a part-time assistant. I would ask Melissa to proofread my work, and she would review my copy and then put it back on my desk with lots of red marks.

I frequently found myself following behind Melissa, asking her if she *liked* the ad copy. "Did it make you want to read the book?" I'd say. Because Melissa understood the Personalities, after a few times of me running after her, she started writing enthusiastic comments in addition to the needed corrections. Occasionally, she even waxed eloquent over the wonderful job I had done. As a Peaceful Phlegmatic, she had learned to get enthused!

If you are a Peaceful Phlegmatic, remember Philippians 4:8: "If anything is excellent or praiseworthy—think about such things."

Express Opinions

When people ask Peaceful Phlegmatics what they would like to do, where they would like to go, or whether they would like coffee or tea, they typically give standard answers like, "I don't care," "It doesn't matter" or "Whatever is easiest." Whereas Powerful Cholerics need to learn to tone down their opinionated nature, Peaceful Phlegmatics need to learn to express their opinions.

After attempting to communicate with the Peaceful Phlegmatic and repeatedly receiving the "whatever" response, most people give up asking and just do what they want to do. While at first this may seem like a suitable solution, it is a short-term fix that creates long-term problems. Let me give you an example of this.

In Chuck's marriage-counseling practice, he has encountered many cases in which the Peaceful Phlegmatic spouse feels worthless, insignificant and unimportant in the marriage. The other spouse, usually a Powerful Choleric, long ago took over the decision making in the home, leaving the Peaceful Phlegmatic to simply take orders and not make waves. While it had been a relief in the early years to not have to "decide," after a decade or two of being treated as an invisible person, the Peaceful Phlegmatic ends up feeling worthless.

If you are a Peaceful Phlegmatic, protect yourself and generate respect from others. Learn to voice your opinions. Maybe you don't need to have an opinion on every issue. Maybe you really do not care about coffee or tea. But there are many issues that you probably really do care about: where you live, what you eat, where you go for vacations. Start by expressing opinions about the things that do matter to you. By doing so, you will gain the respect of others and open up the lines of communication.

Open Up

Unlike Popular Sanguines, who spew out more details about their life than anyone wants to know, Peaceful Phlegmatics need to learn to open up and share what they are thinking and feeling. This is difficult, however, since Peaceful Phlegmatics are proud of their stoic tendencies. But those very cool traits are what shut down avenues of communication, making Peaceful Phlegmatics seem indifferent and apathetic. If you are a Peaceful Phlegmatic, work on sharing your ideas and projecting your voice.

Communicating to Others

Remember, communicating effectively isn't just talking, sharing ideas or speaking to others. Communication is a two-way street. But before we can communicate effectively, we need to know our natural strengths and weakness so that we can capitalize on our strengths and work to overcome our weaknesses. As we work to minimize the distracting communication habits that are a part of our Personality, communication becomes more effective.

One of the best ways to communicate more effectively is to learn to adjust your natural communication style to meet that of the people with whom you are communicating. In chapter 2, we reviewed some of the ways of easily and quickly identifying the Personality types of others. When you identify the Personality of the person with whom you are communicating, either in spoken or written format, you can adjust your approach to them, rather than relying on your natural tendency. You succeed by giving others what they need.

At one seminar I was teaching, a woman who worked in sales shared how understanding this communication concept netted her a $1,500 sale that she believes she would not have gotten otherwise. She is a Powerful Choleric/Popular Sanguine and had an appointment with a Perfect Melancholy. Knowing that Perfect Melancholies are systemically scheduled, task-oriented, and low-key people, she modified her behavior accordingly. To communicate to her potential client that she respected his schedule, she made sure she would be on time by arriving early to the appointment. When he was ready to see her, she entered his office in a more subdued manner than usual. She shook his hand and got right down to business, having all the facts and figures handy.

Without understanding the Personalities, this woman probably would have been late. She might have told him numerous stories about the product and why he should buy it. All of this, in his opinion, would have been a waste of his valuable time. But because she approached him with a desire to meet his needs and communicate on his wavelength, he was all ears. Her respect for his schedule and her professional approach worked, and she won his business.

Whether your communication is professional or personal, you will find it enhanced by following the basic communication tips for your Personality and then changing your approach to meet the needs of others. You cannot change other people, but you can change the way you approach them. Let's look at some simple things we can do, regardless of our Personality, when communicating with people of a differing Personality.

The Popular Sanguine Communicating with Others

Since the Popular Sanguine is a natural talker, the tips for communicating with others involve modifying or limiting all the chatter. So all you talkers, listen up!

Communicating with the Powerful Choleric

When speaking to a Powerful Choleric, you need to stick to the bottom line. When Powerful Cholerics sense that your comments are purposeful and to the point, they will perk up and listen. If you are married to a Powerful Choleric, it may take a while to undo the "tuning you out" pattern that has been in place for years. But, don't give up. If you cut out the extra details and stick to the point, the Powerful Choleric will pay more attention, thereby enhancing communication.

I used to have a neighbor who was a Popular Sanguine. In addition to her Popular Sanguine Personality, she also had some health issues that kept her home most of the time, which made her starved for an audience. If she got hold of you, her constant chatter made it difficult to escape. She was an enjoyable person, and the stay-at-home lifestyle made her a font of neighborhood information, but unless I had 15 minutes to visit with her, I had to rush quickly from my house to the car before she could see me. Often before I'd leave the house, I would peek out the front window to see if she was outside working in her garden.

Picture the Powerful Choleric as the conductor of the orchestra. Never play unless the baton is pointed toward you, and only play the notes as directed. No spontaneous solos!

Communicating with the Perfect Melancholy

When talking to a Perfect Melancholy, you need to be sensitive to the Perfect Melancholy's schedule and level of interest. One day, I was on a radio program when a Popular Sanguine woman called in with a communication problem that she was having with her Perfect Melancholy business partner. She worked in sales and was out in the field all day, while he did the bookkeeping and computer work.

One day, this woman had a particularly great sale and was excited about it. She could hardly wait to share her good news with her partner, expecting that since her sale benefited both of them, he, too, would be enthused. She bounded into his office and loudly exclaimed her success. However, instead of being excited for her, her partner gave her one of those "if looks could kill" kind of looks. She was very confused by his reaction.

I explained to this woman that the Perfect Melancholy is a task-focused person who runs life on a schedule—no exceptions! When she barged into his office unannounced, she disturbed his train of thought and intruded on whatever he was doing. Even though the news was good, it was not received well because of the timing.

I told the woman that the better approach would have been to knock on his door (even if it was open) and then, in her calmest voice, say, "Excuse me. I have some good news to tell you. When would be a good time?" to which he might reply, "Now is fine" or "In 15 minutes. Just let me finish this up." Then she could go to her office, close the door and call a girlfriend with whom she could go into full and energetic detail about the sale while she waited to share the news with her partner.

When you are communicating with a Perfect Melancholy, schedule in advance any lengthy or important things you need to discuss. Be careful not to barge in or interrupt the Perfect Melancholy's own activities or conversation. Respect his or her time and space. Timing is everything!

Communicating with the Peaceful Phlegmatic

When communicating with Peaceful Phlegmatics, you can utilize your natural ability to be positive and encouraging. You can look for the good in Peaceful Phlegmatics, who need to be encouraged for who they are, not just for what others think they should be. Certainly, you can offer encouragement and praise for what Peaceful Phlegmatics do, but they also need to be sure that you are lifting them up for who they are. Learn to show your appreciation for them. Send cards, notes or e-mails. Let them know how much you appreciate them. Bring or send a little gift that you know they will appreciate.

My friend Melody is a Peaceful Phlegmatic. She lives several states away, yet we remain close. Melody and I share an enjoyment of what she calls "fluffy" little romance novels. I am a member of a Christian, inspirational-novel book club, and I get four new books each month. After I read them, I grade them and forward them on to her. So, every few months, she gets a package from me with a selection of books and a note. Because Melody is also the same size I am, at the change of each season, I send her clothes that I am no longer using. Melody knows I have a very busy life, so these simple gestures serve as an encouragement to her and brighten her day—and they make her feel loved and appreciated. They have nothing to do with what she does or does not produce.

My actions just let her know that I am thinking of her and that she is important to me.

As Popular Sanguines, our gift for looking at life through an optimistic filter can be used as an encouragement to others, especially the Peaceful Phlegmatic. It is the little things we do and say that mean so much and build a lasting foundation of respect with a Peaceful Phlegmatic.

The Powerful Choleric Communicating with Others

One of the great strengths of Powerful Cholerics is their ability to think and act quickly. However, this very asset is one of the things that often hinder their communications. If you are a Powerful Choleric, you need to learn to slow down if you want to improve your communication skills.

Communicating with the Popular Sanguine

As a Powerful Choleric, when you are talking to a Popular Sanguine, you will need to make an effort to be interested in their colorful stories, rather than viewing these "Sanguine stories" as an interruption. If you stop what you are doing and give the Popular Sanguine a few minutes of focused attention, actively listening to the story and responding to the Popular Sanguine's traumas, you will usually find that the story doesn't actually take all that long. When your storytelling friend has to trail along behind you or chase you down to finish, the story will actually be lengthened by the frequent interruptions.

You also need to be careful not to crush the spirit of the Popular Sanguine. A friend of mine related the story of how she had tried to teach a Popular Sanguine how to act appropriately in a particular situation by blurting out, "Can't you act any way other than childish? You do not need to be the center of attention all the time!" Unfortunately, my friend cannot count that Popular Sanguine among her friends any longer. While my friend had been trying to help, she used poor communication that crushed the spirit of the Popular Sanguine.

Communicating with the Perfect Melancholy

When you are speaking with a Perfect Melancholy, time is a factor as well. Perfect Melancholies are detail-oriented people and their thought processes are very complex. While you will not have to listen to too many of their stories (Perfect Melancholies are not storytellers by nature), you will need to allow them time to share their thoughts and ideas. You will need to resist your natural tendencies to listen just long enough to get the gist of the topic and then move on—either physically or emotionally, for that "moving on" will effectively shut down communication.

Dodi, a Perfect Melancholy/Peaceful Phlegmatic, told me about a Powerful Choleric boss she had when she was teaching. This principal once asked the teachers for their ideas and input on policy decisions. After they went to lots of trouble and work researching and thinking through the issues, he tuned them out, ignored their input and did what he wanted. Obviously, this made the teachers justifiably angry and resentful.

Communicating with the Peaceful Phlegmatic

When you are communicating with Peaceful Phlegmatics, time is again a factor! Because Peaceful Phlegmatics do not speak in rapid-fire commands and often take longer to process their thoughts than other Personalities, you will be inclined to dismiss them and shut them out. In this case, you need to work on developing patience and good listening skills.

If you are a Powerful Choleric, make an effort to give Peaceful Phlegmatics evidence that their ideas and thoughts are important. Keep in mind that your natural tendencies to bark commands and speak your mind are especially damaging to the Peaceful Phlegmatic. Holly, a Powerful Choleric, found that this was a problem in her communications to a Peaceful Phlegmatic that took place after her husband's mother died. This is her report:

> I am a Powerful Choleric with some Popular Sanguine, and my husband is a Peaceful Phlegmatic. Despite knowing and loving this man for more than 26 years, there are times when I am absolutely clueless as to what is going on inside his head, as he doesn't share much and typically his expression—or lack thereof—doesn't provide many hints.

My husband's mother had been ill and in rapidly declining health. She died on a weekend I was out of town, and the funeral was scheduled for the morning of the day my husband needed to travel out of state to present a seminar at a large national medical convention. The logistics of the week were a nightmare and prevented us from having much time to talk in the first couple of days following his mother's death. His usual stoic, silent approach to life became even more stoic and more silent.

At the time, I did not have any understanding of the Personalities, so I just blurted out my bottom-line thoughts: "If you'd just allow yourself to have a good cry, you'd feel much better." As an afterthought, I added, "How are you doing? I don't know what to tell people when they ask me how you are doing." The minute the words came out of my mouth, I knew I had crossed a line. I saw a flash of hurt flit across his face and then quickly disappear. It was such a brief expression of emotion that had I been looking away, I would have missed it.

I apologized, but the damage was done. The next day, I received an e-mail in which he told me that I had significantly added to his pain by implying that he was not grieving properly. He ended his note by saying that he didn't believe I had meant to hurt him intentionally, but that he couldn't imagine what I had hoped to accomplish by saying what I did. He added that when I am faced with the death of one of my own parents, he hopes he doesn't do anything to further or compound my pain.

The Perfect Melancholy Communicating with Others

Listening is a natural skill for Perfect Melancholies, as they like to process information. However, Perfect Melancholies will need to work on what they say and how they say it, depending on to whom they are speaking. Their nature is geared toward perfection. This makes it easy for them to notice flaws, often using the identification of a fault as a conversation opener—something like, "I noticed that you have a tear in your hem."

Communicating with the Popular Sanguine

When a Perfect Melancholy is talking to a Popular Sanguine, this combination is especially problematic, since the former specializes in criticism and the latter craves praise. If you find yourself in this position, look for opportunities to compliment the Popular Sanguine. Make an effort to open your conversations by saying a word of praise to him or her.

Popular Sanguines are used to having people laugh at their stories, which will often sound foolish to you, the practical and sensible Perfect Melancholy. So remember that you will open lines of communication with Popular Sanguines if you respond openly to their humor by laughing.

I have held a particular conference at the same hotel for 14 years in a row. Over the years, I have had numerous salespeople at the hotel take care of my business. Usually we get along great, and I feel as if they are my "new best friends." However, one year I did not click with my salesperson, because I thought she did not like me. She was efficient and did her job well, but I did not enjoy working with her.

Once I realized this, I tried to figure out the problem. I closely observed our next few interactions. It soon hit me that this salesperson *never* laughed at any little comment I made or a quip I threw in—this salesperson did not think I was funny. I do not generally think of myself as someone who is funny, but I realized that I was used to having others laugh with me as we talk. So I was glad when the salesperson was promoted for her efficiency and moved on. I suddenly wished that everyone on staff understood my needs. Maybe I need a note in my file: "Marita is a Popular Sanguine. She needs you to laugh when she says something funny."

The bottom line is that if you are a Perfect Melancholy, make an effort to respond openly to the humor of the Popular Sanguine.

Communicating with the Powerful Choleric

When you are communicating to Powerful Cholerics, remember their to-do list. Their time is very valuable to them. While you may have done lots of research on a topic and have unlimited knowledge, Powerful Cholerics are not the folks with whom to share it. Give them the bottom line—the essentials. If they ask questions, answer them with a sound bite and then take a breath, allowing them to jump in. If they do not jump in, take over or move on, and then offer supporting details. Let them know that you have additional information if they would like it. Do not answer questions they did not ask.

I met the owners of the Bible software that we sell at CLASS when my company had a booth next to them at the annual Christian Booksellers Association Convention. While I had several versions of Bible software, I had never really found any particular one that I really liked, so I was interested in their product. The Popular Sanguine sales-man, Rick, kept coming over to our booth and talking to me, encourag-ing me to come try their software.

When I finally had the time toward the end of the show, Rick's Perfect Melancholy partner was in the booth. I was really interested, so I went over and asked for a demo, even though Rick wasn't there. Boy, did I get one! All I wanted to know was how the thing worked and whether I needed to read a manual or watch a video to learn how to use it. I want-ed to put my hands on it and try it. However, this Perfect Melancholy man, probably the one who developed it, went on and on about how this software would allow me to commune with God. He told me the Bible would come to life for me, that I would find new ways to spend time in God's Word and make it a part of my life.

He walked me through all kinds of features, while internally I was tapping my foot, eager to get my fingers on the keyboard and play around—which never happened. Had he understood the Personalities, he would have known, after watching me for three days in the next booth, that I have quite a few Powerful Choleric traits. I did not need a feature-by-feature rundown. I just needed a few brief instructions before I made my own decision.

Fortunately, Rick gave me a basic program as a gift at the end of the show. I took it home and installed it on my computer. I did not need to read any instructions or watch a video. I love it. I use it almost daily. Now, we sell so much of this company's software that they have made me a special CLASS edition.

Communicating with the Peaceful Phlegmatic

When you speak to a Peaceful Phlegmatic, you need to rein in your ability to spot negatives. Watch for positives and freely offer praise. Words do not cost you anything, so give them away. If you do this, you'll notice a dramatic change in your interactions with Peaceful Phlegmatics.

The Peaceful Phlegmatic Communicating with Others

Communication does not come naturally for the Peaceful Phlegmatic. They are natural listeners, but true communication requires both sides, giving and taking. So for the Peaceful Phlegmatic, the advice for improving communication all involves what to say and how to say it.

Communicating with the Popular Sanguine

When you are communicating with Popular Sanguines, remember that they are inherently creative people. They have ideas popping out all the time. Some of their ideas you will like, while some you will think are nonsense (as some are). When they have an idea you think has merit, get excited about it. This may feel phony at first, but you will see that it reaps rewards in the communication department.

Your excitement might include a vocal exclamation over an idea's value. You could then share the idea with others, giving the Popular Sanguine full credit for creating the idea. You could show physical approval by slapping them on the back or by hugging them enthusiastically, as Popular Sanguines like touch. Remember, you can't embarrass them, and they like being the center of attention.

Jeff used to work for CLASS when our offices were in California. As a Peaceful Phlegmatic, he learned well how to deal with me, a Popular Sanguine. Every time I developed a new brochure or came up with a new idea that I brought to him for review, he would put on a big smile and exclaim, "Another opportunity to praise you!" Despite the fact that I knew he was placating me, I still loved his response.

Communicating with the Powerful Choleric

When you are talking to a Powerful Choleric, try to speak more quickly than your usual pace. Practice reading a paragraph and time yourself. Then read it again and try to cut 25 percent off of your reading time.

Then read it again, aiming for a 50 percent decrease. You will find that you can probably get the sentences read in half the time. Make a note of that pace, and try to use it when talking to the Powerful Choleric. Give them only the basics, the bottom line. Respond to the Powerful Choleric as though you were on a witness stand, and "let your 'Yes' be yes, and your 'No' be no" (Jas. 5:12).

As a Peaceful Phlegmatic, Debbie has learned to think through in advance what she wants to tell a Powerful Choleric. By doing this, she can give him or her succinct information and be ready to answer any questions. This prevents signals of impatience often sent out from the Powerful Choleric. She found this technique to be especially helpful in dealing with her Powerful Choleric boss!

Communicating with the Perfect Melancholy

Conveying something to Perfect Melancholies is quite different altogether, since they are not in a rush like Powerful Cholerics. Perfect Melancholies appreciate facts, so when speaking to them, offer facts that you can back up with documentation. This is especially important in work situations. Prepare in advance. Think through information and develop research documentation—or at least a resource list—to have on hand for Perfect Melancholies. This will satisfy their need for facts and help you feel prepared. You may never need to share the document, but the fact that you have it will validate what you are saying.

Making Adjustments

All of us, regardless of our specific Personality, have areas in which our communication is easy and we operate out of our strengths. And all of us have areas in which we can improve. After you begin to identify your own Personality and work to improve yourself, work on identifying the Personality type of others and then adjust what you say and how you approach them. Give it a try. Be ready to enter the amazing world of effective communication!

CHAPTER 9

WORKPLACE

You pick your friends and you pick your spouse, but when you are hired for a job, you are plunked into a group of people that you might never have chosen as friends. And yet, you are expected to get along with all of them. For this reason, there are very few places where the understanding of the Personalities is more important than in the workplace. Knowing the Personality of your boss, coworkers and customers can make the place where you spend most of your waking hours tolerable, if not downright pleasant.

Additionally, if you are in a job that conforms to your Personality, you will be much happier. As part of her graduate degree in psychology, Georgia Shaffer was required to do original research for her thesis. She had recently spent an unpleasant summer developing a software system for DuPont, so she decided to survey more than 170 people who were systems programmers, analysts, engineers, project leaders or managers in the area of data processing to determine if there was a direct correlation between job satisfaction and the Personalities. The results of Georgia's research supported her hypothesis: Those who worked in jobs that used the natural strengths of their Personality scored much higher on job satisfaction.

In turn, it has been shown that when people enjoy their jobs, they tend to be more productive, are absent less, and are less likely to move to another job. For example, in Georgia's study, people who were extroverted (Popular Sanguines and Powerful Cholerics) were quite pleased to be in positions that enabled them to have a great deal of interaction with people. Those with more introverted characteristics (Perfect Melancholies and Peaceful Phlegmatics) were satisfied to be in jobs that kept them more isolated from other people.

Applying the Personalities in the Workplace

Before I had to enter the workforce, if I did not get along with someone I just didn't hang out with him or her. But once I had a job, there were difficult people with whom I had to interact—whether or not I liked them. However, because I had been steeped in the Personalities, I was able to easily identify these people's basic Personality and adjust my expectations of them and the way that I approached them. I found that this gave me a huge advantage. In each job, once I figured out my boss's Personality, I knew what to expect from him (or her).

My early jobs were all in food service. I was a waitress all through high school and college—jobs in which getting along with the customers had a direct impact on my income. Because I could figure out the customers, I was able to banter with those who were Popular Sanguines, treat the Powerful Cholerics with respect and jump when they asked for something, tone down my approach with the Perfect Melancholies, and be friendly with (but not bother) the Peaceful Phlegmatics. This was a huge boon to my pocketbook.

As a boss, I find the ability to quickly peg a person's basic Personality to be an ongoing asset. When I have a job opening, I think of which Personality will be the best fit for that position, and I pretty much hire accordingly, although sometimes I hire a person whom I think is not the right Personality for the job but is clearly the one God sent for that position.

I have recently rewritten the job descriptions for my staff. While some management gurus advise creating a job description and then hiring the person to fill it, I adjust the job description to fit the person who is in it. For example, I currently have Pam, a Popular Sanguine, in a general office/administrative assistant position. I knew when I hired Pam that her computer skills were minimal, but she was pleasant and willing to work the hours we needed at the salary we could afford to pay.

Pam has been with us for a year, and while her computer skills have definitely improved and she has been an eager student, the computer is clearly not her gift. But as a Popular Sanguine, she *is* gifted on the phone. Pam is great working with the hotels we use for our various events. She gets all the initial details squared away. While Linda, our Executive Director, still reviews all the contracts, Pam saves her a great deal of time and energy by doing all the footwork.

Pam's phone skills also make her great with the customers. During the hours she works, Pam is number one on the phones. We save the problem calls for Pam. She returns the cranky-customer calls—customers are fans by the time she hangs up with them. Her cheery disposition even comes across in e-mails. While she cannot update the website, she can craft an e-mail response that keeps a customer happy.

Knowing this about Pam, I adjusted her job description to keep her operating in her strengths. She had been thinking of quitting, but her skills are important to our team. With her adjusted job description, one that maximizes her strengths, she is happier—and is staying with our company.

Behavioral-based hiring is a trend in human resources. An article in *American Way Magazine* on the topic states that some companies "understand that you cannot transform a curmudgeon into a cheerleader, or a brilliant headstrong loner into a team player."[1] While the best option is to hire the right Personality for the job, why not make adjustments after the fact? With the cost of training, isn't it worth making employees happy by allowing them to work in their strengths rather than forcing them to do something that goes against their giftings?

TEAMBUILDING THE PERSONALITIES WAY
STEVE ROBBINS

My career has been primarily within the industrial world of machinery manufacturing in which touchy-feely things are not usually considered to be compatible with the likes of drafting, computers, engineering or CAD-CAM machining. Yet even in these environments, good relationships are

Continued on next page

Continued from previous page

key to business growth. The rule holds true from intradepartmental to interdepartmental to long-term relationships with suppliers and customers.

A few years ago, I transferred into a new group that consisted of two other men. The team leader is an off-the-chart Popular Sanguine, the other man is a Powerful Choleric, and I am a mix of Perfect Melancholy/Peaceful Phlegmatic. The team was not producing well, and there were daily disagreements between the two other men, usually regarding lack of organization, forgotten promises to customers, and poor sales performance as a whole. It wasn't long before I wondered if I had made the right move.

However, having learned the Personalities, I decided to apply these concepts to our situation. I began to teach the other men the Personalities—without actually labeling them as such—and pointed out the inherent weaknesses and strengths we each had. I then began to suggest that the roles and jobs be restructured based on each of our strengths.

It took some time, but eventually we made the changes. Because our commissions are based on sales, the Powerful Choleric is now in charge of keeping track of them. He is like a bloodhound to money. (Amazing how many records were slipping through the cracks when the Popular Sanguine was doing it!) On the other hand, the Popular Sanguine team leader is now fully in charge of customer interface, because he, by far, has the best customer rapport. I, as the Perfect Melancholy, have taken on the role of designing forms, formulating reports, putting the processes in place, researching and so on.

Four years later, the results have been beyond my expectations. Sales have skyrocketed. We have been recognized in one of the national trade journals as an outstanding department, and we have gained recognition with some of the nation's largest companies as having set the standard for the kind of work we do. The situation has changed from being chaotic to being the best work situation in my entire career.

How did this happen? Simply put, I put into practice the knowledge I had gained through my study of the Personalities. It could not have happened if we had not incorporated the concepts of the Personalities into our workplace.

Understanding the Personalities and their role in the workplace will help make work something you look forward to, rather than something you dread. This will be helpful if you are an employee who needs to get along with people at work or needs to make an adjustment in your responsibilities for more job satisfaction, or if you are an employer looking to fill your positions with the right people in order to build a strong team. Each Personality type has qualities that make it more naturally suited to certain job roles, and each Personality type also has areas of concern. Let's look at these Personalities in the workplace.

Popular Sanguine

Natural Role: Creative Person

Because the Popular Sanguine is a naturally creative person, he or she will be the happiest in a job that allows for a diversity of tasks, interaction with people, and room for creativity.

Sylvia is one of our Certified Personality Trainers who has used her knowledge of the Personalities in selecting her team members. When she opened her present real-estate company, Sylvia knew that she had to have help. As a Powerful Choleric/Popular Sanguine who was single and a new empty-nester, Sylvia had made herself busy beyond reason and was working 16-hour days. When her business suddenly took off and the workflow became uncontrollable, she knew that she needed someone who could go behind her and pick up the pieces—someone who was flexible and comfortable with a myriad roles and tasks.

Enter Brooke. During the interview process, Sylvia determined that Brooke was a Popular Sanguine/Peaceful Phlegmatic combination. Brooke had worked in retail for many years, and although she had been in management positions, retail had never really been a fit for her. She was bored and not working up to her potential. The Powerful Choleric managers who worked alongside her often hurt her feelings and made her feel inadequate by not offering praise for her skills.

Sylvia knew that Brooke was exactly what she was looking for, and so she hired Brooke as her personal assistant—but with a different take on what the job usually entails. From the beginning, they had an understanding that no two days would be the same. Brooke's job would be to do whatever was required—mow Sylvia's lawn, paint the bathroom, buy groceries, plan meals, pick out Sylvia's clothes for the day, put up real estate signs, hire companies to maintain rentals, feed the cat, keep the books, go to the bank, assist as needed when Sylvia had a public speaking engagement—plus all the normal real-estate assistant's duties.

Brooke loves the job! The Popular Sanguine part of her loves the approval she gets from being master of so many jobs! She jokes about her resume including stylist, lawn maintenance service provider, painter, housekeeper, trainer, junior editor, speaker, and real-estate assistant. It's the perfect job for her!

I wonder if Brooke would like to come work for me?

Skills and Abilities

Due to their natural outgoing nature, Popular Sanguines are the best choice when you need someone up front to make the initial contact with people or if you need someone to create enthusiasm and excitement. The Popular Sanguine's encouraging and uplifting Personality will also ensure that the office staff has fun. This describes Zoë perfectly.

While Zoë was not naturally a technical person, as a Popular Sanguine she loved teaching software programs to students at a business college. She enjoyed being the center of attention when explaining concepts, and she made class interesting and funny by incorporating stories from her previous workplace experiences. Many of the middle-aged students were especially nervous about using a computer, but Zoë was able to put them at ease. Many students praised her teaching style, but she didn't think she had a style—she was just being herself.

After three years, the job had become very repetitive, and Zoë was bored teaching the same subjects. So, she decided to look for a new job. Michael, her Perfect Melancholy husband, tried to help her without understanding Zoë's Personality and how that played into her job satisfaction. He enjoyed his work as a computer programmer, so he suggested she stay in the Information Technology (IT) industry. After all, if he liked IT, so would she—plus, at that time, jobs in that field were plentiful.

Zoë changed jobs and worked for an international IT company as a customer support administrator. Unfortunately, this required her to sit for hours processing orders on the computer—and not speaking to anyone! The customers were overseas and all communication was done by e-mail. Her coworkers did not provide much social interaction either—it was a small office with only a few staff members, and Zoë felt isolated. Her boss was a Perfect Melancholy lady who sat next to her but didn't talk because she was concentrating on her work. It wasn't long before Zoë couldn't handle the solitude anymore. After one year, Zoë was in such a state of distress that she realized she had to leave that job to keep her sanity.

Now Zoë understands her Personality and knows that for her to be happy at work, she needs interaction with people and a job that allows her be a cheerleader.

Tendencies

While Popular Sanguines can be an asset to any team, they are likely to be easily distracted or forgetful. Jessica, a Popular Sanguine, works in our shipping department. She comes into the office when she gets out of school each day. She is a hard worker and does a good job packing the mail orders that we have accumulated throughout the day. However, when Erin, her Peaceful Phlegmatic supervisor, is not there, Jessica tends to chat away with friends—her cell phone precariously perched between her ear and shoulder. She needs someone to talk to as she packs boxes.

If this happened only once in a while, it would not be a problem—after all, I am a Popular Sanguine boss. But we started getting complaints that the orders were incomplete or just plain wrong. Knowing that Jessica needed human interaction and that she liked talking on the phone, we made an adjustment in her duties. Now, she is not allowed to talk on the cell phone at work, but she can answer the office phone and take a product order—or pass the call on to the appropriate party. While she is on the phone, she is focused on the task at hand, and then she can put her energies into packing the order correctly once she hangs up.

Presentation Style

The general presentation style of Popular Sanguines is humorous. Even at a job interview they want to make people smile, and they often make others laugh without really trying.

While competing for the job of Miss Kentucky 2001, Monica Hardin, a 19-year-old Popular Sanguine/Powerful Choleric, committed a huge pre-interview faux pas. The stakes are high in competing for a state title: The winner of "Miss Kentucky" has the opportunity to win a $12,000 cash scholarship and wonderful prizes. The winner also earns about $40,000 during her year of service as a contract employee for the Commonwealth of Kentucky's Agricultural Department by promoting the anti-smoking "No Ifs, Ands, or Butts" program to school students across the state. And let's not forget that Miss Kentucky will compete for the Miss America title—in that competition, the winner receives a $40,000 scholarship, plus a six-figure speaking/appearance contract for one year.

But back to Monica's story. During pageant week, the contestants are housed in one of Transylvania University's dorms. The girls are shuttled around by chaperones to various appearances, lunches and rehearsals during pageant week. After lunch one day, Monica had some down time to prepare for the important interview portion of the competition. Wearing jeans and a T-shirt, no makeup, and with curlers in her hair, Monica began working on her responses to the questions the judges might ask. After she had been studying hard for a while, she decided that she needed a few minutes of fresh air to clear her head. She stepped outside the dorm just as a car was pulling up in front of the dorm that was filled with what she thought to be some of her fellow contestants.

Excited to see her new "best friends," Monica immediately started doing a little dance, waving and sticking her tongue out at the car. However, after the car pulled up to the front door, to her horror, Monica discovered that the people in the vehicle were none other than the judges who had just come back from their lunch break! They could not help themselves—they burst out laughing. Monica, red faced, also laughed and headed back into the dorm as quickly as she could dance there!

Two hours later, she really wowed the judges in the interview—even though they had seen her "immature" side—and ended up winning the Miss Kentucky crown. Thankfully, it was only after the crowning that one of the judges summed up the incident by reminding her how important it is to be "on" and "professional" at all times when working toward an important goal.

Warnings

If you have ever worked with Popular Sanguines, you know that they can appear to be too happy or cute, which often makes it hard for them to come across as serious or believable. This was the case for Stephanie. She told me this story:

When I was in my early 20s, I managed the shoe department of an upscale ladies' store in Alabama. So when I moved to Florida, it seemed logical to accept a position as the manager trainee of a new shoe store that was opening in the mall.

Since the owners were former high school band instructors who had no experience in retail, I felt that I should just move right in and show them everything I knew. They were older, kind of stern, unsmiling and not very outgoing. I, on the other hand, was comfortable, friendly to the customers, happy and making "new best friends" daily. It seemed to be a perfect fit.

One day, I was called to the back of the store and was, gasp, fired! I was told that I was "just too happy, too excited, too quick." My young heart was crushed. I didn't understand what I could have done wrong.

Today, I know that the owners were Perfect Melancholy/ Powerful Cholerics who were bothered by my outgoing persona and my being too comfortable in their store. They had in mind a quieter, more introverted person who would slowly take the reins, while I thought I was taking charge and letting them know I could handle things!

The story has a happy ending, however. My next position suited my Personality to a "T." I was hired as one of the first women in the country to sell cars! The savvy owner and general manager of the forward-thinking dealership had me take a battery of personality tests, which showed me to be perfect for the job. Since I was happy and cute, people wanted to buy cars from me. My new straight-commission job afforded me four times the income as the previous job had. Through the devastation of being fired, I was propelled into the knowledge of how to make a living in what was then a man's world.

Also, when working with Popular Sanguines, it is best not to put them in charge of the money. Chuck is often amazed that I have had no major financial mishaps, because money handling is not my forte.

Powerful Choleric

Natural Role: Leadership Person

Powerful Cholerics naturally gravitate toward positions of leadership. They'd rather be the chief than an Indian. Case in point is Derek, a Powerful Choleric/Popular Sanguine who is always looking for the next challenge. Unless he is crazily busy, he feels unproductive. He is an excellent businessman and sportsman and involves himself in many organizations. Of course, these organizations are always ones in which Derek has a vested interest.

As a Formula 4000 race car driver, Derek recently took over an executive position on the committee because "nothing was happening." Of course, he not only offered to be in a leadership role, but he also offered to do the press releases, the drivers' updates for every meeting, the coordination with the engine manufacturers, and any other correspondence necessary. Now, this wouldn't be a problem except that Derek doesn't type and doesn't know how to open an e-mail or send one in reply. Of course, this meant that these duties would fall to his Perfect Melancholy wife. Spending hours at the end of a dictaphone machine is not her idea of fun—and to make matters worse, she doesn't even particularly like motor racing!

On committees, Powerful Cholerics only want to participate if they are in charge. I know of one woman who was asked to head up a program. She agreed as long as she didn't have to have a committee!

Skills and Abilities

Powerful Cholerics shine in the workplace when they are motivating people to action, controlling the plans and keeping up productivity. They have an amazing ability to quickly size up a situation and give clear instructions as to how to solve the problem at hand while making sure the group sees the immediate gain.

These skills were certainly needed when Susan was sent to Australia to take over the management of a U.S. ministry that had been undermined by an unscrupulous manager. Immediately upon arrival, she was whisked from the airport to the office. There she faced the auditors, attorneys and office workers, who informed her that the previous manager had closed down all the accounts, taken all the bank information, and informed the creditors and contributors that the ministry was closing.

Had she been anything other than a Powerful Choleric, she probably would have quit and boarded the next plane home. However, her skills were exactly what was needed for the situation, and she quickly went into full-scale, takeover mode—controlling all the plans and productivity. Giving directions to the other workers, she got to work and made the necessary contacts to counteract the previous manager's actions.

Four years later, Susan has not only overcome the barriers she'd faced at the beginning, but she has also grown the ministry to a place where it is active in every section of Australia. The ministry's television program is seen in every major city, they have bought land and built a home office—financed and paid for entirely by the Australians—and they have instituted monthly meetings and annual conferences in each state.

FROM A T-SHIRT SEEN IN A MAIL-ORDER CATALOG
"Team Effort: A lot of people doing what I say."

Because such leadership positions are natural for Powerful Cholerics, I like to have them on my team and happily hand over the control of those areas in which they excel. While Powerful Cholerics often butt heads over authority, once you understand the Personality and know a particular Powerful Choleric well enough to comprehend his or her unique skills, it makes life so much easier to simply accept that and allow the Powerful Choleric to operate in his or her strengths.

Tendencies

With the great—and obvious—strengths of the Powerful Choleric, people who are 50 percent (or more) of this Personality need to be aware of how they often come across to others: too impulsive and intimidating. Because Powerful Cholerics are uniquely gifted in crisis situations, their snap decisions, even though they are usually right, can seem impulsive to others and often intimidate those with less confidence. If you are a Powerful Choleric, keeping this "intimidation" factor in mind is important for getting along in the workplace.

When Susan first arrived in Australia, because she was operating in her areas of strengths—seeing the great challenge ahead of her and tackling the problems—she did not realize how her actions were affecting the team. Without understanding that her coworkers needed to share their ideas for how to solve the ministry's problems, she plowed ahead and got the job done. An awareness of this tendency would have probably given her more sensitivity and brought greater understanding and camaraderie among her coworkers. Yet behind the bossiness was the fear that if she didn't take control immediately, her coworkers—many of whom were older than she—would not see her as a leader, and therefore not give her the cooperation that she so desperately needed in order to be successful.

A Powerful Choleric reading this might defend Susan's actions by arguing, "But she got the job done. She had success." Yes, she had success, but her impulsive actions made that success harder, and her youth and perceived brashness caused many long-time, knowledgeable staff members to quit. This left Susan to struggle with customs, rules and regulations that were foreign to her. Had she worked to involve these individuals, seek their expertise and win them over, her success would have been won by the team instead of her having to carry so much of the burden alone.

Presentation Style

If you are a Powerful Choleric, realize that while your natural demeanor is authoritative and convincing, this strength can make less-confident people cower in your presence.

Betty is one of our strong leaders at CLASSeminar. When we teach the module on the Personalities, Betty teaches the Powerful Choleric part and doesn't work to soften her natural Personality, as she is acting as a living visual aide. Her intensity often scares the people who get placed in her small group. Of course, they only come and tell me this after they have been in Betty's group for a while and realize that she really has a heart of gold and cares about the people in her group. When her small-group members report to me, it is because they now love her!

When considering the way Powerful Cholerics present themselves, realize that when they are intensely involved in something, they may look or sound angry to others around them. Cybil shared her own rude awakening with me:

> I learned this the hard way while watching the videotape of an orientation session. While giving my presentation, I felt energized, earnest and passionate about what I was saying. But when I saw myself on videotape, my first thought was, *What am I so angry about? I look and sound totally ticked off!* Until that moment, I had not realized how much of a discrepancy was possible between how I thought I was presenting myself and how others were actually seeing me.

Warning

Powerful Cholerics are always looking for the next challenge and the next opportunity. Because of this, they often get bored with daily tasks—even when that involves maintaining the programs that they themselves instituted. If you want to keep Powerful Cholerics motivated in the workplace, give them new challenges and let them work their magic in solving problems.

Powerful Cholerics typically do not do well in positions that require them to solve personnel problems. The reason for this is because Powerful Cholerics combine being blunt with a fear of showing emotions (except anger), which tends to only cause more problems. A Powerful Choleric's leadership motto might be "Lead, follow, or get out of my way." Not the slogan you want hanging on the wall above your Human Resources specialist's desk!

If you are a Powerful Choleric, you need to be aware that if you are not the boss, and that if you do your job too well, you can become a threat to the boss. Some bosses will do whatever they can to undermine the work of Powerful Cholerics or replace them with someone who may not do the job as well but doesn't make them look bad.

Perfect Melancholy

Natural Role: Detail Person

When accuracy is important, the Perfect Melancholy is the one for the job. Chuck worked for the State of New Mexico for several years in the role of inspector. This position suited him well. He was a part of a team that traveled the state inspecting the facilities that provided mental health services to children. The team, consisting of a therapist, a social worker and a nurse, reviewed patient charts and treatment plans at each facility and then inspected each facility for issues of cleanliness and safety. The team studied personnel files to make sure licenses were current and that only those with a "cleared" status were allowed to be alone with the children. Different team members—either the therapist, the social worker or the nurse—served as the team leader for specific facilities.

Josh, a Peaceful Phlegmatic, was the social worker member of the team, and he was the team leader for a residential treatment center in the southern part of the state. When Josh resigned one year after Chuck started working with him, Chuck was given the team leader position for that particular facility. When he took the team to inspect this facility that had been under Josh's care, he was overwhelmed with how much was wrong!

This facility had been in operation for years with the same leadership team. When Chuck reviewed the old records, he saw that Josh had given them such a clean bill of health that the regular inspections had been waived for two years. How had they gotten into such a mess? Had the directors suddenly become lax?

The directors were shocked when Chuck announced that the team was sanctioning the facility and that the directors would be required to present a corrective action plan within weeks. The directors insisted that they were doing what they had always done, and that Josh had been happy.

What had changed? The Personality of the inspector. Josh did more of a sweeping overview, while Chuck went over every detail. These inspections are important because they ensure that only qualified workers are working with the children, and they prevent known abusers from gaining employment at the facility. When the details matter, the Perfect Melancholy is the one for the job.

Skills and Abilities

Due to their penchant for details, Perfect Melancholies are perfect for jobs that require accurate planning and recordkeeping. They are ideal for jobs in which keeping the financial records straight is important.

Wayne is a contract auditor, which perfectly suits his Perfect Melancholy Personality. Because of his accuracy, he has saved his company millions of dollars. One time, in a cost-cutting measure, his company decided to change it's system from one that required thorough inspections to one in which they simply spot-checked the records. In many cases, this meant merely asking employees if they had the proper documents rather than asking to see the documents and then review them. Wayne knew that this plan defeated the entire idea of auditing. He went to the management and told them that this new system was like asking a bank robber if he or she had robbed a bank. Because Wayne had a history of excellence and accuracy, the management listened to his well-thought-out concerns. Ultimately, they scrapped the new system.

Another trait of Perfect Melancholies is that they tend to be sensitive to the needs of others and are able to get their coworkers to see long-range goals. Curt runs the radiology department for a large hospital. Each morning, the radiology department staff was scheduled to begin their day at 7 A.M., but Curt noticed that one of the X-ray technicians was constantly late for work. Being a Perfect Melancholy, Curt decided to call the employee into his office to discuss the problem. He found out that she was always late because she had to get her child to school and that the school's drop-off time and her work time conflicted.

Because this technician was good at her job and it was in the best interest of the department to keep her, Curt adjusted her work schedule to allow for her to take care of her child's needs. She now comes in on the late shift, an hour later than everyone else, and stays an hour later than everyone else. This has ended up saving the department in overtime costs, as she is able to take care of the end-of-day loose ends that were causing the other employees to stay after their shift ended. Curt's sensitivity saved a good employee and saved his department money.

Tendencies

Perfect Melancholies are naturally detail-oriented, and because of this they can easily become distracted by trying to have everything just right and can become too critical of others. My friend Rachael works for a man like this. Her boss, Matt, wants everything done "just so," and he has no tolerance for mistakes. When those under his direction make an error, he gets frustrated and angry at their "incompetence"—ignoring the hundreds of things they have done right. Matt's own boss frequently tells him to lighten up.

Because Rachael understands the Personalities, she gets along with Matt and makes allowances for his immature behavior. Recently, when Matt's direct assistant quit, Rachel took over some of her duties. Matt seemed glad that his old assistant had left: "She was just too sensitive," he said. Rachael had to smirk internally when she heard Matt say this, as she knew that his problem was being too critical, not that his assistant was too sensitive.

My friend Christine, a Perfect Melancholy, says this about her struggle not to be too critical:

> I find it really difficult to give praise to my staff. I have read lots of books on people skills and made a decision that every day I will give each team member a compliment during his or her shift. I have found that praising their work skills, when I know they are often able to do much better, is really challenging. I feel that if I praise my staff for an 80 percent effort, they'll feel that that is an acceptable standard, instead of reaching for a higher level of achievement.

If you are a Perfect Melancholy, be aware of your propensity for criticism, and make a conscious effort to watch for the good and praise it.

Presentation Style

When you interact with Perfect Melancholies, you will find that they come across as accurate and sincere. This is because they want things done correctly.

Georgia is on our teaching team at our Personality Training Workshops. As a Perfect Melancholy, she provides balance to the Popular Sanguine/Powerful Choleric Personality that my mother and I share. Georgia also has a Masters Degree in Psychology, which gives her a professional perspective that we do not have.

When we do the Personality Training Workshops, Georgia always wants to review her notes before it is her turn to teach. She questions me as to exactly what time she will be on so that she can be prepared. As a Popular Sanguine, I want to poke her and say, "Oh, Georgia, you know this backward and forward. You don't need to study your notes. You don't even need notes!" But I know that she has a Perfect Melancholy Personality, which means that it is important to her to be accurate.

Noel is also a good example of a Perfect Melancholy Personality. He is the manager of a hardware store in Australia, and he always runs a tight ship. He makes sure that the store is well presented and neatly arranged. He hates awkward shaped things that just don't fit on the shelves right—after all, how do you get coils of rope and wire to stay neat or sheets of shade cloth to stay cut straight? He often asks aloud, "Why can't the staff cut a straight line?"

Noel's Perfect Melancholy nature does not contribute to a fun working environment at the store. Everything can feel fairly subdued. Fortunately, after learning about the Personalities, Noel has learned to hire staff members who are Popular Sanguines, who do create some fun and who interact well with the customers and other staff. Of course, the Popular Sanguines drive Noel crazy at times with the amount of work they *don't* get done because they are busy chatting.

For the Perfect Melancholy, if it's worth doing, it is worth doing right.

Warning

If you work with Perfect Melancholies, you know that their desire for correctness, combined with their deep thinking, can make them appear intellectual and remote. As a result, others often feel less intelligent in their presence. And of course, there's the danger that the Perfect Melancholy will get lost in the details.

Derek and Christine owned several childcare centers. With about 150 children at these centers, they were busy places. Derek and Christine had leased these businesses to various operators, but at one point were considering running the centers themselves. They asked Derek's brother Errol—a Perfect Melancholy who can never understand why creating a new chart or form won't fix any problem—to give them a brief overview and analysis of expected profitability if they opted to run the centers themselves. Errol produced a 20-page report that was filled with details delineating the advantages and disadvantages.

As Errol is not a parent, he had to ask Christine—an experienced mother of three—for some needed information. How many nappies (diapers) is a child likely to use in a day? How often do children need to drink, and how much will they drink? What do they like to eat, and how often? How much toilet paper are they likely to use? Errol gave Christine a thorough list with questions such as these. Christine had a good laugh (out of his earshot) before she diligently gave him some answers.

Needless to say, the vision of the projected number of diapers a week was too overwhelming for Errol to contemplate. After looking at all the numbers, Derek and Christine decided not to change the relationships they had with the centers' operators.

Peaceful Phlegmatic

Natural Role: Support Person

One of the great things about Peaceful Phlegmatics is that they do not need to be in the spotlight. They are content to be the support system.

I have mentioned Linda, our executive director. When I think of the good qualities of the Peaceful Phlegmatic, I think of Linda. She is the epitome of a Peaceful Phlegmatic who is living in her strengths.

While Linda has learned to lead, she is an ideal support person. At our CLASSeminar, Linda graciously sits up front when my mother or I are doing the teaching. She unpacks all our notes or props and has them ready for us so that we can simply walk in and start. She sits at a table slightly behind us and hands us props or supplies when we need them. She never looks bored, though she has heard the same information dozens of times. She laughs appropriately, makes note of any funny lines we come up with, and records how long each session actually takes. At the conclusion of each session, she packs up the materials so that they are in order the next time we need them.

At the end of the three-day seminar, Linda efficiently cleans up our workspace and packs our box of supplies to be shipped home with the remaining books and other supplies. Typical of a Peaceful Phlegmatic, Linda is totally capable up on the stage herself, but she is content to be behind the scenes—a perfect support person.

Skills and Abilities

As mentioned previously, Peaceful Phlegmatics are versatile people—and an asset to any team. They are uniquely gifted in areas in which none of the other Personalities excel. For instance, Peaceful Phlegmatics have a calming nature that often helps their coworkers in the group feel relaxed and comfortable. As peacemakers, they easily find the middle ground, stay calm in the midst of chaos, and do not overreact to negative situations.

Brooke, an assistant to a real-estate agent, exhibits these qualities. Most people think that realtors make a living by selling homes, but the reality is that they only make money when they bring the transaction to a *close*. This means that they must correctly line up hundreds of little details while simultaneously dealing with the different temperaments and Personalities of the players involved—from buyer and seller to title companies, attorneys, appraisers, home inspectors and insurance agents.

Recently, Sylvia, the real-estate agent for whom Brooke worked, had a million-dollar home under contract in which Murphy's Law (if anything can go wrong, it will) was reigning. The $10,000 earnest money deposit was lost by the attorney; one inspection showed that the roof of the house needed a total replacement while another showed that the roof was in good repair; and the neighbor had built a lovely brick planter filled with flowers that encroached on the property line by three inches— and the Perfect Melancholy buyer wanted those three inches!

Tempers flared on all sides, and the stress was mounting. As a Powerful Choleric with Popular Sanguine tendencies, Sylvia knew that dealing well with these Personalities and situations was beyond her capability, so she turned to her assistant, Brooke, who was, blessedly, half Peaceful Phlegmatic. Brooke was easily able to speak to all the parties and soothe their concerns. Hour after hour, day after day, she sweetly handled each concern while Sylvia stayed in the office and ranted and raved from her desk about their difficult Personalities!

Because Brooke was able to find a middle ground and stay calm in the midst of chaos, the transaction successfully closed and the commission check is now in the bank! Brooke was duly rewarded for her efforts.

Tendencies

Brooke is a Peaceful Phlegmatic who is functioning in her strengths. However, it is often easy for those with this Personality who have not worked at maturity to be too undisciplined and indecisive.

Vanessa is a Peaceful Phlegmatic who started working in a hardware store while she was in high school. She was shy and quiet, but she was also studious, capable, efficient and good with customers. The store's owners began training her in different roles. A faithful employee, Vanessa stayed there for many years. Her longevity at the store gave her expertise in a variety of areas, and new staff looked to her for guidance and leadership.

The owners wanted to reward her for her faithful service and promoted her to Team Leader, a position that required her to direct staff, deal with company representatives to place orders, and supervise junior staff. Vanessa was hesitant to take on the role, even though it offered much more money. However, not wanting to appear ungrateful, Vanessa decided to take the new position.

After a period of time, the owners found that some things were going really well at the store, but others weren't—especially those things that pertained to Venessa directing the staff. Vanessa would not discipline lazy or incompetent employees, was reluctant to ask the members of her staff to do the boring jobs, and would not make the tough decisions necessary to develop the best team and generate the best business results. When the owners gave Vanessa their appraisal of her performance, they offered her additional training and gave her suggestions on how to deal with the staff. Yet even after this training, Vanessa still felt that she couldn't overcome her fear of upsetting or offending her coworkers.

Presentation Style

Peaceful Phlegmatics come across as believable and pleasant. Their tone is consistent and steady. This is great—unless they are in a position in which they need to project, display authority, or demand respect.

Linda, our executive director, has had to work on her presentation style. She often listens in her car to some of voice coach Roy Hanschke's audio recordings (which we recommend at the CLASSeminar) and practices projecting her voice on her way to work. All day, as she talks to customers, clients and vendors on the phone, she works on projection and vocal variety. You can clearly tell a difference in Linda's voice when she is practicing what Roy has taught her to do.

Warning

While Peaceful Phlegmatics who are functioning in their strengths are a joy to work with, there are some things about them that are troublesome. They may come across as too low key—even dull or lazy. With their even, balanced approach, Peaceful Phlegmatics can appear unenthusiastic and unconvincing. And they are not the ones to count on for motivation.

Liz found this to be true of a Peaceful Phlegmatic designer who worked with her to help her create a line of children's clothing. She shared this story:

> Wade was possibly the most wonderful man I have ever known. He loved his wife as well as all of his coworkers, and he treated everyone with such a gentle kindness that every woman there wished he was her husband! I would personally watch him interact with his wife and think, *If I can't have a husband like that, I don't want one.* It wasn't that he was so physically attractive, but that he was just so *good.*
>
> The only problem was that during the holiday season when we would face daily production deadlines, Wade was *never* in a hurry. In order to get the job done and shipped on time, he would have to stay at work until it was completed, but that meant that he would stay hours after everyone else had left, slowly yet contentedly strolling around the shop. Of course, as a Powerful Choleric owner, I was pulling my hair out, worrying that the job wouldn't get done on time!
>
> On the few occasions when we didn't make it and the order was shipped out late or cancelled, it appeared to be of no real emotional concern to Wade. But it wasn't his bottom line that was affected. No, it was mine—the Powerful Choleric's.
>
> As wonderful as Wade was, and as much as I loved him, he could certainly make me crazy!

As you look around your place of work, the groups in which you are a member, or the committees on which you serve, take note of how the

Personalities play into happiness on the job, successful team-building, and good relationships with clients and customers.

The Rubber Meets the Road

What are the Personalities that you work with? Now that you understand these Personalities, how will you apply this information to improve your relationship with your coworkers and make your workplace more functional?

If you are the boss, you can make some changes that will allow your staff to function in the areas in which they are more naturally gifted. These changes will make you happier—and make everyone else happier and more efficient. For example, when you have an opening, think through what the Personality needs of the job are. If you place a classified ad for the position, word the advertisement in such a way that it attracts the person with the correct Personality for the job.

If you are in a job that is not suited to you, study your Personality. What do you need from a job in order to have satisfying work? Think about what you need to do to find a job that fits who you are. Now, do it. After all, you spend more waking hours at work that any other single place. Wouldn't it be nice to be happy there?

Note

1. Samuel Greengard, "A Perfect Match," *American Way Magazine,* May 15, 2005, p. 52. http://www.peopleanswers.com/news/article_20050515.html (accessed February 2006).

CHAPTER 10

SPIRITUAL LIFE

By now, you have seen that our Personalities influence virtually every aspect of our lives. It should be no surprise, then, that our Personalities impact our spiritual life as well. It was a great comfort to me when I first began to understand the implications my Personality had on the way my spiritual life played out—and I trust you will find these insights enlightening for your life as well.

Throughout my life, I'd heard friends, speakers, preachers—and even my dad—say that in order for people to grow spiritually and develop a deeper faith, they must have a time of daily meditation. Preferably, this would be an hour spent each and every morning in devotions, quiet time or, better yet, recording volumes of written prayers as proof of strong faith and spirituality. (My father had adopted this form of daily devotion—upon his death, we found notebook after notebook of his prayers.) And I had also heard it said that if people want to grow spiritually, they need to read the whole Bible—from Genesis to Revelation—in one year.

When I looked at my life, I realized that I didn't do any of those things. I knew that I must be going about my Christian faith all wrong. So I bought the Bibles divided into daily readings for the year, purchased prayer journals, and prayed aloud personal promises so that I could fulfill this daily devotional time commitment. But each time, I would fail.

I felt inadequate in my spiritual journey and guilty because of my lack of self-discipline. I felt like a second-class citizen of the Christian community. Yet at the same time, I felt close to God. I prayed to God—often. I didn't write my prayers in notebooks, but I did pray in my head. Even when I hadn't read my mandated passage of Scripture for the day, my prayers were answered and I felt at peace with God's guidance and presence in my daily life.

As I have traveled around the country and spoken on this topic, I have found that many people share these same struggles. Many people have bought into this same idea of what makes a person spiritual and have tried similarly structured study times and Bible studies. When they ultimately fail, it often leaves them feeling even farther away from God.

A Gospel for All

Often, when we hear the glowing testimonies of people who have found success by using a specific system, we all try the same system and then feel inadequate when we don't have the matching results. We feel that the failure must be because of a flaw in us, not in the proven plan. But as you will see in this chapter, the Personalities come into play here. There are different tools and techniques that will work more effectively for one Personality type, while others will work better for someone of a different type. If one approach worked for everyone, we would only need one Gospel, but instead, God gave us four! Interestingly, each of the Gospels has a different approach that lines up in such a way as to appeal to each of the Personalities.[1]

Luke is the Gospel for the Popular Sanguines. Luke was known as the "beloved physician" (Col. 4:14), and in his Gospel he stresses the concept of Jesus as "Savior" (see Luke 1:31-33). Popular Sanguines connect especially to these concepts of being beloved and of relating to Christ as their personal Savior. Luke fills his Gospel with details of relationships, angels, and the pageantry that Popular Sanguines love—making Luke the longest of the four Gospels.

Powerful Cholerics connect more to the Gospel of Mark, in which Jesus is portrayed as a servant. Mark is the shortest of the Gospels, and Powerful Cholerics appreciate how he gets right down to the bottom line. It is a book of action and power, not of lengthy discourse, that depicts

Jesus as the mighty and authoritative Son of God. In fact, the book of Mark uses the word "immediately" more frequently and contains more stories of miracles and exorcisms than any of the other Gospels.

Matthew, which focuses more on Jesus as Lord and King, is the Gospel for the Perfect Melancholies. Matthew was a reformed tax collector, and his book is filled with numbers—2 sons, 3 servants, 10 virgins (see Matt. 21:28-32; 25:1-30). It is a book of order and discipleship that was written with a mathematical cadence that only a Perfect Melancholy would notice.

The Gospel of John was written by "the disciple whom Jesus loved" (John 21:20)—just how every Peaceful Phlegmatic would want to be referenced. In John's Gospel, Jesus is portrayed as the Son of God and the only source of eternal life. It is a book of assurance, love, peace and trust, and it does not contain a genealogy or any record of Jesus' birth, childhood, temptations, transfiguration or Great Commission.

Personality and Spiritual Life

If God gave each of us our own version, doesn't it stand to reason that we can approach Him out of the core of how He made us? As I have studied this topic, I have found that our Personalities affect a variety of aspects of our spiritual lives, including the type of church we are attracted to, our view of God, our preferred worship experience, our spiritual strengths (the spiritual concepts that we are most naturally drawn to), the tools and techniques that help us grow closer to God, and even our spiritual gifts—really, our entire spiritual experience.

Andrea shared this story with me about her Personality and her worship experience:

> When our pastor's upcoming sermon topic fit a slower-paced music service, the two Perfect Melancholies on our worship planning team were in heaven. I, however, had experienced incredibly difficult circumstances in the week leading up to this particular service, and my soul longed for a happy, upbeat service where I could just sing jubilantly and let all the sadness go

away. By the second song of the service, I found myself feeling depressed. I felt rotten, and my desire to sing and praise left me. I did not feel close to God. As I sang the introspective songs, I actually felt farther away from Him and the realness of my sin almost overwhelmed me.

As I sat in my pew, I realized that as a Popular Sanguine, I feel closer to God and more able to tell Him that I am sorry when I am upbeat and praising Him. The Perfect Melancholies, on the other hand, feel that they are worshiping when they are able to look deeply at themselves and confess their imperfections to Him. As I now reflect on what took place, I realize that no particular style of worship service is correct. Since every Personality connects to God differently, we must allow for different kinds of songs so that everyone can feel connected to God, and not make others feel bad when our particular style might not fit them.

With these differences in mind, we will next look at some of the areas that I find have the most relevance for people: view of God, spiritual strength, growing closer to God, and spiritual gifts. And since the ultimate form of maturity is to become like Christ with the strengths of all four Personalities and the weaknesses of none, we will conclude by examining the Personality of Jesus to determine how we can become more like Him. [2]

View of God

When I began to study the various attributes of God, I found it amazing that He is so multidimensional. I believe that God knows each of us and each of our individual Personalities. After all, we are wired the way that we are because that is the way He made us! With all of our varied filters through which we view life, God knew that we would also see Him differently based on our individual Personalities—what I like to think of as the colored glasses through which we view life. While there are many different facets of God, based on our own filters we see the side of Him that is the most natural and comfortable for us.

Popular Sanguine

Popular Sanguines easily comprehend the idea that God wants nothing but the best for them—like a loving father. They embrace the view of God that is presented in Matthew 7:11: "If you sinful people know how to give good gifts to your children, how much more will your heavenly *Father* give good gifts to those who ask him" (*NLT*, emphasis added). Popular Sanguines love getting gifts and do not feel the need to earn them.

I was blessed to have a father who modeled God's love to me—even before he was a Christian himself. However, Popular Sanguines who did not have such a relationship with their fathers may have trouble embracing this aspect of God. If their fathers were hard on them or expected a lot out of them, they may view God as being the same way. For these individuals, viewing God more as a best friend—someone with whom they can fellowship—can be more beneficial. As Paul states, "He is the one who invited you into this wonderful *friendship* with his Son, Jesus Christ our Lord" (1 Cor. 1:9, *NLT*, emphasis added).

Powerful Choleric

A big part of being a Christian is about giving God control of our lives. However, a Powerful Choleric wants the control! As a result, Powerful Cholerics often view God as someone with whom they must battle for control, even though Scripture states that this is futile: "We humans keep brainstorming options and plans, but GOD'S purpose prevails" (Prov. 19:21, *THE MESSAGE*). Rather than trying to do it on their own, Powerful Cholerics should heed the advice given in James 4:14-15:

> You don't know what will happen tomorrow. What is life? You are a mist that is seen for a moment and then disappears. Instead, you should say, "If the Lord wants us to, we will live and carry out our plans" (*GOD'S WORD*).

Proverbs 20:24 addresses God's dominion over all: "The Lord decides what a person will do; no one understands what his life is all about" (*NCV*). And Philippians 4:13 points out the need for Christ's power: "For I can do everything with the help of Christ who gives me the strength I need" (*NLT*). Yet Powerful Cholerics keep making plans.

Perfect Melancholy

Of all the Personalities, Perfect Melancholies are the most likely to underline the verses in their Bible—if they dare underline on the tissue-paper-thin pages—that address fear of God. Some of these verses might include:

> Thou shalt *fear* the LORD thy God; him shalt thou serve, and to him shalt thou cleave, and swear by his name (Deut. 10:20, *KJV*, emphasis added).

> And remember that the heavenly Father to whom you pray has no favorites when he judges. He will judge or reward you according to what you do. So you must live in reverent *fear* of him during your time as foreigners here on earth (1 Pet. 1:17, *NLT*, emphasis added).

Melanie, a Perfect Melancholy, viewed God as more of a Being to be revered in a fearful kind of way and felt that she had to watch her *P*s and *Q*s. She states, "I have an almost constant nagging feeling that I am doing something wrong, but I can never put my finger on it. If God were to come back today, I fear He would be disappointed with me because there are things in my life that are not perfect. I feel like sometimes my behavior makes Him sad. I want Him to say, 'Well done good and faithful servant,' but I feel like instead He may say, 'What were you thinking?'"

Lois, also a Perfect Melancholy, had the same view of God. She states, "I felt for a long time that I had to be almost perfect before God would answer my prayers. And if my prayers weren't answered, it had to be my fault—a lack of faith on my part or something. To this day, I still struggle to see God as one who will love me in spite of my imperfections."

Michelle has also struggled with viewing God as a loving father. She says, "As a child, God always seemed out of my reach. I would sing about Him being so big and so mighty that there was nothing He couldn't do. But those words felt hollow to me, because there was something God could not do: be so real that I could touch Him. Now I know genuine love from an ever-patient and forgiving Father that I see, feel and know personally in my life."

Peaceful Phlegmatic

The view of God that Peaceful Phlegmatics are most naturally attracted to is one in which God is characterized as a place of comfort and rest:

> May our Lord Jesus Christ and God our Father, who loved us and in his special favor gave us everlasting *comfort* and good hope, *comfort* your hearts and give you strength in every good thing you do and say (2 Thess. 2:16-17, *NLT*, emphasis added).

> Moses said this about the people of Benjamin: "The Lord's loved ones will lie down in safety, because he protects them all day long. The ones he loves *rest* with him" (Deut. 33:12, *NCV*, emphasis added).

God is so multifaceted that there is an element of Him for each of us. He is a loving Father. He is a best friend. He is someone for whom we should have reverence, or fear. He does want to be in control of our lives. He is a place of comfort and rest. Our individual Personality causes us to more quickly embrace the part of God that is most like us.

Spiritual Strengths

Throughout the pages of the Bible, there are many basic spiritual themes that are often repeated. Some of the most prevalent ones are related to grace, knowledge, justification and the sovereignty of God. Each of these themes—which I call spiritual strengths—represents a strong suit of each Personality.

Popular Sanguine: *Grace*

Popular Sanguines generally have no trouble with the idea that God loves them—after all, they naturally feel that everyone likes them, so why wouldn't God? To Popular Sanguines, grace is a natural extension of God's love. Some of the verses expressing this concept that resonate with Popular Sanguines are the following:

> And if He chose them by *grace*, it is not for the things they have done. If they could be made God's people by what they did, God's gift of *grace* would not really be a gift (Rom. 11:6, *NCV*, emphasis added).

> And all need to be made right with God by His *grace*, which is a free gift. They need to be made free from sin through Jesus Christ (Rom. 3:24, *NCV*, emphasis added).

To see why Popular Sanguines have such an affinity toward grace, we first need to have a basic understanding of what grace is. I remember memorizing a definition of grace from my junior church days: "Grace is God's unmerited favor." While that is a nice, short definition, it really does not explain a lot. Perhaps a better explanation is found in *New Unger's Bible Dictionary:*

> Grace thus rules out all human merit . . . any intermixture of human merit violates grace. . . . Grace thus obviates any obligation to gain merit, and the law as a merit system is no longer applicable to a believer, since he is no longer "under law, but under grace."[3]

This definition points out the elements of grace to which Popular Sanguines are drawn: They do not have to do anything to earn God's favor. Despite their imperfections, they have Christ's merit and Christ's standing. For me, as a Popular Sanguine, the idea of grace is summed up in the signature line I have on my office e-mails: "It is my hope that I live my life in such a way that when I stand at the pearly gates, I will be told that I was 'too forgiving' rather than 'too judgmental.' That is how I hope others will treat me." I am always in need of grace, so I freely give it.

Powerful Choleric: *Justification*

The inherent Personality of the Powerful Choleric—whose motto mirrors the "Just Do It" Nike ads—embodies the spiritual strength of justification and works. Production is important to Powerful Cholerics—it is how they determine their own value and the value of others. Likewise, they show their love for God through their works. James addresses this idea of justification in these passages:

> But someone will say, "You have faith; and I have works." Show me your faith without your works, and I will show you my faith by my works (Jas. 2:18, *NKJV*).

> You foolish man, do you want evidence that faith without deeds is useless? You see that a person is justified by what he does and not by faith alone. . . . As the body without the spirit is dead, so faith without deeds is dead (Jas. 2:20,24,26).

Because "justification" is not a word we typically toss around, I want to make sure that we all have a basic understanding of this spiritual strength. There is some discrepancy regarding the true meaning of this word, but for purposes of demonstrating how the Powerful Choleric's faith is put into action, we can use the following explanation from *Easton's Illustrated Bible Dictionary*: "Good works, while not the ground, are the certain consequence of justification."[4] For the Powerful Choleric, faith and works are seen as one and the same.

Andrea, one of our Certified Personality Trainers, is about half Powerful Choleric. Learning how her Personality impacts her faith helped her understand why she enjoys volunteering for so many activities at church. She says:

> When I am working on a project for church, I find myself praying more and depending more on the Lord for guidance. When

I am leading worship, I always pray to God before the service and let Him know that I cannot sing and lead without His help. I know that when I am doing things for God, I am also learning more about Him, which makes me feel closer to Him.

The area of spiritual strength for Powerful Cholerics is justification and works, showing their love for God by doing.

Perfect Melancholy: *Knowledge*

Perfect Melancholies, who tend to be deep thinkers, are attracted to the spiritual strength of knowledge. Perfect Melancholies carry their love of details, facts, charts and systems into their Christian lives as well. While Popular Sanguines typically accept God's love for them at face value, never questioning it, Perfect Melancholies always want to know the "why."

This was the case for Daniel. He is a systematic theologian who has studied so much *about* God that he can quote virtually any verse of Scripture in several English translations as well as the original Hebrew and Greek. His knowledge of the intricate details about Bible stories, along with his ability to explain their contexts, makes him a superb story-teller. Whether he's preaching to adults or to children, he can keep them spellbound for hours with keen insights.

But when it comes to daily living, Daniel often feels disappointed by God. When his father died unexpectedly, knowledge *about* God wasn't helpful, and he felt let down that God would miss such an important detail in his life—keeping his father alive—after all the time he'd spent devoted to details about God. Ultimately, Daniel did give up asking the big "why" and moved beyond, but not before he'd spent months wandering around in depression.

One of the key verses addressing this quest for knowledge is Proverbs 2:1-6:

My child, listen to me and treasure my instructions. Tune your ears to wisdom, and concentrate on understanding. Cry out for insight and understanding. Search for them as you would for lost money or hidden treasure. Then you will understand what it means to fear the LORD, and you will gain knowledge of God. For the LORD grants wisdom! From his mouth come knowledge and understanding (*NLT*).

While only the Perfect Melancholy is naturally drawn to knowledge, when we look at the definition of knowledge, we see that it is truly something we should all strive to attain. *The Holman Bible Dictionary* describes knowledge this way:

> The Bible speaks often about human knowledge. Knowledge of God is the greatest knowledge and is the chief duty of humankind. . . . This knowledge of God is not simply theoretical or factual knowledge; it includes experiencing the reality of God in one's life and living one's life in a manner that shows a respect for the power and majesty of God.[5]

While the other Personalities cannot understand why anyone would want to take up that much brain space, the Perfect Melancholy is attracted to knowledge simply for the sake of knowing.

Peaceful Phlegmatic: *Sovereignty of God*

Peaceful Phlegmatics are the exact opposite of Powerful Cholerics—they prefer to stay in the background and tend to be indecisive. Because of this, Peaceful Phlegmatics have an easy time in accepting the sovereignty of God in their lives. Now, while the concept of the sovereignty of God is fairly easy to grasp, it is, again, not a word we use every day. So I will call on the experts to explain its meaning here: *Easton's Illustrated Bible Dictionary* states that the sovereignty of God is "His absolute right to do all things according to his own good pleasure."[6]

Two important verses that address the issue of relying on God's sovereign control rather than our own are the following:

> Moreover, because of what Christ has done we have become gifts to God that he delights in, for as part of God's sovereign plan we

were chosen from the beginning to be his, and all things happen just as he decided long ago (Eph. 1:11, *TLB*).

The God who made the whole world and everything in it is the Lord of the land and the sky. He does not live in temples built by human hands. This God is the One who gives life, breath, and everything else to people. He does not need any help from them; he has everything he needs. God began by making one person, and from him came all the different people who live everywhere in the world. God decided exactly when and where they must live (Acts 17:24-26, *NCV*).

It is from this mind-set that the Peaceful Phlegmatic happily functions with a *que sera, sera* attitude—whatever will be, will be.

Growing Closer to God

As Christians, we all desire to grow in our spiritual life and have a closer relationship with God. But what works for one person may not work for another. This is why many of the popular methods for helping people grow in their spirituality—such as reading through the Bible in a year or recording prayers in a journal—produce more spiritual guilt than spiritual growth. So let's next look at what methods work best for each of the different Personality types.

Popular Sanguine

If you were to take a look at the Personality chart (see page 16) and draw a diagonal line through the squares from the top right to the bottom left (through the Powerful Choleric and the Peaceful Phlegmatic squares) and then think about the programs that are out there to help people grow in their spirituality, you would soon realize that these programs are designed for those to the bottom and right of that line. In other words, these programs are designed for those who have some Perfect Melancholy traits and either some Powerful Choleric traits (supplying the drive to follow through) or some Peaceful Phlegmatic traits (providing the needed appreciation of the structure and system). For Popular Sanguines, who naturally struggle with routine, these systems create frustration rather than faith.

It's not that Popular Sanguines *can't* grow closer to God; it's just that they shouldn't expect to follow the same pattern as the other Personalities. For example, trying to read through the Bible in one year—whether it's so many verses, pages or chapters per day—almost *never* works for Popular Sanguines. This can be discouraging—it certainly was for me when March would come and January's reading was still unfinished—but it is important for Popular Sanguines to realize that they are *not* a failure. The problem lies with those who would market such a program as the *only* way for *every* Personality to enjoy God's Word!

If you are a Popular Sanguine, there are a number of other tools that you can use to help you dig into God's Word without having to keep a schedule. One that has helped me greatly is *The Narrated Bible*[7] or the *My Time with God* devotional.[8] In addition, you may want to consider joining a small study group. Attending such a group will give you the accountability you need to spend time in God's Word—to save face, you will read the verses and do the homework!

Another option—especially if you are a Popular Sanguine who has a good dose of Powerful Choleric in you—is to start a Bible study that meets your needs. You do not need to feel qualified to teach in order to lead this group, as there are many wonderful studies out there that only require someone to facilitate the group. My mother and I wrote one such study: *The Journey to Jesus*.[9] We crafted this study in such a way that the homework portion is versatile, and therefore works for all Personalities. Within the book, we encourage people to do as much or as little as they want—after all, a little time in God's Word is better than none!

Popular Sanguines may also find that reading Christian fiction is a good way for them to absorb biblical truth into their life. Other Personalities often turn their noses up at this as shallow and a waste of time, but I recommend it to Popular Sanguines. While it should not be the only source for a person's spiritual growth, a good novel written by a reputable author can teach passively. And research has shown that when people read fiction, they read with their hearts—they get truth without even realizing it.

I once heard a speaker give this statement: "I seldom spend 15 minutes talking to God, but I seldom spend 15 minutes without talking to Him." I now quote this statement frequently, for it perfectly reflects the prayer life of the Popular Sanguine—while they may not do the scheduled, written prayers, they do talk to God all day long.

Powerful Choleric

Like Popular Sanguines, Powerful Cholerics are outgoing and energized by people, and thus they do well in developing their spiritual lives with other people. However, because Powerful Cholerics are more task-focused, they easily get frustrated with the molly-coddling and pettiness that often takes place in small-group settings. They get bored with the people who have to tell all about their personal lives and think that these chatty ones should stick to the program. They want to just get to the task at hand and not waste time on trivial matters.

For Powerful Cholerics, a prayer partner or two is a good solution to this problem. I get together regularly with two or three friends to pray for our husbands and our marriages. We affectionately refer to our prayer time as the "Praying Wives Club." Several of us have a large portion of Powerful Choleric in our Personality mix, and the hour or two that we set aside to pray works well for our schedules and our lives. Because our group is limited in number and not open to guests, we can be in control. We adjust our meeting time to fit our needs to avoid the static confinement of a usual Bible study. I find this intimate group works well for my Powerful Choleric side.

Edna Ellison has written several excellent Bible studies that I recommend for Powerful Choleric women. They are called the Friend to Friend Series, and the current titles include *Friend to Friend: Enriching Friendships Through a Shared Study of Philippians, Friendships of Purpose: A Shared Study of Ephesians* and *Friendships of Faith: A Shared Study of Hebrews.*[10] These studies are designed to be completed together with a friend and are perfect for Powerful Cholerics who want to spend time in God's Word without the complications inherent in group study dynamics.

Short devotional books with clear concepts are another good option for Powerful Cholerics, as they typically do not have the time for involved studies and do not like the little devotional books that tell a cute story and then have a brief biblical application tacked on at the end. And because Powerful Cholerics like information but want it quickly, Bible research software can be a great tool for them. When I sit in a chair or lie in my bed with my beautiful, heavy, leather Bible with tissue paper thin pages, somehow, I just want to go to sleep. But each time I use my software, I find myself wishing that I had more time to study further. The software makes it more interactive—I am participating, not just reading—and allows me to go deeper and deeper into God's Word. If you are a Powerful Choleric and you do not use Bible software, try it. You'll like it!

Powerful Cholerics are also the most goal-oriented of the Personalities, and they can use this tendency in their spiritual lives as a way to grow closer to God. Wendy, a Powerful Choleric, found that she could use her goal-oriented nature to set heavenly goals instead of earthly ones. She says, "By connecting to my God-given goals rather than my personal to-do lists, I find that I am content with being who I am. My greatest quest is to know more of God each day in a way that is powerful, significant and inspiring. While I still have other goals, I am now not driven by them. Instead, I am driven by doing what God wants in my day. Invariably, the success and accomplishment follows and is more than I imagined it would be."

Just as "doing" and "action" are central to the Personality of Powerful Cholerics, so the techniques that work the best in developing their spiritual life are participatory, not passive.

Perfect Melancholy

As noted previously, most Bible reading and study programs were created with the Perfect Melancholy in mind. So while the Popular Sanguine needs encouragement to keep studying God's Word and having a daily devotional time, the Perfect Melancholy needs to relax! I find that this admonition, from Oswald Chambers's classic devotional book *My Utmost for His Highest*, is appropriate for the Perfect Melancholy:

Your god may be your little Christian habit, the habit of prayer at stated times, or the habit of Bible reading. Watch how your Father will upset those times if you begin to worship your habit instead of what the habit symbolizes—I can't do that just now, I am praying; it is my hour with God. No, it is your hour with your habit. There is a quality that is lacking in you. Recognize the defect and then look for the opportunity of exercising yourself along the line of the quality to be added.[11]

Diana told me there was a time in her life when she would have suspected Oswald Chambers of heresy for the above views on Christian habits. She writes:

I can still see pastors and youth leaders—no doubt all of them Perfect Melancholies themselves—earnestly exhorting us never to miss our time of prayer and Bible reading. And the earlier in the day we did it, the better. This fit in well with my Perfect Melancholy lifestyle. For years, I had my routine down pat: awaken to the alarm, shower, and then sit in my rocking chair with a cup of tea with my Bible and my book/chapter/verse reading chart.

My printed prayer list featured daily prayers as well as requests for each day of the week. I divided the world into seven regions so that I could cover the earth in a week. If I missed a day, I tried to make up for it the following morning by praying both days' lists. Fortunately, along the way I read authors such as Chambers and realized the error of my approach. I was acting as if my entrance to heaven depended on my daily performance! I realized that what I really wanted to experience was God Himself and His marvelous grace, not just check off my devotional accomplishments.

Praise God that I've been delivered from that! However, I still do like to pray and read my Bible on something of a schedule. Right now, I'm halfway through the book of Ezekiel, and I should reach Daniel by next Thursday!

Because Perfect Melancholies function so well within a structured environment, it is easy for them to allow a time of Bible reading to be more about discipline and knowledge and less about God—more of a routine than a relationship. But life is not always structured, and this can sometimes cause problems for Perfect Melancholies if they are not willing to relax their routines.

Michelle told me the following story on how the situations in her life taught her to focus more on God and less on habit:

I grew up as a pastor's daughter and attended a Christian school, so my devotional time was pretty regimented. At home, church and school, everything related to my time with God was prepackaged and performed right on schedule. Although this made it very easy for me to do my Bible studies and have my quiet times on schedule, I realized that I was just going through the motions.

There was not a lot of heart and soul connected to my spiritual actions. My prayer time at that time was simply a notebook filled with requests, the date they were answered, and a few shallow thoughts. There was something comforting and stable in the routine, but nothing that facilitated growth or a deeper relationship with God. In fact, I found that my routines eventually created a detachment from the God that I was designed to love deeply as a Father.

When I went through a divorce several years ago and suddenly had to face the scary reality of raising my daughter as a single mom, a friend recommended that I start doing daily devotionals to lighten up my spiritual relationship with God. I began to journal out my thoughts and prayers and write songs of praise to God. I found that as I moved away from the cookie-cutter structure of scheduling everything in my devotional time, and toward a more carefree thought process, I could connect more to God. I let God speak to me when He wanted to, and I let myself take a moment to speak to Him—even if it wasn't on my schedule.

I became more vulnerable to my humanity and God's deity. Through open journaling, I found a God who was there for me in the prayers I was writing. As I poured out sentence after sentence of heartache in my paper journals or on my computer, I heard God's voice answering my prayers loud and clear. Some days His answer would be words of comfort; other days, it would be words of hope.

Now that I am more open and less bent on being perfect, I realize just how precious my time is with God. I almost missed out on one of God's blessings—time with Him—because I was trying fit God into my schedule instead me fitting into His more perfect timing. Now, instead of waiting for a specific prayer time, I find myself jotting down prayers, singing my songs of praise, and simply connecting with God in unscheduled ways throughout the day that would defy my "natural" Perfect Melancholy tendencies.

Another tip for Perfect Melancholies who are seeking to grow closer to God is to allow their ideals to be tempered by wisdom, knowledge and compassion. In the search for knowledge, it is easy for Perfect Melancholies to get too wrapped up in reading books and attending seminars in search of the perfect way to connect with God. They can become so absorbed with the technique that they forget about God.

Finally, because Perfect Melancholies do not function well with noise and activity, they need to find a quiet place to develop communion with God. Georgia says, "I like to be alone with God. I feel especially close to Him in my garden. Spending time in God's creation pulls me away from the distractions of life and enables me to hear His still, small voice. As I sit in my garden, my problems in life fall away, and I am filled with God's peace."

Peaceful Phlegmatic

I believe Peaceful Phlegmatics must be God's favorite Personality, because they take to heart the Great Commandment to "love the Lord your God with all your heart and with all your soul and with all your mind . . . [and] love your neighbor as yourself" (Matt. 22:37). Peaceful Phlegmatics bask in God's presence while the other Personalities are busy "doing" and "being." In addition to spending time with God, Peaceful Phlegmatics value relationships and other people.

Jack is a Peaceful Phlegmatic who serves as a deacon in a church that has an average attendance of 850 people for the regular services. Jack finds that relationships with people are very important. He writes:

> I always feel that I can learn and grow the most when I'm in a group in which everyone participates and shares. It seems like you build a more honest relationship with not just the other people in the group, but also with God. When the lesson is just taught or led by someone who acts like he or she has the final answer on what is right, all you get is "church answers," but when everyone shares equally, it's more like you're getting "heart answers." That's why I think home Bible studies are so good, because people relax more and kick back. When people are comfortable, they'll share more openly. I like to hear what people think inside—how they feel about something. I've seen too many people that have rituals and act like now that they've gone to church, they've "done their duty" for the week instead of being comfortable with having God everywhere with them all day long.

Although Peaceful Phlegmatics generally appreciate traditions such as Communion, Advent and Easter Sunrise Service, a rigid regime with a lot of dos and don'ts tends to paralyze them. Peaceful Phlegmatics are the only Personality that consistently indicates that the tool that most helps them in their Spiritual life is "pondering" Scripture. Since Peaceful Phlegmatics enjoy thinking about what a particular passage means and how to apply it to their lives (rather than just checking off a spiritual to-do list), they don't do well with scheduled reading plans. It makes little difference to them if it takes them three years to work through a one-year Bible plan. Bev shared the following with me about her Peaceful Phlegmatic husband:

> I am a Popular Sanguine married to a Peaceful Phlegmatic. My husband is a very quiet man who isn't vocal about his faith.

There is not a lot of pomp and circumstance in his walk with God, but he is ready 24 hours a day to help if someone in the family needs assistance. When I was leading a Parenting Group for those with teenagers at a church we attended, he was happy to be in the background, making sure that we had coffee and snacks ready at break time. I recently asked him, "What is your peak energy time if someone calls and needs help?" He said, "It doesn't matter, day or night. If something needs to be done, I could do it and do it well." He is there for others in the same way that God is there for us—he is steady, loving and extremely dependable!

An additional tip for Peaceful Phlegmatics who are seeking to grow closer to God is for them to have accountability partners and make commitments that are intentional, not legalistic. Pastor Steve, a Peaceful Phlegmatic himself, says, "My best advice for Peaceful Phlegmatics is to vary your routine. We Peaceful Phlegmatics tend to enjoy the variety as long as we are consistently spending time with our Lord."

Spiritual Gifts

When we look at the concept of spiritual gifts alongside the idea of the four Personality types that we have discussed throughout this book, we find that each Personality's strengths have a predisposition toward specific spiritual gifts. Scripture says that each person is uniquely gifted in areas of spiritual significance (such as teaching, giving and serving). I have often found that these gifts are simply extensions of the inherent personality traits in a person. Of course, it is important to note that God bestows some gifts that appear in a person regardless of his or her personality type—but this seems to be the exception rather than the rule.

The ideas surrounding the concept of spiritual gifts can be controversial. However, instead of going into the debate on spiritual gifts, my goal here is simply to point out some of the connections between the four Personality types and the various spiritual gifts that are mentioned in Scripture. To begin this discussion, let's look at the following helpful definition of the spiritual gifts from *New Unger's Bible Dictionary*:

[Spiritual Gifts] means any extraordinary faculty, which operated for the furtherance of the welfare of the Christian community, and which was itself wrought by the grace of God, through the power of the Holy Spirit, in special individuals, in accordance, respectively, with the measure of their individual capacities, whether it were that the Spirit infused entirely new powers, or stimulated those already existing to higher power and activity.[12]

The Bible touches on the topic of spiritual gifts in four different areas of the New Testament: Romans 12:3-8; 1 Corinthians 12:1, 4-11,28-30; Ephesians 4:3-6,11-12; and 1 Peter 4:11. Note that the passage from 1 Peter only mentions two specific gifts—speaking and serving: "Anyone who *speaks* should *speak* words from God. Anyone who *serves* should *serve* with the strength God gives so that in everything God will be praised through Jesus Christ" (4:11, *NCV*, emphasis added). However, all of the gifts listed in the passages from Romans, 1 Corinthians and Ephesians can be summarized into those two groupings.[13] So, to start looking at how spiritual gifts connect to the Personalities, let's divide all of the spiritual gifts we will talk about into one of those two groups. (Note: Because I have chosen to quote the following Scripture passages using the *New Contemporary Version* of the Bible, I am also listing the more traditional term associated with each gift.)

Speaking

Prophecy (Prophet)
"We all have different gifts, each of which came because of the grace God gave us. The person who has the *gift of prophecy* should use that gift in agreement with the faith" (Rom. 12:6, *NCV*, emphasis added).

Tell the Good News (Evangelist)

"And Christ gave *gifts* to people—he made some to be apostles, some to be prophets, some to *go and tell the Good News*" (Eph. 4:11, *NCV*, emphasis added).

Caring For and Teaching (Pastor/Teacher)

"Anyone who has the *gift of teaching* should teach" (Rom. 12:7, *NCV*, emphasis added).

"And Christ gave *gifts* to people—he made some . . . to have the work of *caring for* and *teaching* God's people" (Eph. 4:11, *NCV*, emphasis added).

Speak with Wisdom (Word of Wisdom)

"The Spirit gives one person the *ability to speak with wisdom*, and the same Spirit gives another the *ability to speak with knowledge* (1 Cor. 12:8, *NCV*, emphasis added).

Leader (Leadership)

"Anyone who has the *gift of being a leader* should try hard when he leads (Rom. 12:8, *NCV*, emphasis added).

Able to Govern (Administration)

"In the church God has given a place . . . [to] *those who are able to govern*" (1 Cor. 12:28, *NCV*, emphasis added).

Serving

Serving (Server)

"Anyone who has the *gift of serving* should serve" (Rom. 12:7, *NCV*, emphasis added).

"Christ gave those *gifts* to prepare God's holy people for the *work of serving*, to make the body of Christ stronger" (Eph. 4:12, *NCV*, emphasis added).

Help Others (Helps)
"Then God has given a place to those . . . who can *help others* (1 Cor. 12:28, *NCV*, emphasis added).

Show Mercy (Mercy)
"Whoever has the *gift of showing mercy* to others should do so with joy" (Rom. 12:8, *NCV*, emphasis added).

Giving
"Whoever has the *gift of giving* to others should give freely" (Rom. 12:8, *NCV*, emphasis added).

Ability to Know the Difference/Discernment
"And [the Spirit] *gives* to another the *ability to know the difference* between good and evil spirits" (1 Cor. 12:10, *NCV*, emphasis added).

Faith
"The same Spirit gives *faith* to one person" (1 Cor. 12:9, *NCV*, emphasis added).

Speak with Knowledge (Knowledge)
"The same Spirit gives another the ability to *speak with knowledge*" (1 Cor. 12:8, *NCV*, emphasis added).

Encouraging Others (Exhortation)
"Whoever has the *gift of encouraging others* should encourage" (Rom 12:8, *NCV*, emphasis added).

You might notice the connection between these spiritual gifts and the Personalities right away. In general, Popular Sanguines and Powerful Cholerics have the gift of speaking while Peaceful Phlegmatics and Perfect Melancholies have the gift of serving. However, the connection between the Personalities and spiritual gifts has even greater shades of complexity.

After years of working with many different people, I have found that the Popular Sanguine and the Powerful Choleric Personalities (and especially people with this exact combination) often have the gifts of prophecy, telling the Good News, caring for and teaching others, and speaking with wisdom. In the same way, the Powerful Choleric and Perfect Melancholy Personalities (and especially people with this exact combination) often tend to have two spiritual gifts in common: leadership and the ability to govern. The Perfect Melancholy and Peaceful Phlegmatic Personalities (and especially people with this exact combination) often have the spiritual gifts of serving, helping others, showing mercy, and giving. And finally, the Peaceful Phlegmatic and Popular Sanguine Personalities (and, again, especially people with this exact combination) often have the spiritual gifts of discernment, faith, speaking with knowledge, and encouraging others.

For most people, there is a strong connection and alignment between their Personality type and their spiritual gifts, as I have outlined. However, there are times when God will draw the needed spiritual gifts out of someone in whom the basic skills or strengths do not yet exist. In these cases, perhaps there is a work that needs to be completed, and in these times God can supernaturally equip someone to get the job done. Having a greater awareness of your strengths and your spiritual gifts together is a liberating way of more fully understanding your purpose in life.

The Personality of Jesus

Christians are always striving to be Christlike. In fact, it's what makes us followers of Christ—we seek to exhibit the attributes of Christ by studying His life and by trying to live in our strengths. And yet, many of us probably still wonder what being Christlike really means for us. However, when we look at Jesus Christ and His Church—all of us—with the new knowledge and understanding of the Personalities, how this is accomplished becomes clearer.

To reach the goal of becoming more Christlike, we first need to examine the personal stories of Jesus' life as told in the Gospels in order to understand His Personality more fully. And when we carefully scrutinize the life of Christ through these stories, we discover an important fact: Christ's own Personality contained the *strengths of all four Personalities* and the *weaknesses of none*. In this final section, we will look at a few of the aspects of Christ's life that fit into each Personality type.

Jesus Was a Popular Sanguine

When we look at the stories of Christ as told in the Gospels, we can quickly see that Christ was a Popular Sanguine![14] When He was born, He entered the world with a celebration! Appropriately, both the powerful and the lowly—the kings and the shepherds—brought Him gifts, and the light show of the night of His birth must have surely rivaled a Fourth of July celebration.

And then Jesus began His ministry with another party! His first miracle was turning water into wine at the wedding in Cana. He was a magnetic leader, and people followed Him from city streets to rooftops and from the plains to the mountaintops. He always drew a crowd, and His stories and parables were spellbinding to His thousands of followers.

Jesus was also an optimist. In Mark 10:27, He says, "With man this is impossible, but not with God; all things are possible with God." In addition, much of Jesus' ministry took place on mountaintops, in synagogues, and in the streets of various cities in Palestine. Physically, Popular Sanguines tend to have an unlimited supply of energy that they call into service when needed, and in Jesus' three-year ministry, He covered the span of many lands with the energy of a Popular Sanguine.

Jesus Was a Powerful Choleric

While it certainly appears that Jesus was a Popular Sanguine, He also shared many of the strengths of the Powerful Choleric.[15] Jesus was a born leader. He led with power and purpose, and He had very clear goals. Jesus knew why He had been sent to Earth, and every major accomplishment and every small activity that He took part in drove Him toward His ultimate goal.

Jesus was a man of action. He turned water into wine. He healed the sick and cast out demons. He prepared a meal for thousands. He boldly went into the Temple and turned over the tables of the moneychangers, crying "Is it not written: 'My house will be called a house of prayer for all nations?' But you have made it a 'den of robbers'" (Mark 11:17). Jesus often did not stop to rest as He traveled and ministered to the people from place to place. He was not afraid of a good fight and was always willing to confront and debate the Pharisees and teachers of the Law to show them the error in their thinking.

There are many occasions in the Gospels when Jesus got straight to the point. For instance, when His disciples asked Him "who is the greatest in the kingdom of heaven" (Matt. 18:1), He used strong and brief sentences to answer their question. When the Pharisees asked Him which of the Laws were the most important, He got right to the point by using two brief sentences to capture the bottom line of all the Laws: "Love the Lord your God with all your heart and with all your soul and with all your mind. . . . Love your neighbor as yourself" (Matt. 22:37,39).

Jesus delegated His authority well, which is also a Powerful Choleric strength. Under His authority, the disciples went out and were able to heal the sick and cast out demons. And to the generations of believers that would follow, He handed down the Great Commission—a command that each of us are still carrying out to this day.

Jesus Was a Perfect Melancholy

Because Jesus lived a perfect life, it would stand to reason that He would certainly be a Perfect Melancholy.[16] Not only was Christ perfect Himself, but He also inspired and encouraged His followers to strive for perfection! He was organized and detailed, as is evidenced by His specific instructions to His disciples about which cities they should visit, how they should carry money, and even what kinds of clothes they should wear. Jesus lived His life according to a plan and meticulously carried out that plan to fulfill the will of the Father.

Jesus spent a great deal of time alone in order to recharge Himself and spend time in fellowship with God the Father. At the beginning of His ministry on Earth, He went alone into the wilderness, where He was tempted by the devil for 40 days. After a busy day of teaching His followers, He would often retreat to the sanctuary of a mountaintop or withdraw into the wilderness. And on the night that He was betrayed and then arrested by the soldiers, He was praying by Himself in the Garden of Gethsemane.

Christ also cared deeply for people, which is another excellent Perfect Melancholy trait. He had a heart for the outcasts of society: the impoverished, the lepers, the prostitutes, and the sinners. He cared for every single person and even took time to care for the little children. He never shied away from emotions or tears. And, like a young genius prodigy (a common trait in Perfect Melancholies), at the age of 12 He amazed all the teachers in the Temple with His wisdom and understanding of the Law.

Jesus Was a Peaceful Phlegmatic

Jesus also had many of the strengths of Peaceful Phlegmatics.[17] He was a man of service and compassion. He was willing to do the lowly tasks and was never too busy or focused on His goals that He neglected to care for the people around Him. He played with the children, held the hand of a little girl, and grieved with a family. He took time to look people in the eye and love them.

Jesus was also humble. He took time out of His day to wash the feet of His disciples—a lowly task that was typically relegated to a servant or a slave. One of His most poignant remarks in all of Scripture is when He instructed His disciples, "If anyone wants to be first, he must be the very last, and the servant of all" (Mark 9:35). Jesus is our lord and king, and yet He took the time to put on humility and complete the tasks of a servant.

Christ was a man of peace, which is one of the primary strengths of the Peaceful Phlegmatic. In fact, one of His many names is the "Prince of Peace." He taught His disciples, "Do not resist an evil person. If someone strikes you on the right cheek, turn to him the other also. And if someone wants to sue you and take your tunic, let him have your cloak as well" (Matt. 5:39). He told His disciples to forgive others "not seven times, but seventy-seven times" (Matt. 18:22). Wherever He traveled, He brought hope and comfort to the people He met. Through all these things, we see that He owned the strengths of the Peaceful Phlegmatic.

Becoming Like Christ

In Jesus, we see that becoming Christlike means striving for the strengths of all the Personalities while letting go of all the weaknesses. It is an impossible task, but what we see in Jesus is a goal to strive for. Our own Personalities are the raw person that God made us to be, but if we continue to remain open to the Holy Spirit's shaping of our lives, we can move from raw to refined and from weaknesses to strength. Each day we study the life of Jesus in Scripture, we can make a conscious effort to live more like Jesus. Each day we accept Jesus and make Him the Lord of our lives, we can "put off [our] old self, which is being corrupted by its deceitful desires; to be made new in the attitude of [our] minds; and to put on the new self, created to be like God in true righteousness and holiness" (Eph. 4:22-24).

When we are all living Spirit-filled lives and we come together in our strengths, we as a group are like Christ. This is how we, as Christians, are intended to function. No one has every skill or strength. But as we come together, we make a whole and are complete in Him. Whether the group we are referring to is the entire Christian community, a specific church body, a parachurch organization, or a group of Christians banded together to support a specific cause, we are always more effective together. Some of us are activists, some are lovers, some are encouragers, some are students of the Word, some are intercessors, some are compassionate, some are leaders. Wherever our individual Personalities fit, there is a place for each and every one of us!

I remember hearing a speaker say, "If we both think the same, one of us isn't needed." In the Body of Christ, we each play a vital role. We are all needed. Perhaps this is what Paul meant when he wrote about the Church having one body with many parts:

> The body is one unit and yet has many parts. As all the parts form one body, so it is with Christ. By one Spirit we were all baptized into one body. Whether we are Jewish or Greek, slave or free, God gave all of us one Spirit to drink. As you know, the human body is not made up of only one part, but of many parts.

So God put each and every part of the body together as he wanted it. How could it be a body if it only had one part? So there are many parts but one body. An eye can't say to a hand, "I don't need you!" Or again, the head can't say to the feet, "I don't need you!" The opposite is true. The parts of the body that we think are weaker are the ones we really need. God's purpose was that the body should not be divided but rather that all of its parts should feel the same concern for each other. If one part of the body suffers, all the other parts share its suffering. If one part is praised, all the others share in its happiness. You are Christ's body and each of you is an individual part of it (1 Cor. 12:12-14, 18-22,25-27, *GOD'S WORD*).

When we accept Jesus as our Savior, we become a new creature in Christ. The power of the Holy Spirit is deposited into our lives, and He begins to shape us, smoothing out the rough edges of our weaknesses. It is not that our Personality changes or that we lose whom God originally created us to be, but that we start to use our Personality strengths that have been waiting to be cultivated and matured.

In Ephesians 4:22-24, we are told to "put off [our] old self . . . and put on the new self, created to be like God in true righteousness and holiness." When we surrender to Jesus, He begins to transform us into our authentic selves, exposing and removing the destructive parts of our weaknesses and helping us move toward unity in Him. By understanding our Personality's strengths and weaknesses, we can develop our lives in accordance to the glorious riches found in Christ Jesus. Ultimately, as we work on our Personality, we become more Christlike.

I hope that as you have read this book, you have determined to grow, to mature, to live in your strengths—to be more like Christ!

Notes

1. Special thanks to Kathryn Robbins for her original research on the connection between the four Gospels and the Personalities. http://www.stonesofglory.com/kathrynrobbins.html.
2. For a more thorough treatment of this subject, see Marita Littauer, *Your Spiritual Personality* (San Francisco: Jossey-Bass, 2005).
3. *The New Unger's Bible Dictionary* (Chicago, IL: Moody Publishers, 2006), s.v. "grace."

4. *Easton's Illustrated Bible Dictionary* (Austin, TX: WORDsearch Corporation, 2005), s.v. "justification."

5. *The Holman Bible Dictionary* (Nashville, TN: Broadman and Holman, 1998), s.v. "knowledge."

6. *Easton's Illustrated Bible Dictionary*, s.v. "sovereignty."

7. F. LaGard Smith, *The Narrated Bible* (Eugene, OR: Harvest House Publishers, 1984).

8. *My Time with God: 15 Minute Devotions for the Entire Year* (Nashville, TN: Thomas Nelson, 2003).

9. Florence Littauer and Marita Littauer, *Journey to Jesus: Looking for God in All the Right Places* (Tulsa, OK: Hensley Publishing, 2004).

10. Edna Ellison, Friend to Friend Series (Birmingham, AL: New Hope Publishers, 2002).

11. Oswald Chambers, *My Utmost for His Highest*, (Uhrichsville, OH: Barbour Publishing, 2006), May 12th reading.

12. *The New Unger's Bible Dictionary*, s.v. "spiritual gift."

13. I am grateful to my friend Judy Wallace for allowing me to benefit from her original research on this topic. Judy has done a more in-depth study that can be found in her book, *In His Presents* (Texarkana, AR: Baptist Publishing House, 2002).

14. See Matthew 2:1-11; 9:19-24; Mark 9:23; John 2:1-11; 6:1-14; 18:8,20.

15. See Matthew 9:37; 10:34; 22:37; Luke 2:46; 4:1-13; John 5:17; 8:14; 21:25.

16. See Matthew 5:48; 10:1-23; 14:23, 26-36; Mark 1:35,40; 6:1; 10:16; Luke 5:15-16; John 11:35.

17. See Matthew 8:5-6; 12:9-10; 19:16-23; 28:1-10; Mark 10:21-22; Luke 2:46-47; 12:27; John 13:5-14; 14:12.

WIRED THAT WAY
PERSONALITY PROFILE

This following Personality Profile was adapted from the *Wired That Way Assessment Tool*, a resource that contains this Personality Profile test, detailed word definitions, additional charts and graphs (to help define each Personality type) and a detailed description of how to understand your Profile score.[1]

Instructions

Read each of the four words on each horizontal line (numbered across, not down). Although it helps to know the word definitions listed in the *Wired That Way Personality Profile*, for this test, try thinking of the word in the broadest sense possible when making your selection.

Select the one word that most accurately describes who you naturally are. Do not include any learned behaviors. For example, if you had to take a class or read a book to learn a certain behavior, do not include that behavior on the profile, as it does not represent who you naturally are. In the same way, if you have been forced to take on a role for your job and now function that way fairly naturally, do not check that word. If you are unsure of which word to choose, ask your family members or friends. Those who live and work with you day in and day out—who see you at your best and worst—will often know you better than you know yourself. People often have a lot of baggage tied up in who they think they are, so input from others can be helpful.

Ideally, check only one word in each four-word grouping. However, if no words feel right, skip that line. If there are two words that seem equal and you cannot decide between the two, select both of them. Although using this method will not add up perfectly to the total of 40 as the Profile was designed, you will get the most accurate results. Once you have selected the appropriate words that describe who you are naturally, transfer your selections to the scoring sheet and add up the number of check marks in each vertical column. This will indicate your basic and secondary Personalities.

Your Personality Profile

In each of the following rows of four words across, check the one or two words that most often apply to you. Continue through all 40 lines. If you are not sure which word best applies to you, ask a spouse or a close friend, or think of what your answer would have been when you were a child—the answer that most applies to your natural personality. Use the word definitions on the next page for the most accurate results.

STRENGTHS

1 ❑ Adventurous	❑ Adaptable	❑ Animated	❑ Analytical
2 ❑ Persistent	❑ Playful	❑ Persuasive	❑ Peaceful
3 ❑ Submissive	❑ Self-sacrificing	❑ Sociable	❑ Strong-willed
4 ❑ Considerate	❑ Controlled	❑ Competitive	❑ Convincing
5 ❑ Refreshing	❑ Respectful	❑ Reserved	❑ Resourceful
6 ❑ Satisfied	❑ Sensitive	❑ Self-reliant	❑ Spirited
7 ❑ Planner	❑ Patient	❑ Positive	❑ Promoter
8 ❑ Sure	❑ Spontaneous	❑ Scheduled	❑ Shy
9 ❑ Orderly	❑ Obliging	❑ Outspoken	❑ Optimistic
10 ❑ Friendly	❑ Faithful	❑ Funny	❑ Forceful
11 ❑ Daring	❑ Delightful	❑ Diplomatic	❑ Detailed
12 ❑ Cheerful	❑ Consistent	❑ Cultured	❑ Confident
13 ❑ Idealistic	❑ Independent	❑ Inoffensive	❑ Inspiring
14 ❑ Demonstrative	❑ Decisive	❑ Dry humor	❑ Deep
15 ❑ Mediator	❑ Musical	❑ Mover	❑ Mixes easily
16 ❑ Thoughtful	❑ Tenacious	❑ Talker	❑ Tolerant
17 ❑ Listener	❑ Loyal	❑ Leader	❑ Lively
18 ❑ Contented	❑ Chief	❑ Chartmaker	❑ Cute
19 ❑ Perfectionist	❑ Pleasant	❑ Productive	❑ Popular
20 ❑ Bouncy	❑ Bold	❑ Behaved	❑ Balanced

WEAKNESSES

21 ❏ Blank	❏ Bashful	❏ Brassy	❏ Bossy
22 ❏ Undisciplined	❏ Unsympathetic	❏ Unenthusiastic	❏ Unforgiving
23 ❏ Reticent	❏ Resentful	❏ Resistant	❏ Repetitious
24 ❏ Fussy	❏ Fearful	❏ Forgetful	❏ Frank
25 ❏ Impatient	❏ Insecure	❏ Indecisive	❏ Interrupts
26 ❏ Unpopular	❏ Uninvolved	❏ Unpredictable	❏ Unaffectionate
27 ❏ Headstrong	❏ Haphazard	❏ Hard to please	❏ Hesitant
28 ❏ Plain	❏ Pessimistic	❏ Proud	❏ Permissive
29 ❏ Angered easily	❏ Aimless	❏ Argumentative	❏ Alienated
30 ❏ Naive	❏ Negative attitude	❏ Nervy	❏ Nonchalant
31 ❏ Worrier	❏ Withdrawn	❏ Workaholic	❏ Wants credit
32 ❏ Too sensitive	❏ Tactless	❏ Timid	❏ Talkative
33 ❏ Doubtful	❏ Disorganized	❏ Domineering	❏ Depressed
34 ❏ Inconsistent	❏ Introvert	❏ Intolerant	❏ Indifferent
35 ❏ Messy	❏ Moody	❏ Mumbles	❏ Manipulative
36 ❏ Slow	❏ Stubborn	❏ Show-off	❏ Skeptical
37 ❏ Loner	❏ Lord over others	❏ Lazy	❏ Loud
38 ❏ Sluggish	❏ Suspicious	❏ Short-tempered	❏ Scatterbrained
39 ❏ Revengeful	❏ Restless	❏ Reluctant	❏ Rash
40 ❏ Compromising	❏ Critical	❏ Crafty	❏ Changeable

Personality Scoring Sheet

Transfer all of your Xs to the corresponding words on the following Personality Scoring Sheet, and then add up your totals. For example, if you checked "animated" on the profile, check it on the scoring sheet below. (Note: The words are in a different order on the Profile and the Scoring Sheet.)

STRENGTHS

	Popular Sanguine	Powerful Choleric	Perfect Melancholy	Peaceful Phlegmatic
1	❑ Animated	❑ Adventurous	❑ Analytical	❑ Adaptable
2	❑ Playful	❑ Persuasive	❑ Persistent	❑ Peaceful
3	❑ Sociable	❑ Strong-willed	❑ Self-sacrificing	❑ Submissive
4	❑ Convincing	❑ Competitive	❑ Considerate	❑ Controlled
5	❑ Refreshing	❑ Resourceful	❑ Respectful	❑ Reserved
6	❑ Spirited	❑ Self-reliant	❑ Sensitive	❑ Satisfied
7	❑ Promoter	❑ Positive	❑ Planner	❑ Patient
8	❑ Spontaneous	❑ Sure	❑ Scheduled	❑ Shy
9	❑ Optimistic	❑ Outspoken	❑ Orderly	❑ Obliging
10	❑ Funny	❑ Forceful	❑ Faithful	❑ Friendly
11	❑ Delightful	❑ Daring	❑ Detailed	❑ Diplomatic
12	❑ Cheerful	❑ Confident	❑ Cultured	❑ Consistent
13	❑ Inspiring	❑ Independent	❑ Idealistic	❑ Inoffensive
14	❑ Demonstrative	❑ Decisive	❑ Deep	❑ Dry humor
15	❑ Mixes easily	❑ Mover	❑ Musical	❑ Mediator
16	❑ Talker	❑ Tenacious	❑ Thoughtful	❑ Tolerant
17	❑ Lively	❑ Leader	❑ Loyal	❑ Listener
18	❑ Cute	❑ Chief	❑ Chartmaker	❑ Contented
19	❑ Popular	❑ Productive	❑ Perfectionist	❑ Pleasant
20	❑ Bouncy	❑ Bold	❑ Behaved	❑ Balanced

Totals Strengths

WEAKNESSES

Popular Sanguine	Powerful Choleric	Perfect Melancholy	Peaceful Phlegmatic
21 ❑ Brassy	❑ Bossy	❑ Bashful	❑ Blank
22 ❑ Undisciplined	❑ Unsympathetic	❑ Unforgiving	❑ Unenthusiastic
23 ❑ Repetitious	❑ Resistant	❑ Resentful	❑ Reticent
24 ❑ Forgetful	❑ Frank	❑ Fussy	❑ Fearful
25 ❑ Interrupts	❑ Impatient	❑ Insecure	❑ Indecisive
26 ❑ Unpredictable	❑ Unaffectionate	❑ Unpopular	❑ Uninvolved
27 ❑ Haphazard	❑ Headstrong	❑ Hard to please	❑ Hesitant
28 ❑ Permissive	❑ Proud	❑ Pessimistic	❑ Plain
29 ❑ Angered easily	❑ Argumentative	❑ Alienated	❑ Aimless
30 ❑ Naive	❑ Nervy	❑ Negative attitude	❑ Nonchalant
31 ❑ Wants credit	❑ Workaholic	❑ Withdrawn	❑ Worrier
32 ❑ Talkative	❑ Tactless	❑ Too sensitive	❑ Timid
33 ❑ Disorganized	❑ Domineering	❑ Depressed	❑ Doubtful
34 ❑ Inconsistent	❑ Intolerant	❑ Introvert	❑ Indifferent
35 ❑ Messy	❑ Manipulative	❑ Moody	❑ Mumbles
36 ❑ Show-off	❑ Stubborn	❑ Skeptical	❑ Slow
37 ❑ Loud	❑ Lord over others	❑ Loner	❑ Lazy
38 ❑ Scatterbrained	❑ Short-tempered	❑ Suspicious	❑ Sluggish
39 ❑ Restless	❑ Rash	❑ Revengeful	❑ Reluctant
40 ❑ Changeable	❑ Crafty	❑ Critical	❑ Compromising

Totals Weaknesses

Combined Totals

Tallying Your Score

Once you've transferred your answers to the scoring sheet, added up your total number of answers in each of the four columns, and added your totals from both the strengths and weaknesses sections, you can determine your dominant Personality type. You will also be able to determine what Personality combination you possess. For example, if your score is 35 in Powerful Choleric strengths and weaknesses, you will be almost all Powerful Choleric. But if your score is 16 in Powerful Choleric, 14 in Perfect Melancholy, and 5 in each of the others, you're a Powerful Choleric with strong Perfect Melancholy traits. You will also be able to determine your least dominant Personality type. As you read and work with the material in this book, you'll understand how to put your strengths to work for you, how to compensate for the weaknesses in your dominant type, and how to understand the strengths and weaknesses of other types.

Note

1. The *Personality Profile,* created by Fred Littauer, is from *After Every Wedding Comes a Marriage* by Florence Littauer, copyright (c) 1981, Harvest House Publishers. Used by permission. Do not duplicate.

ADDITIONAL RESOURCES

For information on becoming a Certified Personality Trainer, or to purchase any of the Personality resources, please visit www.theperson alities.com, or call 800-433-6633.

For additional information on the basic study of the Personalities, please read *Personality Plus: How to Understand Others by Understanding Yourself* by Florence Littauer (Grand Rapids, MI: Fleming Revell, 1992).

For an in-depth study of the Personalities in marriage, please read *Personality Plus for Couples: Understanding Yourself and the One You Love* by Florence Littauer (Grand Rapids, MI: Fleming Revell, 2001).

For an in-depth study of the Personalities and parenting, please read *Personality Plus for Parents: Understanding What Makes Your Child Tick* by Florence Littauer (Grand Rapids, MI: Fleming Revell, 2000).

For additional information on the Personalities and communication, please read *Communication Plus: How to Speak So People Will Listen* by Florence Littauer and Marita Littauer (Ventura, CA: Regal Books, 2006).

For an in-depth study of the Personalities in the workplace, please read *Personality Puzzle* by Florence Littauer and Marita Littauer (Grand Rapids, MI: Fleming Revell, 2003).

For an in-depth study of how the Personalities affect spiritual life (especially spiritual gifts), please read *Your Spiritual Personality: Using the Strengths of Your Personality to Deepen Your Relationship with God* by Marita Littauer (San Francisco: Jossey-Bass, 2005).

OTHER BOOKS BY MARITA LITTAUER

Communication Plus
How to Speak So People Will Listen
(Marita Littauer and Florence Littauer)
Ventura, CA: Regal Books, 2006

Tailor-Made Marriage
When Your Lives Aren't One Size Fits All
(Marita Littauer and Chuck Noon)
Grand Rapids, MI: Kregel Publications, 2006

The Praying Wives Club
Gather Your Girlfriends And Pray for Your Marriage
(Marita Littauer and Dianne Anderson)
Grand Rapids, MI: Kregel Publications, 2006

Making the Blue Plate Special
The Joy of Family Legacies
(Marita Littauer, Florence Littauer and Lauren Littauer Briggs)
Colorado Springs, CO: Cook Communications, 2006

Your Spiritual Personality
Using the Strengths of Your Personality to Deepen Your Relationship with God
San Francisco: Jossey-Bass, 2005.

But Lord, I Was Happy Shallow
Lessons Learned in the Deep Places
(Marita Littauer, General Editor)
Grand Rapids, MI: Kregel Publications, 2004

The Journey to Jesus
Looking for God in All the Right Place
(Marita Littauer and Florence Littauer)
Tulsa, OK: Hensley Publishing, 2004

Love Extravagantly
Making the Modern Marriage Work
(Marita Littauer and Chuck Noon)
Minneapolis, MN: Bethany House, 2001

You've Got What It Takes
Celebrating Being a Woman Today
Minneapolis, MN: Bethany House, 2000

Come As You Are
How Your Personality Shapes Your Relationship With God
(Marita Littauer and Betty Southard)
Minneapolis, MN: Bethany House, 1999

Talking So People Will Listen:
You Can Communicate with Confidence
(Marita Littauer and Florence Littauer)
Ann Arbor, MI: Vine Books, 1998

Getting Along with Almost Anybody
The Complete Personality Book
(Marita Littauer and Florence Littauer)
Grand Rapids, MI: Fleming Revell, 1998

Personality Puzzle
Reduce Conflict and Increase Productivity by Understanding the Four
Personality Types
(Marita Littauer and Florence Littauer)
Grand Rapids, MI: Fleming Revell, 1992

Too Much is Never Enough
Behaviors You Never Thought Were Addictions: How to Recognize and
Overcome Them: A Christian's Guide
(Marita Littauer and Gaylen Larson)
Nampa, ID: Pacific Press Publishing Association, 1994

Giving Back
Creative Ways to Make Your World a Better Place
San Bernardino, CA: Here's Life Publishers, 1991

Homemade Memories
Strengthening Our Ties to Family and Friends Through Creative Hospitality
Eugene, OR: Harvest House Publishers, 1991

Shades of Beauty
The Color-Coordinated Woman
(Marita Littauer and Florence Littauer)
Eugene, OR: Harvest House Publishers, 1982

ABOUT THE AUTHOR

As the daughter of popular speaker, author and nationally recognized personality expert Florence Littauer, Marita has been under Florence's direct tutelage for more than 45 years. Marita is known through her personal speaking ministry and her expertise in personal and professional relationships. She has been speaking professionally for more than 25 years for church, school and business groups, and is the author of 17 books. Additionally, she has firsthand experience in the value of utilizing the Personalities in the workplace.

Marita is the President of CLASServices Inc., an organization that provides resources, training and promotion for Christian speakers and authors. Through the CLASSeminar, which has been offered throughout the United States since 1981, Marita has trained thousands of men and women to develop speaking and writing skills. Many of the concepts presented at the CLASSeminar can be found in her book *Communication Plus* (which is co-authored with her mother). She is a member of the National Speakers Association and is a frequent guest on television and radio programs throughout the country.

**For more information on the ministry
of Marita Littauer, please visit
www.maritalittauer.com or call 800-433-6633.**

Make the most of
WIRED THAT WAY
and **YOUR COMPREHENSIVE PERSONALITY PLAN**
with these resources

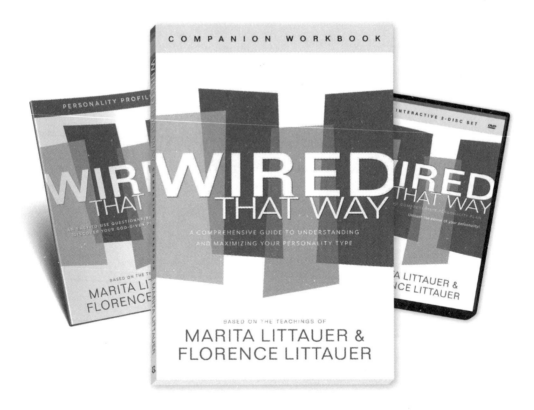